Identity, Learning, and Decision Making in Changing Organizations

Identity, Learning, and Decision Making in Changing Organizations

CHARLES RANSOM SCHWENK

QUORUM BOOKS
Westport, Connecticut • London

Library of Congress Cataloging-in-Publication Data

Schwenk, Charles Ransom, 1952–
    Identity, learning, and decision making in changing organizations / Charles Ransom Schwenk.
        p. cm.
    Includes bibliographical references and index.
    ISBN 1–56720–468–6 (alk. paper)
    1. Organizational learning.   2. Organizational change.   3. Knowledge management.
    I. Title.
    HD58.82.S394   2002
    658.4'038—dc21   2001019870

British Library Cataloguing in Publication Data is available.

Library of Congress Catalog Card Number: 2001019870
ISBN: 1–56720–468–6

First published in 2002

Quorum Books, 88 Post Road West, Westport, CT 06881
An imprint of Greenwood Publishing Group, Inc.
www.quorumbooks.com

Printed in the United States of America

(∞)™

The paper used in this book complies with the
Permanent Paper Standard issued by the National
Information Standards Organization (Z39.48–1984).

10 9 8 7 6 5 4 3 2 1

Copyright Acknowledgments

The author and publisher gratefully acknowledge permission to use the following materials:

Mindfulness by Ellen J. Langer. Copyright © 1989 by Ellen J. Langer. Reprinted by permission of
Perseus Books Publishers, a member of Perseus Books, L.L.C.

"How Shall the Self Be Conceived?" by Anthony R. Pratkanis and Anthony G. Greenwald, in
Journal for the Theory of Social Behavior, 15 (1985): 311–329. Copyright © Blackwell
Publishers Ltd/Executive Management Committee of JTSB.

Contents

Acknowledgments

Thanks to Susan Rhodes for her help in this work. Her comments were essential in clarifying my ideas on this topic and others. She also read through multiple drafts of the manuscript. Barry Anderson helped a great deal with the conceptual work upon which this book is based and provided valuable input on an earlier draft of the book. D. K. Holm patiently read through an earlier draft of this book and encouraged me to see the project through. John Pierce also deserves mention for his amazingly careful and thorough reading of a later draft. David Duncan's critique helped me to revise the section of Chapter 3 describing his work with the Clark Fork Coalition, though we still disagree on the wisdom of his views. Casey Bailey provided information that enriched the section of Chapter 5 dealing with devil's advocacy.

I must also acknowledge a larger debt of gratitude. Isaac Newton once said that if he saw further than others, it was because he stood on the shoulders of giants. There are some people whose work has shaped my thinking. Standing on their shoulders offered me a much better view of the territory I will explore in this book. My vision doesn't equal Newton's but my gratitude does.

Introduction

I will begin with three pieces of common knowledge. The world is changing, the pace of change is accelerating, and individuals and businesses must adapt. Michael Hammer and James Champy, authors of the influential book *Reengineering the Corporation* (1993) have suggested that the unprecedented changes of the last few decades require us to throw out much of the received wisdom of 200 years of industrial management. Microsoft's Bill Gates has argued that business is moving "at the speed of thought," and this requires a fundamental shift in our thinking. In a recent prize-winning book, *Competing on the Edge* (1998), management consultant Shona Brown and Stanford Professor Kathleen Eisenhardt have shown that the ability to adapt rapidly and effectively to change is essential for survival in high-tech companies like Intel, Cisco Systems, and Sun Microsystems. Companies in high-tech industries can be divided into the quick and the dead.

No one can deny that change is happening more rapidly now than at some times in the past. However, I think the image of change accelerating like a runaway train is misleading and needlessly frightening. It springs from a view common in the 1970s, when I first began to teach management, that change was rapid in the seventies but that it was relatively slow in the 1950s and glacial at the turn of the last century. One implication of this view is that the pace of change would accelerate through the rest of the century and beyond. It seemed that the pace of change would one day exceed our ability to cope with it. Another implication was that since the pace of change at the end of the second millennium is unprecedented, the knowledge and wisdom of the past is irrelevant in dealing with the problems caused by this change.

However, I am not sure now that the pace of change was slower in 1900 than it is in 2000. Thomas Edison's inventions alone produced social changes in the early 1900s as profound as those produced by the innovations in electronics, communications, and other technologies that shape our lives today.

If you want to find a period of great technological, economic, and social change, consider the sixth century B.C. Technological changes related to transportation and warfare, along with increased trade and communication, ended the isolation of many parts of the world and called into question existing ideas, values, and religions. New ideas arose in response to these changes.

In the Middle East, Zoroaster described all of creation as a war between two primal forces, light and darkness. In Greece, Heraclitus taught that there is no fixed reality, only change and that fire is the fundamental element in the universe. In China, Confucius laid down a new standard of behavior and government, while in India Buddha developed a method for the realization of anicca (impermanence) and anatta (no-self) and Mahavera, founder of the Jains, developed new spiritual concepts and disciplines to deal with the problems of the Vedic religion. The radically different world views developed by these men reflected the radical changes in their environments.

History is full of profound change and adapting to such change has always been part of the human condition. Radical change can threaten our assumptions about the world and ourselves, and this leads to one final piece of common knowledge: change challenges our identities. In response to this challenge, we rethink and sharpen our definitions of who we are. Unfortunately, this process may bring us into conflict with those who define their identities differently. Since individuals have different interpretations of change and radically different ideas about how they should respond to it, it is not surprising that passionate and sometimes violent disagreements erupt.

Consider the following business-related issues: class action lawsuits against tobacco companies and firearms manufacturers, preemployment drug testing, proposed drastic reductions in industry emissions of greenhouse gases, widespread demands for changes in the role of the World Trade Organization and International Monetary Fund, antitrust prosecution of high-tech companies like Microsoft, prohibitions on the development and use of genetically modified foods, and stringent limitations on the environmental impact caused by mining and logging companies. These issues have two things in common. The first is that people differ passionately about them and the second is that we must develop ways of dealing with them. In order to develop solutions to these problems, we must understand why there are such extreme differences of opinion about them.

When I listen to discussions of these topics, I am struck by the fact that people's views about them are rooted in their identities. What people believe about these issues reflects how they define themselves. It may be that people's beliefs about all the important issues in their lives and work reflect their self-concepts and that the decisions they make on these issues are inextricably bound up with their identities.

This book is about the relationship between self-concepts, identities, and crucial decisions. It deals with a fundamental dilemma that has faced every individual, group, organization, and society throughout human history: how to conceptualize the self and manage individuals to achieve collective action in a changing world. On the one hand, individuals must have clearly defined identities within a working concept of self. These identities direct their actions and provide the basis for a meaningful life. They also allow individuals to define their place in social groups such as organizations and communities and, therefore, provide the basis for collective action.

On the other hand, individuals must not take their own identities and interests too seriously. If they do, they may place their short-term self-interest above the interests of their group, organization, or society. Even worse, they may succumb to mindless identification with a social group. People's self-concepts include roles they play in families, organizations, and societies. If these roles are taken too seriously, individuals may be willing to do whatever is necessary to preserve their social group as they conceive of it. This leads to rigid identification that does not allow the individual or social group to adapt to the demands of a changing environment. Leaders often encourage strong identification with the groups and organizations they run. However, organizations and societies that promote mindless identification are prone to engage in the kind of self-destructive struggles and conflicts that have caused suffering and death throughout the history of our species.

In this book, I will make these basic arguments:

1. My "self," which frames all my perceptions, determines my decisions, and shapes my actions, the "I" to which I refer when I say "I think," "I feel," and "I act," is a mental structure or schema.

2. My self-schema is composed of identities linked to relationships with others and membership in groups or organizations. Identity is that aspect of the person that is central, enduring, and distinctive. Any individual includes multiple identities, each with its own set of values, preferences, and ways of framing problems, and multiple social roles within each identity. For example, your work identity might include roles like mentor, manager, or union representative. Important life decisions are made by resolving conflicts between these identities.

3. When a single identity becomes central or dominant in the self-schema, the individual attempts to make it more stable or enduring through autobiographical memory distortion and to make it more distinctive through conflict with those who do not share the identity. This reduces conflict between identities but it also reduces the individual's ability to comprehend complex problems and make effective decisions, especially in rapidly changing and competitive environments.

4. When organizations encourage their members to identify too strongly with their organizational roles, self-schemas become impoverished and the organization's knowledge structure becomes less complex.

5. Through the use of dialogue by organizations, supplemented by devil's advocacy and the mindful use of identities by individuals, self-schemas and organizational knowledge structures can be enriched and clarified, decision-making can be improved, and individuals and organizations can pursue wiser courses of action.

The chapters of the book are devoted to clarifying these basic arguments. Chapter 1 deals with the formation of the self-schema and the role of social identities within it. A social identity describes what is central, enduring, and distinctive in an individual and multiple identities interact in using the self-schema in decision-making. I will discuss identity fixation and self-schema impoverishment, which may occur when a single organizational identity becomes dominant in an individual.

Chapter 2 covers an important process by which people attempt to make their identities appear enduring, autobiographical memory construction. I will describe common patterns of autobiographical memory distortion and illustrate them with a personal example. I will also discuss the ways memory distortion in the service of identity affects decisions.

Chapter 3 deals with the role of polarizing conflict in solidifying identities and making them more distinctive. Here I will outline the ways such identity-based conflicts can promote groupthink, escalating commitment, and the destruction of common resources.

Chapter 4 discusses the concept of organizational knowledge structures and the ways individual identities relate to them. I explain the concept of impoverished knowledge structures and the conditions under which such structures have the most negative effects. The problem of impoverished knowledge structures must be attacked at both the organizational and individual level.

Chapter 5 describes methods for using dialogue and structured conflict within organizations as a way of broadening organizational knowledge structures. Finally, Chapter 6 deals with techniques that promote the wise use of the self-schema. These include internal devil's advocacy, autobiographical memory work, and constructing dialogues.

1

Identities, Organizations, and Adaptation to Change

What a wonderfully complex thing, this simple-seeming unity—the self.
H. G. Wells, *The Sleeper Awakes*[1]

This chapter is about the ways our identities can either expand or limit our ability to make effective decisions and adapt to change. Differences in the ways we define ourselves affect the ways we live our lives, what we find meaningful, and how we understand the world and our place in it.

Globalization has forced many corporations to confront the effects of diverse self-concepts among managers from different cultures. International business researcher Geert Hofstede has studied this topic since the late 1970s. Based on hundreds of interviews of managers from multiple cultures, he has concluded that those from Asian and Western cultures have different views on the role of the individual in businesses and societies. Individualism is thought to be more important to Westerners while collectivism is embraced by Asians. This is obviously an oversimplification, but studies of individual employees and groups of managers suggest that there may be basic differences in social decision-making between cultures.[2] The large conglomerates like the *Keiretsu* in Japan and the *Chaebol* of South Korea represent different ways of organizing individuals and businesses than is common in the United States. It may be that some of the differences in business practices are rooted in different views of the self.

Even within a single Western country, there can be profound differences in identities related to business practice. In the United States for example, entrepreneurs and executives in high-tech or "new economy" companies see themselves differently than those in "old economy" companies. New economy executives see themselves as technological visionaries, pioneers, and revolutionaries while those participating in more traditional businesses see themselves as responsible custodians of the shareholders' interests. This often accounts for the culture clashes that plague joint ventures and strategic alliances between e-commerce companies and more traditional retailers. For example, the Disney company acquired a majority interest in the Internet toy retailer Toysmart and soon became aware of differences in identity and vision between the two companies. When Disney recently closed the Toysmart.com Web site, David Lord of Toysmart said, "Disney is a fine institution that runs its business by the bottom line and we're an Internet company, which means we weren't driven by the bottom line."[3]

These examples suggest that there can be dramatic differences in the way people define their identities and that serious practical problems can result from these differences. Though our identities shape the way we understand and deal with the world, we may not be fully aware of their influence on our behavior. It is even more difficult for us to understand the differences between our identities and those of others. We may not realize how great these differences are or how much they affect people's approaches to important decisions.[4]

In the next section of the chapter, I will briefly discuss philosophical work on the nature of the self. I realize this work may seem far removed from the crucial decisions of daily life and business—more appropriate for an intense discussion between earnest college philosophy majors than for a book on managing in times of increasing diversity and change. However, I think some reflection on the nature of the self makes good practical sense as it can provide insights necessary for effectively managing yourself and others. If you agree, read on. If not, you may wish to skip the next section and move on to the following section entitled "How We Construct the Self-Schema." That section returns to more practical issues, describing the ways our identities are structured and the role they play in social life and decision-making.

KNOWING OURSELVES

It is odd that there is such radical disagreement about the nature of the self, given that the existence of a self seems so obvious. Many people are deeply and firmly convinced that we each possess a self that is the central core of our being. This self is something more than just our thoughts, feelings, or body. It is the real and substantial "I" to which we refer when we say "I think," "I feel," or "I have a body." Few question the apparently obvious fact of their own existence because they mistakenly believe it is self-evident.

Some, like Descartes, argue that my existence is proven by the fact that I think. Thought cannot exist without a thinker. Because Descartes gave one of the clearest statements of this conception of the self, this self is sometimes called the

Cartesian Ego.[5] Gilbert Ryle, an English philosopher writing and teaching at Oxford in the 1940s, called this view the "official doctrine" of most theorists and lay people and labeled it "the dogma of the Ghost in the Machine." According to this dogma, every person has both a body and a mind. Actions of the body are public and can be observed by the self and others. Actions of the mind are private and can only be observed by the self. He argued that this view of the self was first developed by Descartes.[6]

Some professional philosophers currently hold that it is logically and psychologically impossible to describe our thoughts and actions without referring to this "I" or self.[7] These people claim that terms like "thinking" and "feeling" logically imply the existence of a thinking self. They feel this assumption is built into our language. In response to this argument, a great many thinkers, including twentieth-century philosophers like Derek Parfit, eighteenth-century Enlightenment philosophers such as David Hume, and even the Buddha, who lived and taught in India five centuries before Christ,[8] simply observe that it *is* possible for them to imagine thought without a thinking self. They point out that in earlier times, it was commonly believed that the existence of the universe implied the existence of God because a creation requires a creator. Now many people accept the idea that the evolution of the universe can be adequately explained without appealing to the intervention of a thinking deity. Similarly, it is possible to explain how thoughts and decisions evolve in individuals (and in organizations) without appealing to a thinking self.

William James summarized the development of this view (which he called the Associationist Theory) since David Hume. Appendix A, at the end of the chapter, provides a more detailed discussion of this theory. James suggested that the Associationist perspective rests on a useful metaphor for consciousness as a *stream*.[9] According to this metaphor, what we experience as our "selves" are streams of distinct conscious states, each leading to the next without the process needing to be directed by a self. Since this is an important point, I will clarify it further. I am not saying I can prove that the self does not exist in any sense. I am merely saying that there is no evidence that the self I am conscious of, the self I feel, is an observable entity. James's discussion of this concept is included in Appendix B.

It is important to account for the feeling or consciousness of the self in the midst of decision-making and action. Philosophers discussing this topic often use the term "self-consciousness" to describe the intuitive feeling that the self exists. This feeling of a self operating in everyday action is very deep and it forms the basis for most theories of the self used by ordinary people in everyday life.

The role of self-consciousness in day-to-day decision-making has been discussed recently by philosophers and psychologists. For example, in *The Nature of Consciousness* the authors examine how consciousness of self is linked to the conscious use of information in problem solving. This theme is also taken up in the recent book, *The Theater of Consciousness*, in which the author argues that self as a schema, or structure for perception, provides the context for conscious information processing. He later elaborates on the functions of consciousness mediated by the self.[10]

Though Immanuel Kant did postulate the existence of a "transcendental self," he would have agreed with James that our common view of the self is not accurate. Kant said this about the "consciousness of self,"

The unbroken identity of apperception of the manifold that is given in intuition contains a synthesis of representations, and is possible only through the consciousness of that synthesis. The empirical consciousness, which accompanies various representations, is itself various and disunited, and without reference to the identity of the subject.[11]

Kant asserts that our deep, habitual perception of a self is a necessary part of the process by which we organize and understand sensory perception and respond to it. But this self is a *consequence* of the process of organizing perceptions rather than the *cause* of the process.[12]

A single unitary self of the type postulated in microeconomics, for example, presents difficulties in explaining behaviors such as preference reversals. These might be better explained by assuming "multiple selves" within each individual, each with its own preference function.[13]

Cognitive and social psychologists have articulated and progressively refined models that explain human behavior without reference to the concept of self. In these models, human behavior is seen as the result of the interaction between physiological, emotional, and cognitive systems within a social environment. Though some philosophers, such as Charles Taylor, believe these models are inadequate because they do not rest on the concept of self as a cause of behavior, psychologists from William James through the behaviorists through those working within the cognitive perspective have undermined the notion that self is central to the explanation of behavior.[14]

Social science with a behaviorist orientation relied on simple (perhaps simplistic) principles linking reinforcers in the environment to behavior. B. F. Skinner, probably the best known and most controversial representative of behaviorism, explicitly stated that the concept of self is not necessary in a science of behavior.[15] Cognitive psychologists have correctly criticized behaviorists for devoting too little attention to the role of cognitive structures and processes but the cognitive models of behavior do not assume a substantial self either. These models define the self as a schema or cognitive structure that helps social organisms integrate environmental information and respond consistently to the demands of the environment.[16]

A philosopher whose work is consistent with this research is Daniel Dennett. In *Consciousness Explained*, he calls the traditional view of the self the "Cartesian Theater" in homage to Descartes. According to this view, all mental events are observed by a central self that is like the audience in a theater. Our behavior is then controlled by this self. Dennett argues that this concept of self presents too many theoretical problems to be useful as a framework for understanding behavior. These problems include the impossibility of observing the self directly, the problem of the "ghost in the machine," and the fact that we sometimes seem to have multiple "selves" that pull us in different directions.

Dennett argues that our behavior is controlled not by a central self but by a number of loosely coupled perceptual, cognitive, and behavioral subsystems that interact in different ways at different times. Dennett's argument appears to contradict the common experience that we perceive our selves quite readily and are aware of them all of the time. However, he asserts that consciousness of a "self" occurs periodically as the result of certain types of interaction among these systems.[17] Other evidence, included in Appendix C, suggests that our awareness of self varies over time.

The concept of the self-schema, which I will discuss next, provides the basis for understanding the role of identity in decision-making. When we consider an important personal decision, for example, we sometimes feel conflicted about the course of action we should take because the demands of different social roles or identities suggest different choices. When we attempt to make such choices, we evoke the self-schema that functions as a structure or set of rules for deciding between alternative perspectives on a problem. When we make use of the self-schema, we become conscious of our self. I have included some of James' original discussion in Appendix D.

HOW WE CONSTRUCT THE SELF-SCHEMA

Some of the philosophical arguments about the nature of the self discussed above may seem to contradict common sense, but they do show that there are many ways to understand our identities. I want to suggest a conception of the self that is useful in understanding how we make our most important and difficult decisions. It rests on a concept borrowed from the discipline of cognitive psychology, the self-schema.

A schema is a mental construct, a way of thinking that provides a framework for interpreting events and making decisions.[18] The schema is the cognitive structure by which we match abstract concepts to concrete reality. For example, if we want to decide whether one event caused another (say, whether the recent Bridgestone/Firestone tire recall caused a decline in Ford's stock price), we must apply our abstract idea of causality to this particular case. It is our schema for causality that allows us to do this.[19]

Over the last several decades, cognitive psychologists have refined the concept of the schema and linked it to current thinking on perception and decision-making. Ulrich Neisser, in his book *Cognition and Reality*, says we use our schemas

to interpret our perceptions and filter the information coming to us from the outside world.[20] Rumelhart calls schemas "data structures for representing the generic
concepts stored in memory."[21]

Perhaps the best way to explain what schemas are is to say what they are like, to
use analogies. Schemas are like scripts for plays, like lenses, like computer programs, and like maps. Like scripts, they direct our actions. Like lenses, they focus
and filter our perceptions. Like computer programs, they allow us to access information in memory. Like maps, they are symbolic representations of reality that
allow us to find our way in unfamiliar circumstances. We have schemas that structure our perceptions and guide our actions in all important areas of our lives, from
ordering food in a restaurant to performing our roles as parents or employees.

The self-schema is a kind of master-schema that encompasses our schemas for
all aspects of our lives.[22] Our self-schema tells us when we need to play a particular role such as manager, spouse, or teacher. It also explains how roles like these relate to our overall self-image.[23] Self-schemas are perhaps the most basic of the
cognitive structures through which we human beings understand our world.[24] Appendix E contains an article by psychologists Anthony Pratkanis and Anthony
Greenwald dealing with the self-schema.

The structure of the self-schema is complex, too complex to be captured in a
brief discussion or a single diagram. It may be conceived as a network of elements
including memories, beliefs, identities, and roles with complex links between these
elements.[25] Memories, for example, may have different relationships to different
beliefs, supporting some while detracting from others. Individual identities like
the work identity and the family identity may be closely linked in some individuals and completely separate in others.

The self-schema includes both *core* features and *peripheral* features. The core
features are those that are most basic, central, or important to our current image of
who we are.[26] Thus, our core identities are those that are most likely to affect our
decisions in life and work. Peripheral identities are those that are less important to
our current self-image and, therefore, less likely to be reflected in our decisions.

Take Federal Reserve Chairman Alan Greenspan as an example. His life and
decisions are currently dominated by his identities as an economist and public servant, his core identities. He also has peripheral identities such as those associated
with his family, with his religious beliefs, and with his hobbies, including tennis.
These identities play a small role in his analysis of economic conditions and his
decisions on interest rates. Self-schemas change over time and identities that were
once peripheral become more central. When Dr. Greenspan retires, he may find
that his peripheral identities become more central to his life.

Beyond these basic observations, I will not attempt to describe the self-schema
in detail. Instead, I will deal with the self-schema as it operates in decision making. I will focus on the self-schema in use, which is similar to the working self-

concept discussed by Markus and Nurius.[27] If you want to make an important life or business decision, thinking about the decision from the perspective of different identities can suggest alternatives. This view of the self as composed of separate social identities in potential conflict has a number of implications for business decision-making that have been outlined by management researchers Pratt and Foreman.[28] The self-schema and its component identities are represented in Figure 1.1.

When I use the term "identities," I am not talking simply about social roles. We can play roles without really believing in them, but we believe in our identities; we take them more seriously and hold them more deeply. Identities contain social roles, providing structure and meaning for them. Sociologists like Manuel Castells and Anthony Giddens have emphasized this distinction.[29]

Giddens and Castells suggest that individuals have traditionally had a single dominant identity that frames their other identities. However, modernity, and especially globalization, has fragmented our identities and left us uncertain about how they should be integrated. According to Castells, "For a given individual, there may be a plurality of identities. Yet, such a plurality is a source of stress and contradiction in both self-representation and social action."[30] Many people have discussed the problems caused by fragmentation of identities, but in this book I want to emphasize the potential benefits of multiple identities.

Figure 1.1
Identity-Based Self-Schema Used in Social Decision-Making

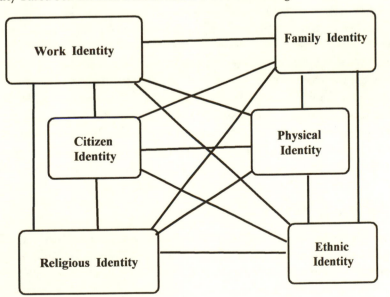

Figure 1.1 lists some of the important identities an individual might hold. For example, one's *work identity* might include the roles of supervisor, project team member, and subordinate. The *family identity* could include roles like parent, spouse, or child. The *citizen identity* would contain roles such as those of voter and member of a political party and political interest groups. A person's *ethnic identity* might involve participation in ethnic social functions and working to advance the social and economic status of his or her ethnic group. The *religious identity* could include the roles of worshiper and teacher. Finally, we all possess a *physical identity* that encompass our gender, age, and state of health.

We play different social roles depending on whether we are male or female, old or young, healthy or disabled. According to philosophers Lakoff and Johnson,[31] many of the abstract concepts that guide our decisions are grounded in simple physical metaphors. People of different ages and genders, having different physical experiences, may have different ways of understanding change.

Identities are evoked by the decisions we face in our daily lives. Making decisions and commitments further defines and shapes identities and the relationships between them. When there are many complex links between identities, more of an individual's knowledge and past experience can be brought to bear on current decisions.

Decisions that have implications for multiple identities are resolved through evaluation of the relationships between identities. For example, the decision to resign from your job may have implications for your work, family, and even citizen identities. You make the decision by considering the relative importance of the different identities, the ways identities support or undermine each other, and the possibility of meeting the demands of multiple identities simultaneously.

When we are faced with a decision, alternate identities within the self-schema generate views of the decision, establish evaluation criteria, and create preferences that often suggest different choices. The final choice is mediated by the self, which is essentially a structure or set of rules for deciding between alternative perspectives on a problem. However, this self is not a substantial, constant part of an individual. It is a construction developed by the individual over time in the context of past decisions and experiences. This construction directs the person's actions.

For those who find this topic especially interesting, as I do, I have included more detailed discussions of the readings I found most useful in Appendix B.

SELF-SCHEMAS AND SOCIAL BEHAVIOR

The self-schema begins to form in infancy and becomes a habitual way of perceiving all experience.[32] Through it, we make sense of our diverse desires and aspirations, organize our memories, monitor our behavior, and define our place in the social world.[33] The development and value of this self at various stages of human development was recognized by the pioneering child psychologist Jean Piaget. Researchers building on his work have argued that children develop an increasingly complex sense of self as they acquire an increasingly sophisticated view of the outside world.[34]

From an evolutionary perspective, the capacity for the development and use of a self-schema is important for the survival of human beings as a species of social animal. The rudiments of a self-schema can be found in higher primates. Primatologists Parker and Mitchell have argued that primates most closely related to human beings (orangutans, gorillas, and chimpanzees) exhibit a number of behaviors related to human self-awareness, including mirror self-recognition, imitation of novel facial and gestural behaviors, and symbol use. Primates that are less closely related to humans (cebus monkeys, macaques, and gibbons) exhibit tool use and a recognition of object permanence, as do humans and higher primates, but lack mirror self-recognition, facial and gestural imitation, and symbol use. This suggests that the rudiments of human self-awareness evolved relatively late in primates.

Parker has shown that rudimentary self-awareness forms the basis for what she calls apprenticeship in foraging and feeding. The ability to learn through apprenticeship allows an individual to acquire behaviors much more effectively and rapidly than he or she could through trial-and-error learning. The ability to compare your own actions to those of your teacher depends on an awareness of yourself as different from the teacher. Thus, self-awareness has survival value in social species and provides the foundation for social learning.[35]

Those in the discipline of cognitive anthropology, building on the early work of George Herbert Mead,[36] see the self as a mental construction that allows individuals to adapt to their culture.[37] For Mead, the most important aspect of the self is that it internalizes the attitudes of others in society in the form of "the generalized other." Individuals' self-concepts also influence their societies. Writing more recently, Cohen suggests that we must understand the consciousness of self in order to really understand human society.[38]

The belief in a consistent self is the basis for personal identity and it could be argued that individuals could not function in a socially acceptable way without it. Such conditions as multiple personality disorder and schizophrenia represent a breakdown in the consistent self-concept. Sass[39] notes that the symptoms of schizophrenia include "self-disturbances," which are breakdowns or distortions of the sense of self. Bandura[40] focuses on the value of "self-efficacy" (people's belief that they can control important outcomes in their lives) in dealing with difficulties. Wood and Bandura note that

Individuals with weakly held self-beliefs are highly vulnerable to change, and negative experiences readily reinstate their disbelief in their capabilities.[41]

Bandura and others would argue that the firm belief in a stable self is necessary for feelings of self-efficacy.

In summary, the self-schema has a variety of functions. These include: (1) providing a structure for organizing memory, (2) enabling individuals to persist in difficult courses of action, (3) enabling individuals to make consistent choices among conflicting desires or demands, (4) enabling individuals to learn by imitation or apprenticeship, (5) making individuals' actions more consistent with those with whom they interact, thereby, (6) making coordinated social action possible.

The self-schema, composed of multiple identities, also provides the framework for moral or ethical decision-making in business. For example, when executives at Mattel decide whether to market a toy that may pose safety concerns, they can frame the decision from the perspective of their work identity, in which case they would consider factors like costs, risks, profits, and the legal risks of unsafe products. Those with children, however, can also frame the decision in terms of their family identity, in which case they would think more seriously about the emotional impact on families of an injury caused by the toy.

When making ethical business decisions, people attempt to listen to the voice of conscience. In a self-schema with multiple identities, the voice of conscience may be the voice of an identity we had considered peripheral. Often, by considering the decision from the perspective of this peripheral identity, we can broaden our perspective. I believe the wise use of multiple identities allows us to make more moral decisions. At a minimum, it allows us to develop creative alternatives for dealing with moral dilemmas. Thus, the wise use of the self-schema may improve business ethics and corporate social responsibility.

Though the self-schema is useful, mindless identification with it leads to reification. By this process, the reality of the self becomes an unquestioned assumption upon which organizational identity is built. This process has implications for the self-schema, which are dealt with in the next section.

HOW WE IDENTIFY WITH ORGANIZATIONS

The previous discussion of the self-schema sets the stage for the treatment of identification. Recent articles by management scholars Ashforth and Kreiner,[42] Dutton, Dukerich, and Harquail[43] and psychologists Hogg and Terry[44] outline the essential features of the identification process. Dutton et al., focusing on the cognitive aspects of identification, view it as a process of self-definition or categorization. Organizational identification is one form of psychological attachment that occurs when members adopt the defining characteristics of the organization as defining characteristics for themselves.[45]

Pratt,[46] and Hogg and Terry,[47] have discussed the psychological processes by which individuals identify with organizations, groups, societies, and ideologies, grounding their work in social identity theory. Social identity theory suggests that individuals construct a self by assuming a number of role identities within social groups and arranging them hierarchically.[48] The self is enacted as these identities are evoked in social situations. As individuals continue to engage in behaviors demanded by the organization, their organizational identities are evoked and their identification with the organization increases.

Self-categorization theory developed from social identity theory and focuses on the way we categorize ourselves and others into social in groups and out groups.[49] The self-categorization process helps individuals define and differentiate their social identities by contrasting themselves, as part of the in group, with those in out groups. Unfortunately, it also reinforces the process of polarizing conflict between those identified with different groups. I will return to this topic in Chapter 3.

An important concept is the strength of identification. Definitions of this concept vary but the strength of identification has at least three dimensions: affective, behavioral, and cognitive.

In the affective dimension, those who are strongly identified with a point of view, group, or organization express its importance to them and are emotionally involved with it. Threats to the object of identification are met with concern, whereas things that enhance this object are valued. As William James[50] suggested, we consider the object of identification to be part of ourselves.

Mael and Ashforth[51] focus on this dimension in their research on identification within organizations. They have developed a scale to measure the strength of members' identification that contains the following items, which members answered on a scale ranging from "strongly agree" to "strongly disagree":

1. When someone criticizes my organization, it feels like a personal insult.
2. I am very interested in what others think of my organization.
3. When I talk about my organization, I usually say "we" rather than "they."
4. My organization's successes are my successes.
5. When someone praises my organization, it feels like a personal compliment.

Those who agree with these statements are considered to be strongly committed.

Second is the behavioral dimension. When we identify with an organization or an organizational role, we spend time in behaviors consistent with the role and rarely engage in behavior that is inconsistent with it. It is possible that a person strongly identifies with a role he or she is rarely able to enact because of the demands of other roles. For example, a teacher may have to spend a great deal of time on administrative chores and be unable to devote time to working with students, which is a more important part of his identity. Such dissonance does not persist, however. It is resolved through changing behavior or identity.

Third is the cognitive dimension. The stronger a person's organizational identi-fication, the more the member's self-concept is tied to his or her organizational membership.[52] When people are strongly identified, their identity affects the way they process information, make decisions, and view outsiders.

Identity specifies what is central, stable, and distinctive about a person. Individuals have multiple identities[53] tied to the groups and organizations with which they are affiliated, and they shift among identities as their role requirements demand.[54] For example, the same individual may possess the identities of a manager, soldier, church member, and family member.

Although it often appears as if our identities are stable and enduring, they do change over time but retain continuity.[55] In other words, they are stable but not fixed. We tend to overestimate the stability of our identities and our self-schema because of biases in memory that will be covered in Chapter 2.

OVERIDENTIFICATION AND SELF-SCHEMA IMPOVERISHMENT

A single, strongly held organizational identity may have benefits to the organi-zation and may also strengthen members' self-concepts.[56] For this reason, individuals often resist changing their identities to meet the demands of those who control organizations and societies because they believe their identities are real and that certain changes violate their integrity. Attempts by administrators to change or ma-nipulate organizational identity may provoke "cognitive opposition."[57] Historically, such resistance has been an important weapon against tyranny and totalitarianism. The American Revolution, for example, was led by people who regarded the sanc-tity of the self and the right to individual liberty as self-evident truths.

Strong identification may also have a dark side. It may lead to an excessive com-mitment to the organization that results in tyrannical leadership, weakening of so-cial identities other than those connected with the organization, unethical behavior on behalf of the organization, and an attempt to suppress diversity of views.[58] Dukerich and her colleagues[59] describe the phenomenon of *overidentifi-cation*, in which the self is diminished and whatever is unique about the individual is constrained by the connection with the organization. For example, strong iden-tification may cause administrators to narrow their range of vision by focusing on particular values, particular items of empirical knowledge, and particular alterna-tives that do not threaten their image of the organization.[60] Gioia and Thomas[61] have shown that during change, top management's identification with the orga-nization affects the way they interpret issues and their choice of strategies to deal with these issues.

One way to explain overidentification with organizations is to focus on people's desire to belong to social groups and conform to their rules. In other words, some of us identify too strongly with our organizations because we have an especially strong need for affiliation and structure. This explanation stresses motivational rather than cognitive factors and there are decades of research to support it.

Social psychologist Stanley Milgram, for example, conducted some rather cold-blooded experiments demonstrating that some people's need for conformity was so strong they would deliver what they believed to be fatal electric shocks to others simply because the experimenter told them to do so.[62] The psychoanalyst Erich Fromm, drawing on the work of Sigmund Freud, wrote about our desire to escape from the burdens of freedom into the psychological safety of conformity in a book aptly titled *Escape from Freedom*.[63] Some people, so-called authoritarians, were thought to be more susceptible to excessive identification and conformity pressure. Psychologist Milton Rokeach, in a book called *The Open and Closed Mind*,[64] described the authoritarian personality and developed a test to measure it.

While the motivational explanation gives a partial account of overidentification, I think there is more to the story. There is also cognitive explanation, which stresses that our mental capacities are limited and that we must have rules and shortcuts to simplify our decisions. We identify with organizations partly because identity gives us clear rules for our behavior and helps reduce the effort involved in thinking and deciding. The more strongly we identify with an organization, the more easily we can decide how to behave within our organizational role. Thus, we are all subject to overidentification, not just those of us who have strong needs for affiliation and conformity.

Under the influence of overidentification, individuals assume that organizational identity has a concrete reality, rather than recognizing that it is simply part of a schema that provides the basis for decisions and actions. Once they believe the organization is real, they begin to cling to it as a source of security. Consequently, threats to the organization will be met with defensive actions designed to preserve the organization's existence rather than being seen as exploratory actions aimed at discovering the ways the objectives of the organization might be served by other means. Sense making will be restricted,[65] biased views and assumptions will not be questioned, groups will be less effective at decision-making,[66] and the dark side of identification will emerge. As part of this process, individuals may revise their memories so that they conform to the views of the dominant coalition in the organization.

Members caught up in this type of identification would feel that any means was justified to achieve the end of organizational survival. Morgan discussed this type of identification in his description of organizations as "psychic prisons," which impose their power on individuals by constraining their world views.[67] Perrow calls this phenomenon institutionalization, in which,

[Organizations] take on a distinctive character; they become prized in and of themselves.... People build their lives around them, identify with them, become dependent on them.[68]

According to Colignon,[69] institutionalization is based on a kind of reification that obscures the agency of individuals and interest groups in organizational outcomes and leads to increased emphasis by the organization's leaders on defining the organization's ideology and ensuring commitment through cooptation of those who may challenge the leaders' definition of the ideology.

But the identification that drives organizational members to cling to the organization and to grasp chances to "save" it in the face of an external threat is based on more than simple reification. It is based on the lifelong habit of personal reification, a process related to what Colignon calls "individualist reification."[70] It is intuitively obvious to most people that organizations are not concrete entities and that errors in judgment result from assuming that they are. The phenomenon of personal reification, however, is more difficult since it involves the counterintuitive claim that our identities are no more real than the organizations we work for and study.

Strong identification may lead to impoverishment of the self-schema through a process McGregor and Little call *identity fixation*.[71] As the work identity expands in importance and the individual spends more time within it, other identities (for example, parent and community member) will shrink and the links between these identities and other elements of the self-schema will fade. Thus, the diversity and complexity of the links will be reduced. I will refer to this reduction as *self-schema impoverishment*. Figure 1.2 shows the difference between a rich and an impoverished self-schema. The self-schema impoverishment with which I am concerned involves the expansion of one identity to the point that it reduces the importance (and the time devoted to the maintenance of) other identities.

As one identity begins to dominate, self-serving attributions that bolster it become more common. Thus, there is less chance that different identities will suggest different attributions that conflict with each other. Individuals may retain multiple identities but still have impoverished self-schemas if they have few connections between these identities. This may happen when people "compartmentalize their lives." This results in a reduction in the number of links between identities in the self-schema.

When strongly identified individuals are faced with decisions, they are unlikely to consider the implications of the decisions from the perspective of multiple identities and they will be unlikely to give adequate attention to the views of those who are not associated with individuals' dominant organizational identities. Memories relevant to other identities are unlikely to be evoked. The information and beliefs evoked by the decision will be biased in ways that preserve the individual's self-image. The effect of this restriction of information processing will be to make the decision seem simpler than it actually is.

For examples of the effects of self-schema impoverishment on decision-making, we can consider the most current; for example, the case of Bill Gates of Microsoft who reacted very defensively to criticism of his company, or an older business ex-

Figure 1.2
Rich and Impoverished Self-Schemas

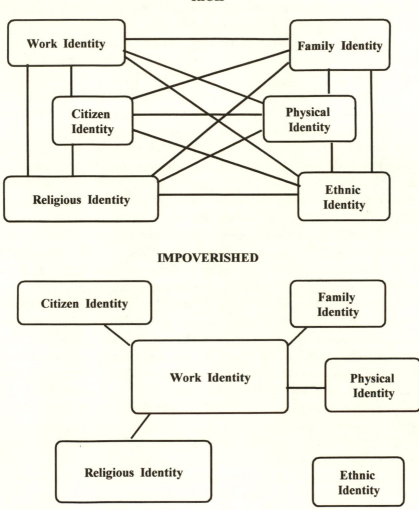

ample like Henry Ford's resistance to changing his company's identity, or a very old example like the Pharaoh's resistance to the exodus of the Israelites. What historian Barbara Tuchman calls the "March of Folly"[72] has continued throughout history so we would expect to find example of identity-based folly in all historical periods.

At Microsoft, the identity of the cofounder, Bill Gates, was intimately bound up with the company's identity. Gates, in clinging to his own identity as the leader of the world's leading software company, adopted a very bellicose and belligerent stance toward the Justice Department in its antitrust investigation. Bill Gates's own testimony, which seemed evasive in the extreme, showed this defensive reaction to threats to his and the company's identity. This may, in the long run, hurt Microsoft as the Justice Department takes a hard line in negotiating the remedy for the company's abuse of its monopoly power.

Earlier in this century, another pioneering innovator, Henry Ford, made a classic mistake when he clung to the identity of the automobile industry that he had created, an identity that involved standardized production and a focus on efficiency to lower cost. Though this approach enabled Ford to produce automobiles that many families could afford, it eventually became outdated as increasingly affluent consumers demanded variety in styling. Ford famously remarked in response to these demands, "they can have any color they want as long as it's black." This insistence on maintaining identity eventually cost Ford its dominance of the automobile industry.

According to the Bible, a very early example of identity-based resistance to change is found in Pharaoh's insistence on his identity as the leader of Egypt. Though Jehovah brought down ten plagues and, through Moses, told Pharaoh they could be stopped by letting the Israelites go, Pharaoh's "heart was hardened" and he refused until his own son was killed by the final plague. This suggests that Pharaoh's identity as a leader overwhelmed his identity as a parent.

When individuals engage in identification based on the unquestioned assumption of the reality of the self and the need to protect and enhance it, they cling to their organizational identity and act as though the environment in which they operate is consistent with it. Strong identification will also affect the way an individual responds to information that challenges the assumptions that form the basis for the identification. Individuals with impoverished self-schemas will have access to fewer of their own alternative points of view so they will be less likely to understand the value of conflicting information and respond positively to it.

Sadly, identity fixation and self-schema impoverishment become increasingly likely as individuals spend more time within their organizations. Juliet Schor, in her 1993 book *The Overworked Americans*[73] demonstrated that Americans devoted more of their time to work in the 1980s than they did in earlier decades. This trend may have accelerated in the 1990s.[74] The danger of fixation on work identities and self-schema impoverishment increases as we devote more of our lives to our organizational identities.

CONCLUSIONS

Strong identification with any social or organizational role will result in an impoverished self-schema that will make it less likely that all important perspectives are considered in decisions. It will make it hard for individuals to even

Figure 1.3
The Cycle of Self-Schema Impoverishment

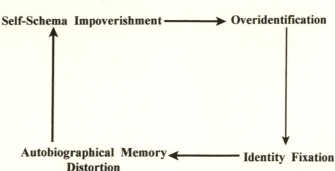

imagine alternative perspectives. An oversimplified self-schema will make individuals susceptible to a variety of biases and self-serving attributions and, ultimately, less able to adapt to change while retaining the benefits of self-schema stability. Figure 1.3 deals with the causes and consequences of an impoverished self-schema.

As individuals become overly committed to social or organizational identities they may developed identity fixation which, along with autobiographical memory distortion, to be discussed in Chapter 2, leads to self-schema impoverishment. Figure 1.3 is incomplete. It does not include group-level processes like groupthink that promote self-schema impoverishment or organizational-level phenomena like knowledge structures. I will discuss these matters in Chapters 3 and 4 and present a figure at the end of Chapter 4, which gives an expanded cycle showing how impoverishment occurs at both the individual and organizational level.

Chapter 2 deals with one of the most important processes by which reification or self-schema impoverishment is maintained, autobiographical memory distortion. If the self and the organization are cognitive constructions, how is it that we come to believe in their reality? Part of the answer has to do with the way we construct autobiographical memories.

Autobiographical memories help us to create and preserve a belief in a consistent and relatively unchanging self and still incorporate the modifications in self-definition required by new information from a changing environment. However, if we confuse our current view of ourselves with the absolute truth, we may be unable to recognize the possibility of other interpretations of the life events leading up to our current self-schema. In the same way, strong, mindless identification with an organization and its mission may lead to autobiographical revision.

NOTES

1. H. G. Wells, *The Island of Dr. Moreau, the Sleeper Awakes*, vol. 2 *The Works of H. G. Wells* (London: Classic Books, 1919), p. 315.

2. Hofstede's studies of employees of multinational corporations showed some systematic differences in attitudes about the self and the collective between some Asian countries and those in the United States, but also substantial differences between individual Asian and Western countries. See G. Hofstede, *Culture's Consequences* (Beverly Hills, CA: Sage Publications, 1980); and G. Hofstede, *Cultures in Organizations: Software of the Mind* (New York: McGraw-Hill, 1997). Wu found some support for the common view of Eastern self-concepts in his study of autobiographical statements by Chinese Confucians. See P. Wu, *The Confucian's Progress: Autobiographical Writings in Traditional China* (Princeton, NJ: Princeton University Press, 1990). Further, Ji, Schwarz, and Nisbett found evidence that Chinese and Americans may attend to and report different types of social behaviors in autobiographical memory. See L. Ji, N. Schwarz, and R. Nisbett, "Culture, autobiographical memory, and behavioral frequency reports," *Personality and Social Psychology Bulletin* 26(2000): 585–593. Choi, Nisbett, and Norenzayan summarized the growing body of evidence suggesting that East Asians may be more sensitive to the broad social context when explaining people's behavior while Westerners are more sensitive to individual traits. See I. Choi, R. Nisbett, and A. Norenzayan, "Causal attributions across cultures: Variation and universality," *Psychological Bulletin* 125(1999): 47–63. Recently, in the journal *Organization Science*, Joo Yup Kim and Sang Hoon Nam have discussed the importance of the concept of "face" in understanding organizational behavior in Asia 9(1998): 522–533.

3. *Wall Street Journal*, May 23, 2000, p. A4.

4. One way to summarize the many views expressed by thinkers in a wide range of Western and Eastern traditions is presented by philosopher Troy Organ, who identifies three fundamentally different and incompatible views of the nature of the self. These include independent substance theories, held by Plato and others, in which the self is conceived as a real entity that exists independently of the body and other elements of the person; dependent substance theories, held by evolutionists and philosophers influenced by Kant, that view the self as a real entity, the existence of which is dependent on the body, mind, or other elements of the person; and relationship theories, held by David Hume, John Dewey, and many Buddhists, which maintain that what we call the self is an emergent property of the interaction of other elements of the individual. See T. Organ, *Philosophy and the Self: East and West* (London: Associated University Press, 1987).

5. D. Parfit, *Reasons and Persons* (Oxford: Oxford University Press, 1984); K. Popper and J. Eccles, *The Self and Its Brain* (London: Routledge, 1977); G. Ryle, *The Concept of Mind* (Chicago: University of Chicago Press, 1949).

6. Ryle, ibid., pp. 11–24.

7. Many prominent contemporary philosophers express this view. See, for example, C. Taylor, *Sources of the Self* (Cambridge, MA: Harvard University Press, 1989), 53–62; T. Nagel, *The Possibility of Altruism* (Oxford: Oxford University Press, 1970); H. Noonan, *Personal Identity* (London: Routledge, 1989).

8. See Parfit, *Reasons and Persons*, pp. 274–280, and D. Hume, *A Treatise of Human Nature* (New York: Meridian Books, 1739/1962). The teachings of the Buddha have inspired much analysis and scholarship in the East and the West. A source for an English translation of the earliest transcriptions of the Buddha's own words is M. Walsh, *Thus Have I Heard: The Long Discourses of the Buddha* (London: Wisdom Publications, 1987).

9. See William James' amazingly insightful and thorough discussion of this topic in the chapters entitled "The Stream of Thought" and "The Consciousness of Self" in *The Principles of Psychology*, 1890/1950, especially pages 224–290 and 350–360.

10. J. Block, O. Flanagan, and G. Guzeldere, *The Nature of Consciousness: Philosophical Debates* (Boston: MIT Press, 1997). B. Baars, *In the Theater of Consciousness* (New York: Oxford University Press, 1997), 157–164.

11. I. Kant, *Critique of Pure Reason* (New York: Anchor Books, 1781/1966), 78.

12. Kant's points were elaborated upon by S. Hurley, *Consciousness in Action* (Cambridge, MA: Harvard University Press, 1998). See pp. 55–87, especially p. 68.

13. G. Ainslie, "Beyond Microeconomics: Conflict among Interests in a Multiple Self as a Determinant of Value," in *The Multiple Self*, ed. J. Elster (Cambridge: Cambridge University Press, 1986), pp. 133–176. A. Etzioni, *The Moral Dimension* (New York: Basic Books, 1988).

14. D. Dennett, *Consciousness Explained* (Boston: Little, Brown, & Co., 1991). C. Taylor, *Sources of the Self* (Cambridge, MA: Harvard University Press, 1989). D. Chalmers, *The Conscious Mind* (Oxford, England: Oxford University Press, 1996).

15. B. Skinner, *Science and Human Behavior* (New York: Free Press, 1953). See Chapter 18 entitled "The Self," pp. 283–297.

16. A. Pratkanis and A. Greenwald, "How shall the self be conceived?" *Journal for the Theory of Social Behavior* 15(1985): 311–329.

17. Dennett, *Consciousness Explained.* See the discussion of the Cartesian Theater on pp. 253–254. Appendix A gives further evidence that the awareness of self varies over time.

18. U. Neisser, *Memory Observed: Remembering in Natural Contexts* (San Francisco: Freeman, 1982); E. Engle and R. Lord, "Implicit theories, self-schemas, and leader-member exchange," *Academy of Management Journal* 40(1997): 988–1010.

19. Kant, ibid., p. 125.

20. U. Neisser, *Cognition and Reality* (San Francisco, CA: W. H. Freeman, 1976), p. 54.

21. D. Rumelhart, "Schemata: The Building Blocks of Cognition," in *Theoretical Issues in Reading Comprehension,* ed. K. Spiro, B. Bruce, and W. Brewer (Hillsdale, NJ: Erlbaum, 1980), 33–58. See p. 34.

22. H. Markus, J. Smith, and R. Moreland, "Role of the self-concept in the perception of others," *Journal of Personality and Social Psychology* 49(1985): 1494–1512; E. Engle and R. Lord, "Implicit theories, self-schemas, and leader-member exchange," *Academy of Management Journal* 40(1997): 988–1010.

23. Some management scholars have discussed identity submaps, which are similar to self-schemas. These provide the "point of self-reference needed to utilize other submaps." M. Fiol and A. Huff, "Maps for managers: Where are we? Where do we go from here?" *Journal of Management* 29(1992): 267–285; p. 278.

24. This cognitive view of the self is difficult to understand. I have found the following discussion by Pratkanis and Greenwald very useful, "How shall the self be conceived?" (*Journal for the Theory of Social Behavior* 15(1985): 311–329).

25. I. McGregor and B. Little, "Personal projects, happiness, and meaning: On doing well and being yourself," *Journal of Personality & Social Psychology* 74(1998): 494–512; see p. 496.

26. McGregor and Little, ibid.; H. Markus and P. Nurius, "Possible selves," *American Psychologist* 41(1986): 954–969, p. 957.

27. Markus and Nurius, ibid., 957–958.

28. M. Pratt and P. Foreman, "Clarifying managerial responses to multiple organizational identities," *Academy of Management Review* 25(2000): 18–42. See p. 19.

29. See M. Castells, *The Power of Identity* (Oxford: Blackwell Publishers, 1997); and A. Giddens, *Modernity and Self Identity: Self and Society in the Late Modern Age* (Stanford, CA: Stanford University Press, 1991).

30. See Castells, *The Power of Identity*, p. 6.

31. G. Lakoff and M. Johnson, *Philosophy in the Flesh: The Embodied Mind and Its Challenges to Western Thought* (New York: Basic Books, 1999).

32. E. Higgins, "The self digest: Self-knowledge serving self-regulatory functions," *Journal of Personality and Social Psychology* 71(1996): 1062–1083.

33. These statements are supported by a number of studies in social psychology. See for example, J. Campbell, P. Trapnell, S. Heine, I. Katz, L. Lavalle, and D. Lehman, "Self-concept clarity: Measurement, personality correlates, and cultural boundaries," *Journal of Personality & Social Psychology* 70(1996): 141–156; T. Strauman, "Stability within the self: A longitudinal study of the structural implications of self-discrepancy theory," *Journal of Personality & Social Psychology* 71(1996): 1142–1153; A. Greenwald and M. Banaji, "The self as a memory system: Powerful, but ordinary," *Journal of Personality & Social Psychology* 57(1989): 41–54.

34. Higgins, 1996, 1064–1065.

35. This point is also supported by A. Bandura, *Social Foundations of Thought and Action* (Englewood Cliffs, NJ: Prentice-Hall, 1986).

36. G. Mead, *Mind, Self, and Society from the Standpoint of a Social Behaviorist* (Chicago: University of Chicago Press, 1934).

37. A. Cohen, *Self Consciousness: An Alternative Anthropology of Identity* (London: Routledge, 1994); A. Cohen and N. Rapport (Eds.), *Questions of Consciousness* (London: Routledge, 1995); G. Erchak, *The Anthropology of Self and Behavior* (New Brunswick, NJ: Rutgers University Press, 1992); W. Goldschmidt, *The Human Career: The Self in the Symbolic World* (Cambridge, MA: Basil Blackwell, 1990).

38. A. Cohen, 1994, p. 22.

39. L. Sass, *Madness and Modernism* (New York: Basic Books, 1992).

40. A. Bandura, *Social Foundations of Thought and Action* (Englewood Cliffs, NJ: Prentice-Hall, 1986).

41. D. Wood and A. Bandura, "Social cognitive theory of organizational management," *Academy of Management Review* 13(1989): 361–368.

42. B. Ashforth and G. Kreiner, "How can you do it?": Dirty work and the challenge of constructing a positive identity," *Academy of Management Review* 24(1999): 413–432.

43. J. Dutton, J. Dukerich, and C. Harquail, "Organizational images and member identification," *Administrative Science Quarterly* 39(1994): 239–263.

44. M. Hogg and D. Terry, "Social identity and self-categorization processes in organizational contexts," *Academy of Management Review* 25(2000): 121–140.

45. Dutton et al., 1994, 242.

46. M. Pratt, "How Do People Identify with Organizations?" In *Identity in Organizations: Building Theory through Conversations*, ed. D. Whetten and P. Godfrey (Thousand Oaks, CA: Sage, 1998), 192–199.

47. Hogg and Terry, 2000.

48. H. Tajfel, "Social identity and intergroup behavior," *Social Sciences Information* 14(1974): 101–118; H. Tajfel and J. Turner, "The Social Identity Theory of Intergroup Behavior," in *The Psychology of Intergroup Relations*, ed. S. Worchel and W. Austin (Chicago: Nelson-Hall, 1986), 7–24.

49. Hogg and Terry, 2000, 123–126.

50. W. James, *The Principles of Psychology* (New York: Dover, 1890/1950).

51. F. Mael and B. Ashforth, "Loyal from day one: Biodata, organizational identification, and turnover among newcomers," *Personnel Psychology* 48(1995): 309–328.

52. Dutton et al., 1994, 242; S. Albert and D. Whetten, "Organizational Identity," in *Research in Organizational Behavior*, ed. L. Cummings and B. Staw (Greenwich, CT: JAI Press, 1985), 263–295.

53. M. Pratt and P. Foreman, "Clarifying managerial responses to multiple organizational identities," *Academy of Management Review* 25(2000): 18–42.

54. S. Scott and V. Lane, "A stakeholder approach to organizational identity," *Academy of Management Review* 25(2000): 43–62. See p. 49.

55. M. Banaji and D. Prentice, "The self in social contexts," *Annual Review of Psychology* 45(1994): 297–332.

56. J. Dutton, J. Dukerich, and C. Harquail, "Organizational images and member identification," *Administrative Science Quarterly* 39(1994): 239–263.

57. L. Gustafson and R. Reger, "Using organizational identity to achieve stability and change in high velocity environments," in *Proceedings of the National Academy of Management Meetings*, 464–468; p. 465. R. Reger, L. Gustafson, S. Demarie, and J. Mullane, "Reframing the organization: Why implementing total quality is easier said than done," *Academy of Management Review* 19(1994): 565–584. See p. 571.

58. B. Ashforth and F. Mael, "The dark side of organizational identification." Paper presented at the Academy of Management Meetings, Las Vegas; J. Dukerich, R. Kramer, and J. Parkes, "The Dark Side of Organizational Identification," in *Identity in Organizations*, ed. D. Whetten and D. Godfrey (Thousand Oaks, CA: Sage, 1998); G. Kunda, *Engineering Culture* (Philadelphia: Temple University Press, 1992); C. Schwenk, "The case for weaker leadership," *Business Strategy Review* 8(1997): 4–9.

59. Dukerich et al., 1998; 251–254.

60. Nobel laureate Herbert Simon discussed this narrowing of focus in his seminal book, *Administrative Behavior*, published in 1945 (New York: Free Press). See p. 210.

61. D. Gioia and J. Thomas, "Identity, image, and issue interpretation: Sensemaking during strategic change in academia," *Administrative Science Quarterly* 41(1996): 370–403.

62. Milgram discusses his research in S. Milgram, *Obedience to Authority: An Experimental View* (New York: Harper & Row, 1974).

63. See E. Fromm, *Escape from Freedom* (New York: Rinehart, 1941).

64. See M. Rokeach, *The Open and Closed Mind* (New York: Basic Books, 1960).

65. K. Weick. *Sensemaking in Organizations* (Thousand Oaks, CA: Sage, 1995).

66. I. Janis, *Crucial Decisions: Leadership in Policymaking and Crisis Management* (New York: Free Press, 1989).

67. G. Morgan, *Images of Organizations* (New York: Basic Books, 1986).

68. C. Perrow, *Complex Organizations: A Critical Essay* (New York: Random House, 1986), p. 167.

69. R. Colignon, "The holistic and individualistic views of organizations," *Theory & Society* 18(1989): 83–123. See pp. 95–98.

70. Colignon, 1989; pp. 100–105.

71. I. McGregor and B. Little, "Personal projects, happiness, and meaning: On doing well and being yourself," *Journal of Personality & Social Psychology* 74(1998): 494–512. See p. 502.

72. B. Tuchman, *The March of Folly* (New York: Knopf, 1984).

73. J. Schor, *The Overworked Americans* (New York: Basic Books, 1993).

74. J. Ciulla, *The Working Life* (New York: Times Books, 2000); B. Robertson, *There's No Place Like Work* (New York: Spence Publishing, 2000).

APPENDIX A:
THE ASSOCIATIONIST THEORY

[From *The Principles of Psychology*, first published by William James in 1890. The material included here is taken from the Dover edition of James's work (New York, 1950), pp. 350–353. The text has been edited for brevity and some footnotes have been omitted.]

Locke paved the way for [this theory] by the hypothesis he suggested of the same substance having two successive consciousnesses, or of the same consciousness being supported by more than one substance. He made his readers feel that the *important* unity of the Self was its verifiable and felt unity, and that a metaphysical or absolute unity would be insignificant, so long as a *consciousness* of diversity might be there.

Hume showed how great the consciousness of diversity actually was. In the famous chapter on Personal Identity, in his *Treatise on Human Nature*, he writes as follows:

There are some philosophers who imagine we are every moment intimately conscious of what we call our SELF; that we feel its existence and its continuance in existence, and are certain, beyond the evidence of a demonstration, both of its perfect identity and simplicity . . . Unluckily all these positive assertions are contrary to that very experience which is pleaded for them, nor have we any idea of Self, after the manner it is here explained . . . It must be some one impression that gives rise to every real idea . . . If any impression gives rise to the idea of Self, that impression must continue invariably the same through the whole course of our lives, since self is supposed to exist after that manner. But there is no impression constant and invariable. Pain and pleasure, grief and joy, passions and sensations succeed each other, and never all exist at the same time . . . For my part, when I enter most intimately into what I call *myself*, I always stumble on some particular perception or other of heat or cold, light or shade, love or hatred, pain or pleasure. I never can catch myself at any time without a perception, and never can observe anything but the perception. When my perceptions are removed for any time, as by sound sleep, so long am I insensible of myself, and may truly be said not to exist. And were all my perceptions removed by death, and could I neither think, nor feel, nor see, nor love, nor hate after the dissolution of my body, I should be entirely annihilated, nor do I conceive what is farther requisite to make me a perfect non-entity. If anyone, upon serious and unprejudiced reflection, thinks lie has a different notion of himself, I must confess I can reason no longer with him. All I can allow him is, that he may be in the right as well as I, and that we are essentially different in this particular. He may, perhaps, perceive something simple and continued which he calls himself; though I am certain there is no such principle in me.

But setting aside some metaphysicians of this kind, I may venture to affirm of the rest of mankind that they are *nothing but a bundle or collection of different perceptions,* which succeed each other with an inconceivable rapidity, and are in a perpetual flux and movement. Our eyes cannot turn in their sockets without varying our perceptions. Our thought is still more variable than our sight; and all our other Senses and faculties contribute to this change; nor is there any single power of the soul which remains unalterably the same, perhaps for one moment. The mind is a kind of theatre, where several perceptions successively make their appearance; pass, repass, glide away and mingle in an infinite variety of postures and situations. *There is properly no simplicity in it at one time, nor identity in different; whatever* natural propension we may have to imagine that simplicity and identity. The comparison of the theatre must not mislead us. They are the successive perceptions only, that constitute the mind; nor have we the most distant notion of the place where these scenes are represented, nor of the material of which it is composed.

But Hume, after doing this good piece of introspective work, proceeds to pour out the child with the bath, and to fly to as great an extreme as the substantialist philosophers. As they say the Self is nothing but Unity, unity abstract and absolute, so Hume says it is nothing but Diversity, diversity abstract and absolute; whereas in truth it is that mixture of unity and diversity which we ourselves have already found so easy to pick apart. We found among the objects of the stream certain feelings that hardly changed, that stood out warm and vivid in the past just as the present feeling does now; and we found the present feeling to be the centre of accretion to which, *de proche en proche*, these other feelings are, by *the judging Thought*, felt to cling. Hume says nothing of the judging Thought; and he denies this thread of resemblance, this core of sameness running through the ingredients of the Self, to exist even as a phenomenal thing. To him there is no *tertium quid* between pure unity and pure separateness. A succession of ideas connected by a close relation affords to an accurate view as perfect a notion of diversity as if there was *no Manner of relation at all.*

All our distinct perceptions are distinct existences, and the mind never perceives any real connection among distinct existences. Did our perceptions either inhere in something simple or individual, or *did the mind perceive some real connection* among them, there would be no difficulty in the case. For my part, I must plead the privilege of a sceptic and confess that this difficulty is too hard for my understanding. I pretend not, however, to pronounce it insuperable. Others, perhaps . . .may discover some hypothesis that will reconcile these contradictions. (Appendix to book I of Hume's *Treatise on Human Nature*.)

Hume is at bottom as much of a metaphysician as Thomas Aquinas. No wonder he can discover no 'hypothesis.' The unity of the parts of the stream is just as 'real' a connection as their diversity is a real separation; both connection and separation are ways in which the past thoughts appear to the present Thought; unlike each other in respect of date and certain qualities—this is the separation; alike in other qualities, and continuous in time—this is the connection. In demanding a more 'real' connection than this obvious and verifiable likeness and continuity, Hume seeks 'the world behind the looking-glass,' and gives a striking example of that Absolutism which is the great disease of philosophic Thought.

The chain of distinct existences into which Hume thus chopped up our 'stream' was adopted by all of his successors as a complete inventory of the facts. The associationist Philosophy was founded. Somehow, out of 'ideas,' each separate, each ignorant of its mates, but sticking together and calling each other up according to certain laws, all the higher forms of consciousness were to be explained, and among them the consciousness of our personal identity. [...]

APPENDIX B:
THE STREAM OF CONSCIOUSNESS

[From William James, *The Principles of Psychology*, 1890/1950, New York: Dover, pp. 237–239.]

Within each personal consciousness, thought is sensibly continuous.

I can only define 'continuous' as that which is without breach, crack, or division. I have already said that the breach from one mind to another is perhaps the greatest breach in nature. The only breaches that can well be conceived to occur within the limits of a single mind would either be *interruptions*, time-gaps during which the consciousness went out altogether to come into existence again at a later moment; or they would be breaks in the quality, or content, of the thought, so abrupt that the segment that followed had no connection whatever with the one that went before. The proposition that within each personal consciousness thought feels continuous, means two things:

1. That even where there is a time-gap the consciousness after it feels as if it belonged together with the consciousness before it, as another part of the same self;
2. That the changes from one moment to another in the quality of the consciousness are never absolutely abrupt.

The case of the time-gaps, as the simplest, shall be taken first. And first of all, a word about time-gaps of which the consciousness may not be itself aware.

[Earlier in this volume] we saw that such time-gaps existed, and that they might be more numerous than is usually supposed. If the consciousness is not aware of them, it cannot feel them as interruptions. In the unconsciousness produced by nitrous oxide and other anaesthetics, in that of epilepsy and fainting, the broken edges of the sentient life may meet and merge over the gap, much as the feelings of space of the opposite margins of the 'blind spot' meet and merge over that objective interruption to the sensitiveness of the eye. Such consciousness as this, whatever it be for the on looking psychologist, is for itself unbroken. It *feels* unbroken; a waking day of it is sensibly a unit as long as that day lasts, in the sense in which the hours themselves are units, as having all their parts next to each other, with no intrustheive alien substance between. To expect the consciousness to feel the interruptions of its objective continuity as gaps, would be like expecting the eye to feel a gap of silence because it does not hear, or the ear to feel a gap of darkness because it does not see. So much for the gaps that are unfelt.

With the felt gaps the case is different. On waking from sleep, we usually know that we have been unconscious, and we often have an accurate judgment of how long. The judgment here is certainly an inference from sensible signs, and its ease is due to long practice in the particular field. The result of it, however, is that the consciousness is, *for itself*, not what it was in the former case, but interrupted and continuous, in the mere time-sense of the words. But in the other sense of continuity, the sense of the parts being inwardly connected and belonging together because they are parts of a common whole, the consciousness remains sensibly continuous and one. What now is the common whole? The natural name for it is *myself, I,* or *me.*

When Paul and Peter wake up in the same bed, and recognize that they have been asleep, each one of them mentally reaches back and makes connection with but *one* of the two streams of thought which were broken by the sleeping hours. As the current of an electrode buried in the ground unerringly finds its way to its own similarly buried mate, across no matter how much intervening earth; so Peter's present instantly finds out Peter's past, and never by mistake knits itself on to that of Paul. Paul's thought in turn is as little liable to go astray. The past thought of Peter is appropriated by the present Peter alone. He may have a *knowledge,* and a correct one too, of what Paul's last drowsy states of mind were as [he] sank into sleep, but it is an entirely different sort of knowledge from that which [he] has of his own last states. He *remembers* his own states, whilst he only *conceives* Paul's. Remembrance is like direct feeling; its object is suffused with a warmth and intimacy to which no object of mere conception ever attains. This quality of warmth and intimacy and immediacy is what Peter's *present* thought also possesses for itself. So sure as this present is me, is mine, it says, so sure is anything else that comes with the same warmth and intimacy and immediacy, me and mine. What the qualities called warmth and intimacy may in themselves be will have to be matter for future consideration. But whatever past feelings appear with those qualities must be admitted to receive the greeting of the present mental state, to be owned by it, and accepted as belonging together with it in a common self. This community of self is what the time-gap cannot break in twain, and is why a present thought, although not ignorant of the time-gap, can still regard itself as continuous with certain chosen portions of the past.

Consciousness, then, does not appear to itself chopped up in bits. Such words as 'chain' or 'train' do not describe it fitly as it presents itself in the first instance. It is nothing jointed; it flows. A 'river' or a 'stream' are the metaphors by which it is most naturally described. *In talking of it hereafter, let us call it the stream of thought, of consciousness, or of subjective life.*[. . .]

APPENDIX C:
VARIATIONS IN THE AWARENESS OF SELF

If the self is a construction, it should be possible to recognize the construction and to step beyond it at times. I will use the research on mystical experiences to support my claim that people often do transcend the self and perceive phenomena without the intermediation of the self.

Before beginning this discussion, it is appropriate to define terms. The experiences that I wish to discuss are called by a variety of names, including ecstatic, religious, and transcendent experiences. There is a *very* long history of research dealing with these experiences. However, I will focus on the studies that have been conducted within the last twenty-five years.

Greeley (1975), Hay and Morisy (1978) and Thomas and Cooper (1978) examined responses to a question on religious experience included in national opinion polls in the United States and Great Britain. The question was worded in a slightly different manner in each survey but basically it asked respondents whether they had ever been aware of a presence or power that was different from their everyday selves. Roughly one third of those polled in all three studies in both countries responded affirmatively to this question. The questions were worded in such a way that a variety of interpretations are possible. Further, it is dangerous to build theory on the basis of a response to a single question. However, with these cautions in mind, it may be said that those responding positively seem to be indicating that they experienced some sort of alteration in their ordinary day-to-day working conceptions of self.

A later study using data from the 1988 General Social Survey showed that over 72 percent of respondents reported having experienced at least one of five mystical experiences at least once in their lives (Levin 1993). Though not all these experiences would involve an alteration of the working concept of self, this study supports the assertion that experiences of this kind are common.

If such experiences represent a pathological breakdown of a person's grasp on the "reality" of their selves, we would expect them to be negatively related to measures of psychological well-being. Indeed, the common view is that such experiences are most common among the poor and disempowered, who are most subject to psychological breakdowns. Analyses by Greeley (1975) and Hay and Morisy (1978), however, show that mystical experiences are more prevalent among those of *higher* socioeconomic status who report *greater* feelings of psychological well-being. This suggests that such experiences may actually represent beneficial insights into alternative views of reality or self.

Hood (1975), drawing on earlier work by James (1902) and Stace (1960), constructed a scale to measure mystical experience. Hood's work, and subsequent research (Caird 1988; Genia 1997; Reinert and Stifler 1993; Stifler, Greer, Sneck, and Dovenmuehle 1993), showed that experiences involving a breakdown of the common experience of a unitary discrete self are quite varied, suggesting that many factors may influence the reporting and interpretation of such experiences. Nonetheless, the reports of such experience, and the fact that they do not seem to be produced by psychosis or psychological breakdown, is consistent with the argument that the "self" is a cognitive construct that may be temporarily altered or suspended in ways that allow for new insights, which alter the self-concept in beneficial ways.

APPENDIX D:
THE CONSCIOUSNESS OF SELF

[From William James, *The Principles of Psychology*, 1890/1950, New York: Dover, chapter 10, pp. 291–298, 309–317.]

Let us begin with the Self in its widest acceptation, and follow it up to its most delicate and subtle form, advancing from the study of the empirical, as the Germans call it, to that of the pure, Ego.

THE EMPIRICAL SELF OR "ME"

The Empirical Self of each of us is all that he is tempted to call by the name of *me*. But it is clear that between what a man calls *me* and what he simply calls *mine* the line is difficult to draw. We feel and act about certain things that are ours very much as we feel and act about ourselves. Our fame, our children, the work of our hands, may be as dear to us as our bodies are, and arouse the same feelings and the same acts of reprisal if attacked. And our bodies themselves, are they simply ours, or are they us? Certainly men have been ready to disown their very bodies and to regard them as mere vestures, or even as prisons of clay from which they should some day be glad to escape.

We see then that we are dealing with a fluctuating material. The same object being sometimes treated as a part of me, at other times as simply mine, and then again as if I had nothing to do with it at all. In *its widest possible sense*, however, *a man's Self is the sum total of all that he CAN call his*, not only his body and his psychic powers, but his clothes and his house, his wife and children, his ancestors and friends, his reputation and works, his lands and horses, and yacht and bank-account. All these things give him the same emotions. If they wax and prosper, he feels triumphant; if they dwindle and die away, he feels cast down—not necessarily in the same degree for each thing, but in much the same way for all. Understanding the Self in this widest sense, we may begin by dividing the history of it into three parts, relating respectively to—(1) Its constituents; (2) The feelings and emotions they arouse—*Self-feelings*; (3) The actions to which they prompt—*Self-seeking and Self-preservation*.

1. The constituents of the Self may be divided into two classes, those which make up respectively—(a) The material Self; (b) The social Self; (c) The spiritual Self; and (d) The pure Ego.

(a) The body is the innermost part of *the material Self* in each of us; and certain parts of the body seem more intimately ours than the rest. The clothes come next. The old saying that the human person is composed of three parts—soul, body and clothes—is more than a joke. We so appropriate our clothes and identify ourselves with them that there are few of us who, if asked to choose between having a beautiful body clad in raiment perpetually shabby and unclean, and having an ugly and blemished form always spotlessly attired, would not hesitate a moment before making a decisive reply. Next, our immediate family is a part of ourselves. Our father and mother, our wife and babes, are bone of our bone and flesh of our flesh. When they die, a part of our very selves is gone. If they do anything wrong, it is our shame. If they are insulted, our anger flashes forth as readily as if we stood in their place. Our home comes next. Its scenes are part of our life; its aspects awaken the tenderest feelings of affection; and we do not easily forgive the stranger who, in visiting it, finds fault with its arrangements or treats it with contempt. All these different things are the objects of instinctive preferences coupled with the most important practical interests of life. We all have a blind impulse to watch over our body, to deck it with clothing of an ornamental sort, to cherish parents, wife and babes, and to find for ourselves a home of our own which we may live in and 'improve.'

An equally instinctive impulse drives us to collect property; and the collections thus made become, with different degrees of intimacy, parts of our empirical selves. The parts of our wealth most intimately ours are those which are saturated with our labor. There are few men who would not feel personally annihilated if a life-long construction of their hands or brains—say an entomological collection or an extensive work in manuscript—were suddenly swept away. The miser feels similarly towards his gold, and although it is true that a part of our depression at the loss of possessions is due to our feeling that we must now go without certain goods that we expected the possessions to bring in their train, yet in every case there remains, over and above this, a sense of the shrinkage of our personality, a partial conversion of ourselves to nothingness, which is a psychological phenomenon by itself. We are all at once assimilated to the tramps and poor devils whom we so despise, and at the same time removed farther than ever away from the happy sons of earth who lord it over land and sea and men in the full-blown lustihood that wealth and power can give, and before whom, stiffen ourselves as we will by appealing to antisnobbish first principles, we cannot escape an emotion, open or sneaking, of respect and dread.

(b) *A man's Social Self* is the recognition which he gets from his mates. We are not only gregarious animals, liking to be in sight of our fellows, but we have an innate propensity to get ourselves noticed, and noticed favorably, by our kind. No more fiendish punishment could be devised, were such a thing physically possible, than that one should be turned loose in society and remain absolutely unnoticed by all the members thereof. If no one turned round when we entered, answered when we spoke, or minded what we did, but if every person we met 'cut us dead,' and acted as if we were non-existing things, a kind of rage and impotent despair would ere long well up in us, from which the cruellest bodily tortures would be a relief; for these would make us feel that, however bad might be our plight, we had not sunk to such a depth as to be unworthy of attention at all. Properly speaking, *a man has as many social selves as there are individuals who recognize him* and carry an image of him in their mind. To wound any one of these his images is to wound him. But as the individuals who carry the images fall naturally into classes, we may practically say that he has as many different social selves as there are distinct *groups* of persons about whose opinion he cares. He generally shows a different side of himself to each of these different groups. Many a youth who is demure enough before his parents and teachers, swears and swaggers like a pirate among his 'tough' young friends. We do not show ourselves to our children as to our club companions, to our customers as to the laborers we employ, to our own masters and employers as to our intimate friends. From this there results what practically is a division of the man into several selves; and this may be a discordant splitting, as where one is afraid to let one set of his acquaintances know him as he is elsewhere; or it may be a perfectly harmonious division of labor, as where one tender to his children is stern to the soldiers or prisoners under his command.

The most peculiar social self which one is apt to have is in the mind of the person one is in love with. The good or bad fortunes of this self cause the most intense elation and dejection—unreasonable enough as measured by every other standard than that of the organic feeling of the individual. To his own consciousness he is not, so long as this particular social self fails to get recognition, and when it is recognized his contentment passes all bounds.

A man's *fame*, good or bad, and his *honor* or dishonor, are names for one of his social selves. The particular social self of a man called his honor is usually the result of one of those splittings of which we have spoken. It is his image in the eyes of his own 'set,' which exalts or condemns him as he conforms or not to certain requirements that may not be made of one in another walk of life. Thus a layman may abandon a city infected with cholera; but a priest or a doctor would think such an act incompatible with his honor. A soldier's honor requires him to fight or to die under circumstances where another man can apologize or run away with no stain upon his social self. A judge, a statesman, are in like manner debarred by the honor of their cloth from entering into pecuniary relations perfectly honorable to persons in private life. Nothing is commoner than to hear people discriminate between their different selves of this sort: "As a man I pity you, but as an official I must show you no mercy; as a politician I regard him as an ally, but as a moralist I loathe him;" etc., etc. What may be called 'club-opinion' is one of the very strongest forces in life.* The thief must not steal from other thieves; the gambler must pay his gambling-debts, though he pay no other debts in the world. The code of honor of fashionable society has throughout history been full of permissions as well as of vetoes, the only reason for following either of which is that so we best serve one of our social selves. You must not lie in general, but you may lie as much as you please if asked about your relations with a lady; you must accept a challenge from an equal, but if challenged by an inferior you may laugh him to scorn: these are examples of what is meant.

(c) By the *Spiritual Self,* so far as it belongs to the Empirical Me, I mean a man's inner or subjective being, his psychic faculties or dispositions, taken concretely; not the bare principle of personal Unity, or 'pure' Ego, which remains still to be discussed. These psychic dispositions are the most enduring and intimate part of the self, that which we most verily seem to be. We take a purer self-satisfaction when we think of our ability to argue and discriminate, of our moral sensibility and conscience, of our indomitable will, than when we survey any of our other possessions. Only when these are altered is a man said to be *alienatus a se.*

Now this spiritual self may be considered in various ways. We may divide it into faculties, as just instanced, isolating them one from another, and identifying ourselves with either in turn. This is an *abstract* way of dealing with consciousness, in which, as it actually presents itself, a plurality of such faculties are always to be simultaneously found; or we may insist on a concrete view, and then the spiritual self in us will be either the entire stream of our personal consciousness, or the present 'segment' or 'section' of that stream, according as we take a broader or a narrower view—both the stream and the section being concrete existences in time, and each being a unity after its own peculiar kind. But whether we take it abstractly or concretely, our considering the spiritual self at all is a reflective process, is the result

---

*"He who imagines commendation and disgrace not to be strong motives on men . . . seems little skilled in the nature and history of mankind; the greatest part whereof he shall find to govern themselves chiefly, If not solely, by this law of fashion; and so they do that which keeps them in reputation with their company, little regard the laws of God or the magistrate. The penalties that attend the breach of God's laws some, nay, most, men seldom seriously reflect on; and amongst those that do, many, whilst they break the laws, entertain thoughts of future reconciliation, and making their peace for such breaches: and as to the punishments due from the laws of the commonwealth, they frequently flatter themselves with the hope of impunity. But no man escapes the punishment of their censure and dislike who offends against the fashion and opinion of the company he keeps, and would recommend himself to. Nor is there one in ten thousand who is stiff and insensible enough to bear up under the constant dislike and condemnation of his own club. He must be of a strange and unusual constitution who can content himself to live in constant disgrace and disrepute with his own particular society. Solitude many men have sought end been reconciled to; but nobody that has the least thought or sense of a man about him can live in society under the constant dislike and Ill opinion of his familiars and those he converses with. This is a burden too heavy for human sufferance: and he must be made up of irreconcilable contradictions who can take pleasure in company and yet be insensible of contempt and disgrace from his companions" (Locke's Essay, book ii. ch. xxviii. § 12).

of our abandoning the outward-looking point of view, and of our having become able to think of subjectivity as such, *to think ourselves as thinkers.*

This attention to thought as such, and the identification of ourselves with it rather than with any of the objects which it reveals, is a momentous and in some respects a rather mysterious operation, of which we need here only say that as a matter of fact it exists; and that in everyone, at an early age, the distinction between thought as such, and what it is 'of ' or 'about,' has become familiar to the mind. The deeper grounds for this discrimination may possibly be hard to find; but superficial grounds are plenty and near at hand. Almost anyone will tell us that thought is a different sort of existence from things, because many sorts of thought are of no things—e.g., pleasures, pains, and emotions; others are of non-existent things—errors and fictions; others again of existent things, but in a form that is symbolic and does not resemble them—abstract ideas and concepts; whilst in the thoughts that do resemble the things they are 'of ' (percepts, sensations), we can feel, alongside of the thing known, the thought of it going on as an altogether separate act and operation in the mind.

Now this subjective life of ours, distinguished as such so clearly from the objects known by its means, may, as aforesaid, be taken by us in a concrete or in an abstract way. Of the concrete way I will say nothing just now, except that the actual 'section' of the stream will ere long, in our discussion of the nature of the principle of *unity* in consciousness, play a very important part. The abstract way claims our attention first. If the stream as a whole is identified with the Self far more than any outward thing, a *certain portion of the stream abstracted from the rest* is so identified in an altogether peculiar degree, and is felt by all men as a sort of innermost centre within the circle, of sanctuary within the citadel, constituted by the subjective life as a whole. Compared with this element of the stream, the other parts, even of the subjective life, seem transient external possessions, of which each in turn can be disowned, whilst that which disowns them remains. Now, *what is this self of all the other selves?*

Probably all men would describe it in much the same way up to a certain point. They would call it the *active* element in all consciousness; saying that whatever qualities a man's feelings may possess, or whatever content his thought may include, there is a spiritual something in him which seems to *go out* to meet these qualities and contents, whilst they seem to *come in* to be received by it. It is what welcomes or rejects. It presides over the perception of sensations, and by giving or withholding its assent it influences the movements they tend to arouse. It is the home of interest—not the pleasant or the painful, not even pleasure or pain, as such, but that within us to which pleasure and pain, the pleasant and the painful, speak. It is the source of effort and attention, and the place from which appear to emanate the fiats of the will. A psychologist who should reflect upon it in his own person could hardly help, I should think, connecting it more or less vaguely with the process by which ideas or incoming sensations are 'reflected' or pass over into outward acts. Not necessarily that it should *be* this process or the mere feeling of this process, but that it should be in some close way *related* to this process; for it plays a part analogous to it in the psychic life, being a sort of junction at which sensory ideas terminate and from which motor ideas proceed, and forming a kind of link between the two. Being more incessantly there than any other single element of the mental life, the other elements end by seeming to accrete round it and to belong to it. It become opposed to them as the permanent is opposed to the changing and inconstant.

One may, I think, without fear of being upset by any future Galtonian circulars, believe that all men must single out from the rest of what they call themselves some central principle of which each would recognize the foregoing to be a fair general description—accurate enough, at any rate, to denote what is meant, and keep it unconfused with other things. The moment, however, they came to closer quarters with it, trying to define more accurately its precise nature, we should find opinions beginning to diverge. Some would say that it is a simple active substance, the soul, of which they are thus conscious; others, that it is nothing but a fiction, the imaginary being denoted by the pronoun I; and between these extremes of opinion all sorts of intermediaries would be found.

RIVALRY AND CONFLICT OF THE DIFFERENT SELVES

With most objects of desire, physical nature restricts our choice to but one of many represented goods, and even so it is here. I am often confronted by the necessity of standing by one of my empirical selves and relinquishing the rest. Not that I would not, if I could, be both handsome and fat and well dressed, and a great athlete, and make a million a year, be a wit, a *bon-vivant,* and a lady-killer, as well as a philosopher; a philanthropist, statesman, warrior, and African explorer, as well as a 'tone-poet' and saint. But the thing is simply impossible. The millionaire's work would run counter to the saint's; the *bon-vivant* and the philanthropist would trip each other up; the philosopher and the lady-killer could not well keep house in the same tenement of clay. Such different characters may conceivably at the outset of life be alike *possible* to a man. But to make any one of them actual, the rest must more or less be suppressed. So the seeker of his truest, strongest, deepest self must review the list carefully, and pick out the one on which to stake his salvation. All other selves thereupon become unreal, but the fortunes of this self are real. Its failures are real failures, its triumphs real triumphs, carrying shame and gladness with them. . . . Our thought, incessantly deciding, among many things of a kind, which ones for it shall be realities, here chooses one of many possible selves or characters, and forthwith reckons it no shame to fail in any of those not adopted expressly as its own. [. . .]

A tolerably unanimous opinion ranges the different selves of which a man may be 'seized and possessed' and the consequent different orders of his self-regard, in an *hierarchical scale with the bodily Self at the bottom, the spiritual Self at the top, and the extracorporeal material selves and the various social selves between.* Our merely natural self-seeking would lead us to aggrandize all these selves; we give up deliberately only those among them which we find we cannot keep. Our unselfishness is thus apt to be a 'virtue of necessity'; and it is not without all show of reason that cynics quote the fable of the fox and the grapes in describing our progress therein. But this is the moral education of the race; and if we agree in the result that on the whole the selves we can keep are the intrinsically best, we need not complain of being led to the knowledge of their superior worth in such a tortuous way.

Of course this is not the only way in which we learn to subordinate our lower selves to our higher. A direct ethical judgment unquestionably also plays its part, and last, not least, we apply to our own persons judgments originally called forth by the acts of others. It is one of the strangest laws of our nature that many things which we are well satisfied with in ourselves disgust us when seen in others. With another man's bodily 'hoggishness' hardly anyone has any sympathy;—almost as little with his cupidity, his social vanity and eagerness, his jealousy, his despotism, and his pride. Left absolutely to myself I should probably allow all these spontaneous tendencies to luxuriate in me unchecked, and it would be long before I formed a distinct notion of the order of their subordination. But having constantly to pass judgment on my associates, I come ere long to see, as Herr Horwicz says, my own lusts in the mirror of the lusts of others, and to *think* about them in a very different way from that in which I simply feel. Of course, the moral generalities which from childhood have been instilled into me accelerate enormously the advent of this reflective judgment on myself.

So it comes to pass that, as aforesaid, men have arranged the various selves which they may seek in an hierarchical scale according to their worth. A certain amount of bodily selfishness is required as a basis for all the other selves. But too much sensuality is despised, or at best condoned on account of the other qualities of the individual. The wider material selves are regarded as higher than the immediate body. He is esteemed a poor creature who is unable to forego a little meat and drink and warmth and sleep for the sake of getting on in the world. The social self as a whole, again, ranks higher than the material self as a whole. We must care more for our honor, our friends, our human ties, than for a sound skin or wealth. And the spiritual self is so supremely precious that, rather than lose it, a man ought to be willing to give up friends and good fame, and property, and life itself.

In each kind of self, material, social, and spiritual, men distinguish between the immediate and actual, and the remote and potential, between the narrower and the wider view, to the detriment of the former and advantage of the latter. One must forego a present bodily enjoyment for the sake of one's general health; one must abandon the dollar in the hand for the sake of the hundred dollars to come; one must make an enemy of his present interlocutor if thereby one makes friends of a more valued circle; one must go without learning and grace, and wit, the better to compass one's soul's salvation.

Of all these wider, more potential selves, *the potential social self is* the most interesting, by reason of certain apparent paradoxes to which it leads in conduct, and by reason of its connection with our moral and religious life. When for motives of honorable conscience I brave the condemnation of my own family, club, and 'set'; when, as a Protestant, I turn catholic; as a catholic, freethinker; as a 'regular practitioner,' homoeopath, or what not, I am always inwardly strengthened in my course and steeled against the loss of my actual social self by the thought of other and better *possible* social judges than those whose verdict goes against me now. The ideal social self which I thus seek in appealing to their decision may be very remote: it may be represented as barely possible. I may not hope for its realization during my lifetime; I may even expect the future generations, which would approve me if they knew me, to know nothing about me when I am dead and gone. Yet still the emotion that beckons me on is indubitably the pursuit of an ideal social self, of a self that is at least worthy of approving recognition by the highest *possible* judging companion, if such companion there be.* This self is the true, the intimate, the ultimate, the permanent Me which I seek. This judge is God, the Absolute Mind, the 'Great Companion.' We hear, in these days of scientific enlightenment, a great deal of discussion about the efficacy of prayer; and many reasons are given us why we should not pray, whilst others are given us why we should. But in all this very little is said of the reason why we do pray, which is simply that we cannot *help* praying. It seems probable that, in spite of all that 'science' may do to the contrary, men will continue to pray to the end of time, unless their mental nature changes in a manner which nothing we know should lead us to expect. The impulse to pray is a necessary consequence of the fact that whilst the innermost of the empirical selves of a man is a Self of the social sort, it yet can find its only adequate *Socius* in an ideal world.

All progress in the social Self is the substitution of higher tribunals for lower; this ideal tribunal is the highest; and most men, either continually or occasionally, carry a reference to it in their breast. The humblest outcast on this earth can feel himself to be real and valid by means of this higher recognition. And, on the other

---

*It must be observed that the qualities of the Self thus ideally constituted are all qualities approved by my actual fellows in the first instance; and that my reason for now appealing from their verdict to that of the ideal judge lies in some outward peculiarity of the immediate case. What once was admired in me as courage has now become in the eyes of men 'impertinence'; what was fortitude is obstinacy; what was fidelity is now fanaticism. The ideal judge alone, I now believe, can read my qualities, my willingnesses, my powers, for what they truly are. My fellows, misled by interest and prejudice, have gone astray.

hand, for most of us, a world with no such inner refuge when the outer social self failed and dropped from us would be the abyss of horror. I say 'for most of us,' because it is probable that individuals differ a good deal in the degree in which they are haunted by this sense of an ideal spectator. It is a much more essential part of the consciousness of some men than of others. Those who have the most of it are possibly the most religious men. But I am sure that even those who say they are altogether without it deceive themselves, and really have it in some degree. Only a non-gregarious animal could be completely without it. Probably no one can make sacrifices for 'right,' without to some degree personifying the principle of right for which the sacrifice is made, and expecting thanks from it. *Complete* social unselfishness, in other words, can hardly exist; *complete* social suicide hardly occur to a man's mind. Even such texts as Job's, "Though He slay me yet will I trust Him," or Marcus Aurelius's, "If gods hate me and my children, there is a reason for it," can least of all be cited to prove the contrary. For beyond all doubt Job reveled in the thought of Jehovah's recognition of the worship after the slaying should have been done; and the Roman emperor felt sure the Absolute Reason would not be all indifferent to his acquiescence in the gods' dislike. The old test of piety, "Are you willing to be damned for the glory of God?" was probably never answered in the affirmative except by those who felt sure in their heart of hearts that God would 'credit' them with their willingness, and set more store by them thus than if in His unfathomable scheme. He had not damned them at all.

All this about the impossibility of suicide is said on the supposition of *positive* motives. When possessed by the emotion of *fear*, however, we are in a *negative* state of mind; that is, our desire is limited to the mere banishing of something, without regard to what shall take its place. In this state of mind there can unquestionably be genuine thoughts, and genuine acts, of suicide, spiritual and social, as well as bodily. Anything, *anything*, at such times, so as to escape and not to be! But such conditions of suicidal frenzy are pathological in their nature and run dead against everything that is regular in the life of the Self in man. [...]

SUMMARY

To sum up now this long chapter. The consciousness of Self involves a stream of thought, each part of which as 'I' can 1) remember those which went before, and know the things they knew; and 2) emphasize and care paramountly for certain one among them as '*me*,' and *appropriate to these* the rest. The nucleus of the '*me*' is always the bodily existence felt to be present at the time. Whatever remembered-past-feelings that *resemble* this present feeling are deemed to belong to the same *me* with it. Whatever other things are perceived to be *associated* with this feeling are deemed to form part of that me's *experience*; and of them certain ones (which fluctuate more or less) are reckoned to be themselves *constituents of* the me in a larger sense—such as the clothes, the material possessions, the friends, the honors and esteem which the person receives or may receive. This me is an empirical aggregate of things objectively known. The *I* which knows them cannot itself be an *aggregate,* neither for psychological purposes need it be considered to be an unchanging metaphysical entity like the Soul, or a principle like the pure Ego, viewed as 'out of time.' It is a *Thought,* at each moment different from that of the last moment, but *appropriative* of the latter, together with all that the latter called its own. All the experiential facts find their place in this description, unincumbered with any hypothesis save that of the existence of passing thoughts or states of mind. The same brain may subserve many conscious selves, either alternate or coexisting; but by what modifications in its action, or whether ultra-cerebral conditions may intervene, are questions which cannot now be answered.

If anyone urge that I assign no *reason* why the successive passing thoughts should inherit each other's possessions, or why they and the brain-states should be functions (in the mathematical sense) of each other, I reply that the reason, if there be any, must lie where all real reasons lie, in the total sense or meaning of the world. If there be such a meaning, or any approach to it (as we are bound to trust there is), it alone can make clear to us why such finite human streams of thought are called into existence in such functional dependence upon brains. This is as much as to say that the special natural science of *psychology* must stop with the mere functional formula. *If the passing thought be the directly verifiable existent which no school has hitherto doubted it to be, then that thought is itself the thinker,* and psychology need not look beyond. The only pathway that I can discover for bringing in a more transcendental thinker would be to *deny* that we have any *direct* knowledge of the thought as such. The latter's existence would then be reduced to a postulate, an assertion that there *must be* a *knower* correlative to all this *known;* and the problem *who that knower is* would have become a metaphysical problem. With the question once stated in these terms, the spiritualist and transcendentalist solutions must be considered *as prima facie* on a par with our own psychological one, and discussed impartially. But that carries us beyond the psychological or naturalistic point of view. [. . .]

APPENDIX E:
HOW SHALL THE SELF BE CONCEIVED?

[From Anthony R. Pratkanis and Anthony G. Greenwald, *Journal for the Theory of Social Behavior*, 15(1985): pp. 311–329.]

The modern history of psychological interest in the self has been marked by two curious phenomena. First, self theorists have shown a fondness for metaphor (see Smith 1984). The self has been likened to a stream (James 1890), a mirror or "looking glass self" (Cooley 1902/1964 and Mead 1934), an acorn becoming an oak (Maslow 1968), an actor on stage (Goffman 1959), a central region of a larger structure (Allport 1961; Claparede 1911/1951; Combs and Snygg 1949/1959; Koffka 1935; Lewin 1936), and, quite recently, a DNA molecule that contains instructions for its own replication and Godel's theorem that asserts its own unprovability (Hofstadter 1979).

Second, the self has periodically become "sidetracked and lost to view" (Allport 1943, p. 451) by academic psychology. The self was held in high esteem during the first decades of psychology's existence as an academic discipline, at the turn of the 20th century. William James devoted 111 pages of his *Principles of Psychology* to the self and Mary Calkins (1912, 1916, 1919) periodically reviewed the self literature. However, the self was subsequently ignored until Allport (1943) reviewed evidence to support the proposition that "ego-involvement, or its absence, makes a critical difference in human behaviour" (p. 459). After the mid-century resurgence of interest, the self returned to academic slumber until about a decade ago. Since about 1975, there has been a strong renewal of interest in the self, including a surge of research activity (see Greenwald and Pratkanis 1984, for a review) and the appearance of several anthologies (e.g., Schlenker 1985; Suls 1982; Suls and Greenwald 1983; Wegner and Wallacher 1980).

Perhaps the metaphors and the fluctuations of interest in the self are related. In part, the metaphors are simply confusing—a point well made by Hilgard (1949), who used the mirror metaphor in likening self-awareness to being "between the two mirrors of a barber-shop, with each image viewing each other one, so that as the self takes a look at itself taking a look at itself, it soon gets all confused as to the self that is doing the looking and the self which is being looked at" (p. 377). Perhaps more importantly, the various self metaphors have not been suggestive of effective research procedures (see Greenwald and Pratkanis 1984, pp. 165–166).

Will interest in the self again soon fade? In the present authors' opinion history is not about to repeat itself. Perhaps the chief indication of a difference from the past is that recent research attention to the self has been accompanied by the development of a new metaphor—the self as an organization of knowledge (Epstein 1973; Greenwald 1980; Loevinger 1976). Further, the organization-of-knowledge metaphor has apparently been successful in guiding the generation of several useful research procedures. In this article we review the recent wave of research on the self, and then discuss the metaphor of the self as an organization of knowledge. Our review leads to a conception of the self as a complex, person-specific, central, attitudinal schema (Greenwald and Pratkanis 1984). We conclude by relating this new conception of the self to the major traditional concerns and questions about the nature of the self.

I. NEW RESEARCH TECHNIQUES FOR THE STUDY OF THE SELF

This section reviews some of the techniques that have been developed in the current wave of research on the self. Each of the seven programs of research that we consider provides a different approach to the assessment of individual differences that have been conceptually related to the self. We start with individual difference measures based on familiar paper and pencil self-report procedures, and progress to ones that make use of procedures and concepts evolved in recent cognitive psychological research (cf. Srull 1984).

Self-Monitoring

Snyder (1974; Snyder and Campbell 1982) identified the high self-monitoring person as one who attends to interpersonal cues and is able flexibly to construct a personal identity consistent with the requirements of a social situation. In contrast, the low self-monitor is relatively inattentive to interpersonal cues and constructs a consistent ("principled") identity that varies little across situations. Consistent with this reasoning, Snyder's (1974) Self-monitoring Scale has been used to predict individual differences in social behavior. For example, high self-monitors (compared to low self-monitors) demonstrate lower attitude-behavior consistency, offer more situational attributions for their behavior, and are more attentive and sensitive to their social environments (Snyder and Campbell 1982).

Public and Private Self-Consciousness

Fenigstein, Scheier, and Buss (1975) defined the public self as consisting of observable self-produced stimuli, such as physique, clothing, grooming, facial expression and speech. The private self, on the other hand, consists of self-produced stimuli that are not publicly observable, such as internal bodily sensations, emotional feelings, thoughts, and self-evaluation. The Self-Consciousness Scale (Fenigstein et al. 1975) provides measures of individual differences in consciousness of these two aspects, and has been successful in predicting individual differences in social behavior (see Carver and Scheier 1981; Scheier and Carver 1983 for reviews). For example, those high in public self-consciousness have been shown to be more sensitive to rejection and to moderate opinion more in anticipation of a future discussion. Those high in private self-consciousness are better able to resist group pressure and the persuasive pressure of a counter-attitudinal role-playing procedure. Scheier and Carver (1983) note that individual differences in social behavior associated with public and private self-consciousness are paralleled by ones that occur in response to situational manipulations of public self-awareness (for example, a camera pointed at the subject) and private self-awareness (for example, having the subject face a mirror), respectively.

Self-Verification, Symbolic Self-Completion, and Self-Esteem Maintenance

Several researchers have demonstrated that maintenance of the self-concept is a motivating force that guides both social behavior and judgment. This principle has roots in earlier work on cognitive dissonance theory (Aronson 1968; Greenwald and Ronis 1978). However, it has been broadly extended in recent work, especially by Swann (e.g. 1983), Wicklund and Gollwitzer (1982), and Tesser and Campbell (1983). Swann's research has shown that social interactions are often structured in a fashion that serves a self-verification function, selectively producing feedback that confirms an existing self-concept. Wicklund and Gollwitzer have shown that symbolic indicators of status (symbolic self-completions) are especially sought in self-defining domains in which a failure or deficiency has recently been suffered. Tesser and Campbell's research has demonstrated the extent to which interpersonal attraction toward highly competent others is governed by considerations of self-esteem maintenance. Competent others are most readily liked and identified with when their competence is in a non-selfdefining performance domain. (See Aronson 1984, Chapter 7, for additional discussion of the manner in which self-esteem maintenance is central to interpersonal attraction.)

The Spontaneous Self-Concept

In a series of recent investigations, McGuire and his associates (see McGuire and McGuire 1982 for details) have elicited contents of the "spontaneous self-concept" by using the open-ended probe, "Tell us about yourself." (See Wylie 1974, for reviews of previous uses of open-ended self-concept measures.) In analyzing children's responses to tell-us-about-yourself, McGuire and Padawer-Singer (1976) found that the most frequently mentioned categories were activities, significant others, and attitudes, followed by demographic characteristics, self-evaluations, and physical features. Among other results obtained by McGuire and colleagues was a variety of evidence for a distinctiveness principle. The spontaneous self-concept is especially likely to include characteristics that distinguish self from others. A critical focus of the spontaneous self-concept work concerns the extent to which self-evaluation is fundamental to the self-concept. McGuire's data have revealed relatively little self-evaluative content, and he has urged a reduction of attention to self-evaluation in self-concept research. In contrast, Greenwald, Bellezza, and Banaji (1985) found that self-report measures of self-esteem were reliably correlated with both amount and affective content of items produced in response to a series of categorized self-concept probes. The question remains an interesting one for further research.

Memory and Judgment Latency Measures

The long-established traditions of using memory and judgment latency to diagnose cognitive structure have recently been applied to self-relevant phenomena by Markus (1977), Rogers (1981), Kuiper (1981), and others. Markus and her associates (e.g., Markus and Sentis 1982) have investigated individual differences in judgment latencies and accessibility of knowledge on such personal dimensions as independence, gender role, and body weight. They have found that subjects judge and retrieve information most efficiently on dimensions that are important to the self-concept. A related finding reported by Kuiper (1981) is that self-descriptiveness judgments are made especially rapidly for trait words that are both extremely high and low in self-descriptiveness. Markus has interpreted her several findings as evidence for the self as a system of schemata, or self-maintaining subdomains of knowledge about the self. The preference of Rogers (1981) and Kulper (1981) has been for a model in which the self is conceived as a favored cognitive category, or prototype (cf. Rosch 1973). In still another cognitive vein, Bower and Gilligan (1979) have interpreted these and similar data as evidence for a representation of the self as a subregion of a propositional semantic network of the sort proposed by Anderson and Bower (1973; subsequently reconceptualized by Anderson 1976).

Depression and Self-Cognition

Much recent research has supported the conclusion that, as a personality type, depressives show distinct variations from the patterns of self-concept content and processing typically displayed by normals. (See, for example, the recent special issue of *Social Cognition*, Kuiper and Higgins 1985.) Kuiper and his associates (e.g., Kuiper and Derry 1981; Kuiper, MacDonald, and Derry 1983) have found that, whereas normals are schematic for (i.e., efficient processors of) evaluatively positive traits, chronic depressives are schematic for evaluatively negative ones. Mild depressives appear to be schematic for a mixture of depressed and non-depressed content, suggesting a cognitive structure in flux.

Another cognitive aspect of the normal-depressive contrast has been studied by Alloy and Abramson (1979), who reported that self-perceptions of depressives are more objectively accurate than are those of normals (see also Lewinsohn, Mischel, Chaplin, and Barton 1980). In their studies, Alloy and Abramson asked depressed and non-depressed subjects to estimate the degree of contingency between their button-press responses and the occurrence of an experimentally manipulated outcome. Normal subjects overestimated the degree of contingency when the outcome was favorable, but underestimated the contingency when the outcome was unfavorable. On the other hand, depressives were more objectively accurate in their judgments, and were not influenced by outcome valence. (To use a concept that is introduced below, it appears that the depressed subjects lack the beneffectance bias that is characteristic of normal self-cognition.)

Multidimensional Scaling of the Self

Breckler, Pratkanis, and McCann (1985) applied the technique of multidimensional scaling to portray individual differences in self-concept in a 2-dimensional trait space that is constructed from trait similarity judgments. This method locates each person near in the trait space to the positions of their self-descriptive traits, and distant from non-descriptive traits. Each subject's location is shown as an open circle, and each subject's concept of a generalized other is indicated by a dot.

The two dimensions are both evaluative, similar to those found in other multidimensional scalings of trait adjectives (e.g., Rosenberg and Sedlak 1972). Consistent with the positive bias in the normal self-concept, self locations are more evaluatively positive than are those of generalized others. Also, subjects recall best (on an unexpected test) and most rapidly identify as self-descriptive those traits that are closest to the self's location in the trait space. These findings support an interpretation of the self as an important reference point in a mental personality space.

II. A NEW METAPHOR: SELF AS ORGANIZATION OF KNOWLEDGE

The approach known as cognitive science is emerging as an important synthesis of recent developments in psychology, linguistics, and artificial intelligence. A central insight of this approach is that intelligent performances depend on highly organized and domain-specific knowledge structures (e.g., Newell and Simon 1963; Hayes-Roth, Waterman, and Lenat 1983). A particular task of cognitive science researchers has been to develop descriptions of these knowledge structures. Thus, hypotheses abound concerning structures identified as images, propositions, categories, prototypes, scripts, frames, schemata, semantic networks, cognitive maps, etc. The growing use of such cognitive-structural concepts in discussions of the self (see Greenwald and Pratkanis 1984, pp. 144–151) indicates a convergence of the study of self with the cognitive science approach. We here review this very important theoretical trend by observing how it has effectively replaced old metaphors for the self with a new and effective one—the self as an organization of knowledge.

In characterizing social knowledge structures, several theorists have found the concept of *schema* particularly useful (see Hastie 1981; Markus 1977; Rumelhart 1984; Taylor and Crocker 1981). A schema is a structure that consists not only of descriptive data (knowledge) about an object or domain, but also rules and procedures for its own operation and further development (Neisser 1976, pp. 55–56). The schema concept has proved particularly useful in recent discussions of the self (see Greenwald and Pratkanis 1984, pp. 146–147) and is the chief structural component of the conception of self toward which the present review is headed. Before attempting a summary statement of that conception (in Section III, below), we first review the two areas of research that have provided the strongest support for the organization-of-knowledge metaphor for the self—the relation of self and memory, and the role of self-evaluation in the organization of self-knowledge.

Self as the Organization of Memory

Early in the twentieth century Claparede (1911/1951) proposed that the self serves as an axis for memory, with events remembered by virtue of their association with self. The self, in other words, was viewed as the bearer of memory's continuity and coherence over periods spanning several decades. This central organizing role of the self in memory has been expressed in a variety of subsequent views, such as those of Koffka (1935), Combs and Snygg (1949/1959), and Allport (1961). A modern rendering of these views is that the cognitive structure associated with the self is, by virtue of its scope and complexity, the major organizing structure that functions in acquiring (encoding) and accessing (retrieving) knowledge.

Recent research on the relation of self and memory supports the conception of the self as an active, central structure of memory. A wide variety of findings indicate that memory functions well when the self is involved in the encoding or retrieval of to-be-remembered items. The results of this recent research can be described in terms of four "self/memory" effects. (See Greenwald 1981, and Greenwald and Pratkanis 1984, for citations of specific studies.)

The self-generation effect. Material that is actively generated by the learner is retrieved more easily than is material passively encountered. For example, Slamecka and Graf (1978) found that subjects showed superior recall for items that had been incompletely presented, but accompanied by a rule for generating the missing information (e.g., synonym: *rapid-f*) compared to a complete presentation (e.g., synonym: *rapid-fast*).

The self-reference effect. Material that is encoded with reference to self is more easily retrieved than is material otherwise encoded. For example, Rogers, Kuiper, and Kirker (1977) found that subjects could better recall trait words that had been judged in relationship to the self (i.e., Does this word describe you?) than ones judged in the context of other tasks.

The ego-involvement effect. Material that is associated with a persisting task is more easily retrieved than is material associated with a completed task. For example, Nuttin and Greenwald (1968) repeatedly found that subjects demonstrate superior retention of information that they expect to encounter again at a future date.

The second-generation effect. Material that is associated or linked to the self is more easily retrieved than is material associated with others. For example, Greenwald, Banaji, Pratkanis, and Breckler (1981) found that subjects were better at recalling nouns that had been used in sentences involving the self-generated names of friends compared to sentences using the names of unfamiliar others.

Of the four effects just described, the self-reference effect has attracted the greatest number of attempts at theoretical interpretation. Greenwald (1981) and Greenwald and Pratkanis (1984, pp. 134–137) have noted that there are three classes of viable interpretations for the self-reference effect. This wealth of interpretations is embarrassing to the extent that it indicates the difficulty of designing experiments that rule out alternative interpretations. It is also possible, however, that the several explanations are *all* correct—that is, that the self is an effective cognitive structure that possesses multiple devices for facilitating both acquisition and retrieval of knowledge.

Self-evaluation as a Basis for the Organization of Self-knowledge

The observation that self-feelings are typically strong and positive has been made by many writers. James (1890) observed that our selves come with a glow and warmth, Cooley (1902/1964) noted that "I" is known primarily as feeling, and Allport (1937) remarked that nothing is more sacred than the beloved ego. Recent theorists no less stress the point that the self engenders strong, passionate feelings (cf. Epstein 1973; Markus and Sentis 1982; C. Rogers 1951; T. B. Rogers 1981). Sherif and Cantril (1947), Rosenberg (1979), and Greenwald and Pratkanis (1984) converge in concluding that this prominence of a feeling component of the self justifies regarding the self as an attitude object. The present treatment extends these previous ones by suggesting that affect, or self-evaluation, plays an important organizing role in self-knowledge. This point will be made in two ways—first, by observing that the self is characterized by cognitive biases that function in part to maintain positive self-affect and, second, by presenting an analysis of human motivation in which maintenance of the sense of self-worth plays a major explanatory role.

Cognitive Biases—The Totalitarian Ego

Greenwald (1980) identified three biases in the self-knowledge of the average normal adult of (at least) the North American culture. This set of biases was labeled the "totalitarian ego" because they resemble those that characterize the functioning of the information control apparatus of a totalitarian dictatorship. (The "totalitarian" characterization was not intended to imply that ego generally is modeled by a totalitarian system. In particular, there is nothing in this conception of ego that corresponds to the coercive terror that is often regarded as the primary characteristic of a totalitarian system.) As the following summaries indicate, ego's biases of egocentricity, beneffectance, and cognitive conservatism are likely to operate to maintain a favorable self-evaluation.

Egocentricity: Judgment and memory tend to be focused on the self. The egocentric character of knowledge is indicated by three well-established research conclusions: (i) Information that is related to self has a privileged position in memory (e.g., the self/memory effects reviewed above); (ii) there is a pervasive tendency to insert self into perceived causal sequences, either as an influencing agent (referred to as the illusion of control, Langer 1975) or as the imagined target of another's actions; and (iii) the self serves as a reference point in social judgments (see above discussion of multidimensional scaling of the self, p. 316).

Beneffectance: This term was compounded from beneficence (doing good) and effectance (competence). It was coined as an umbrella term to cover phenomena previously labeled as self-serving, egocentric, egotistic, and ego-defensive attributions by other writers. These terms collectively label the tendency to perceive oneself as an effective agent in achieving desired (good) ends, while avoiding undesirable ones. Four lines of research have demonstrated the pervasiveness of this bias in the normal personality. These are (i) the tendency to recall successes more readily than failures, (ii) the acceptance of responsibility for successes but not for failures on individual or group tasks, (iii) the denial of responsibility for harming others, and (iv) the tendency to identify with victors and to disaffiliate with losers.

Cognitive conservatism: Conservatism is the disposition to resist change, to maintain that which is established. In perception, basic skills such as object conservation (perceptual constancy) and assimilation (reuse of existing categories) illustrate cognitive conservatism. Such conservative processes are widely regarded as functioning in the service of veridical judgment. Two other conservative (change-resisting) processes, confirmation bias and rewriting of memory, appear to serve the interests of accuracy less well. Confirmation bias takes the form of (i) information-seeking strategies that selectively confirm initial hypotheses, (ii) selective recall of information that confirms previously established beliefs, (iii) selective generation of arguments that support opinions under attack, and (iv) researchers' selective evaluation of their own data as a function of the data's agreement with their hypotheses. Rewriting of memory is evident in (i) systematic misrecall of prior opinions so as to obscure the occurrence of opinion change, (ii) belief that newly acquired facts have had lengthy residence in memory, and (iii) overestimation of the validity of inaccurate memories.

The egocentricity, beneffectance, and conservatism biases are found not only in totalitarian propaganda systems and in normal human cognition but also in the development of effective theoretical paradigms in "normal" science (Kuhn 1970). The association of these biases with the human self is made plausible by findings indicating that the biases are typically increased in strength by procedures that have been identified as "ego-involving" (Greenwald 1980, pp. 610–611), and by the success with which Epstein (1973) and Loevinger (1976) used the metaphor of scientific theory in their discussions of the self.

Pursuing the organization-of-knowledge metaphor, Greenwald (1980) suggested that the egocentricity and conservatism biases function to maintain the integrity of ego's knowledge structure, preserving access to information from the variably distant past while continuing to extend the system's domain. Biases comparable to egocentricity and conservatism can be identified in effectively functioning nonhuman knowledge systems, such as a busy library (Greenwald 1980, p. 613). It is, however, the remaining bias, beneffectance, that most directly serves to maintain positive self-regard.

How might beneffectance-aided positive regard support the functioning of the self as a knowledge system? A plausible answer follows from the observation that positive self-regard facilitates success in many situations in which perseverance is the critical ingredient of successful performance (Greenwald 1980, p. 614; cf. Bandura 1977; McFarlin and Blascovich 1982; Shrauger and Sorman 1977). Also supportive of the suggested relationship involving beneffectance, positive self-regard, and effective action is the previously noted absence of the beneffectance bias in personalities that are classed as depressive. That is, persons who lack both beneffectance and positive self-regard are commonly regarded as being ineffective in many of their endeavors. The positive self-regard that is associated with the totalitarian ego's biases appears, then, to serve the important function of enabling the self's knowledge structure to link with effective action.

Self-Evaluation and Motivational Facets of the Self— Ego Task Analysis

The just-noted relation between positive self-regard and personal efficacy provides a useful starting point for considering the alternative ways in which one's sense of self-worth may be supported. Social psychology has, through its history, developed a wealth of theoretical accounts of the maintenance of self-evaluation. These include cognitive dissonance theory (as presented by Aronson 1968), self-presentation theory (Goffman 1959), impression management theory (Schlenker 1980), symbolic self-completion theory (Wicklund and Gollwitzer 1983), and self-esteem maintenance theory (Tesser and Campbell 1983). Recently, after reviewing research on ego-involvement and self-awareness, Greenwald (1982a) suggested that a synthesis of the diverse analyses of self-evaluation could be achieved by assuming the existence of stable individual differences in the basis for one's sense of self worth. This proposal, identified as ego task analysis, was subsequently elaborated by Greenwald and Breckler (1985) and Breckler and Greenwald (in press).

In terms of ego task analysis, social behavior is guided by a hierarchical structure of tasks. At the top of this hierarchy is an ego task—the task of establishing one's sense of self-worth. Unlike other tasks, ego tasks are not terminated by successes. Rather, the goal of establishing one's self-worth is a lifelong enterprise. Greenwald and Breckler (1985) identified four ego tasks, three of which contribute to establishing self-worth via the evaluations of different audiences. The four ego tasks are referred to alternatively as motivational facets of the self.

The diffuse self: The goal of the diffuse self's ego task is hedonic satisfaction or positive affect. The diffuse self is an unsocialized self, a proto-self that can be understood as developmentally more primitive than the following three.

The public self: For this facet of the self, self-evaluation derives from the favorable evaluations of others—an outer audience. The public self's ego task can be understood as that of public impression management.

The private self-evaluation: Self-evaluation is based on comparison of performance with internal standards—evaluation by an inner audience. The private self's task resembles McClelland's conception of achievement motivation (McClelland, Atkinson, Clark, and Lowell 1953).

The collective self: Self-evaluation is based on achieving the goals of important reference groups. These goals are often identified with important social values. The collective self's ego task is similar to ego-involvement as conceived by Sherif and Cantril (1947).

Greenwald and Breckler (1985) propose that persons develop stable (dispositional) preferences for deriving their sense of self-worth from a particular type of audience—public (outer), private (inner), or collective (reference group). These stable dispositions are referred to as ego task orientations. Public and private ego task orientations correspond approximately to the dispositional dimensions of public and private self-consciousness that are measured by Fenigstein et al.'s (1975) Self-Consciousness Scale. Realization of the potential of ego task analysis must, however, await the development of a more complete set of measures of the dispositional dimensions represented by the four ego task orientations (cf. Breckler and Greenwald in press).

In the present context, ego task analysis provides some detail to the present conception of the self as an important object of evaluation—that is, as an attitude object. Among the functions of the attitudinal knowledge structure associated with the self is that of maintaining the evaluative disposition toward the self. This translates to maintaining self-esteem, or the sense of self-worth. Ego task analysis proposes that maintenance of self-worth is among the strongest and most persistent of human goals. Further, stable individual differences in strategies used to achieve this goal are associated with characteristic differences in motivation to please the various audiences whose standards can provide the basis for self-evaluation.

III. HOW SHALL THE SELF BE CONCEIVED?

This article has sought to document the role of recent research on the self in establishing a new metaphor for the self, as an organization of knowledge. It remains to develop the implications of this metaphor for the conception of self. In particular, we wish to show that the self-as-organization-of-knowledge conception effectively resolves several long-standing enigmas concerning the self. To do this, we answer a series of questions, starting with the one that provided the title of this article.

How Shall the Self Be Conceived?

Our fully spelled-out conception is that *the self is a complex, person-specific, central, attitudinal schema*. This definition stresses four characteristics of the self:

The self is a knowledge structure—a schema, or actively self-maintaining knowledge structure.

The content of this knowledge structure varies from person to person—the schema is person-specific.

The self is a focus of affective regard—the knowledge structure is an attitudinal schema.

The self consists of diffuse, public, private, and collective facets, each contributing (and in different proportions for different persons) to affective self-regard—the attitudinal schema is complex.

Our conception of the self as a complex, person-specific, central, attitudinal schema is, itself, complex. But it need not be unmanageably so. The answer to the next question proposes that the self is constructed from ordinary materials. The self's complexity and person-to-person variability therefore present obstacles, but not ones so potent as to deter study.

Is the Self Ordinary or Unique?

The main ingredients of our definition of the self are attitude and schema, familiar psychological constructs that are well tied to research operations. We thus view the self as ordinary, but it is also undeniably special. It is unique due to the quantity of knowledge it synthesizes and to its complexity. Among the unique properties that presumably emerge from the scope and complexity of the self are the abilities to retrieve knowledge of events of the distant past, and to maintain the coherence of personal experience.

How Shall the Subject/Object Duality of the Self Be Explained?

Previous writers have conceived the self's subject/object duality in terms of the metaphor of a mirror's reflectivity. Unfortunately, the mirror metaphor appears to be debilitating in its failure to differentiate the properties of subject-of-knowledge (self as knower) from those of object-of-knowledge (self as known). A superior conception is achieved by interpreting the self as an active, self-maintaining knowledge structure—that is, a schema. The schema conception encompasses both knowledge content and knowledge process. Thus, subjective aspects of the self can be understood in terms of the process aspect of schema, and objective aspects identified with the content aspect of schema. The schema structure effectively portrays subject/object or process/content duality partly by virtue of the possibility of embodying this duality as computer program/data. (This argument is spelled out at greater length in Greenwald and Pratkanis 1984, pp. 141–144.)

Is the Self Genuine and Stable, or Artificial and Malleable?

Commentators on the process of self-presentation have often regarded the self as plastic, situation-dependent, and chameleon-like (Gergen 1982; Goffman 1959). Such observations obviously tend to undermine the view of the self as a coherent, stable, central cognitive structure. Nevertheless, in conceiving the self as a federation of diffuse, public, private, and collective factions, we hope to accommodate the broad evidence of situational influences on self-presentation, while preserving the conception of a stable, central organization.

Is the Self Unitary or Multiple?

We agree with Epstein (1973, 1980) in regarding the self as a primary organizer, responsible for achieving a typically large degree of unity in one's personal knowledge structure. The ordinary unity or coherence of the self is particularly compelling when contrasted with pathologies, such as Korsakoff syndrome (see

Butters and Cermak 1980; Jacoby and Witherspoon 1982) and multiple personality, in which coherence and unity appear to be lacking. At the same time, we endorse Allport's (1961) observation that "unity of personality is only a matter of degree, and we should avoid exaggerating it" (p. 386). The distinction among diffuse, public, private, and collective facets of the self provides one way of describing multiplicity without abandoning unity. This view of the self's unity should not be mistaken as an advocacy of the idea of total unity within the person. Rather, we see the self's unity as no more than an island of coherence within a larger psychic sea (Greenwald 1982b).

A Final Comment: The Self as Historically Bound Knowledge Structure

The self evolves historically during a person's lifetime. This evolution is due in part to culturally assisted growth in the self's knowledge content. Because the contribution of culture is free also to evolve, it is certain that the self has evolved greatly in history. In the last half-millennium, scientific understanding has become an increasingly potent contributor to culture. And, in just the present century, understanding based on the works of Freud and Piaget has brought once-mysterious mental processes into the range of ordinary understanding. As understanding of self's processes thus increases, the introspectively inaccessible (process) aspects of the schema-self are converted to accessible content. The present surge of research attention to the self should produce further understanding that will diffuse gradually into culture and thus into collective mental content. Research on the self, then, is fated to alter the picture that it describes.

NOTE

This article is a synthesis and updating of material presented in previous papers by Greenwald and Pratkanis (1984), Greenwald and Breckler (1985), and Greenwald (1980, 1981, 1982a). Its preparation was aided by a grant from National Science Foundation, BNS 82–17006, and by support from the Graduate School of Industrial Administration, Carnegie-Mellon University. The authors thank Marlene E. Turner for helpful comments. Address correspondence to Anthony R. Pratkanis, Graduate School of Industrial Administration, Carnegie-Mellon University, Pittsburgh, PA 15213 or Anthony G. Greenwald, Department of Psychology, Ohio State University, 404C West 17th Avenue, Columbus, OH 43210.

2

Promoting Identity Stability: Autobiographical Memory Construction

> Who controls the past controls the future. Who controls the present controls the past.
>
> —George Orwell, *1984*[1]

Hillary Clinton was labeled an "outsider" when she first announced her candidacy for the Senate from the state of New York. Though she showed little interest in the state prior to that time, she subsequently revealed that she had always had a deep interest in issues affecting New Yorkers and even in the state's sports teams. She moved to New York and began to use the word "we" when talking to New Yorkers. Some cynics suggested that she had revised her memories to fit her new identity. If she has, I can sympathize because I know that I have reconstructed my own memories to fit new identities. Research suggests that this sort of personal memory revision is rather common.

Our identities are constantly evolving and changing but we want to make them more stable and permanent. In this chapter I will describe the way we do this through autobiographical memory construction. We can remember only a small number of the events in our lives and we select those that seem most relevant to defining who we are. Our selection creates distortions and biases in memories. If we can reduce these biases, we can make organizational and personal decisions more effectively. Shona Brown and Kathleen Eisenhardt provided support for this claim in their 1998 study of computer firms. They demonstrated that the most effective managers in rapidly changing environments learn more from the past than others. As the authors state, "Wise use of the past diminishes risk and frees resources to focus on new ideas."[2]

We simplify our memories to make them more consistent with our dominant identity. The psychoanalyst Erik Erikson, who developed the concept of the "identity crisis," discussed memory modification in his analysis of Martin Luther's struggle to define his identity. Erikson said,

By accepting some definition as to who he is, usually on the basis of a function in an economy, a place in the sequence of generations, and a status in the structure of society, the adult is able to selectively reconstruct his past in such a way that, step by step, it seems to have planned him, or better, he seems to have planned it.[3]

In chapter 1, I suggested that autobiographical memory is revised as we take up new identities and that the revision serves to convince us that our lives have always been progressing toward our current mix of identities. In this chapter, I will discuss research on the distortion of memories and use my own autobiographical memories to illustrate the processes of identity-based memory distortion.

The term "autobiographical memory" refers to people's recollections of events that occur in their lives, whether or not these recollections are written down or recorded. Memories of significant decisions you have made are part of your autobiographical memory, which is why autobiographical memory has implications for management decisions.

Those who engage in a moment's honest introspection will realize that their memories of important life events are not entirely accurate. A bit more reflection suggests that there are patterns in memory distortion and that these distortions are usually "self-enhancing" (that is, they tend to clarify and enhance an individual's view of self). Research on autobiographical memory distortion supports these points.[4] It is obvious that such distortions limit our ability to draw accurate conclusions from our experiences, to profit from past mistakes, and to acquire wisdom. The extent and nature of the damage, however, is not as obvious.

Research on the accuracy of autobiographical memory has explored the causes and consequences of distortions. In a sense, this research is part of a long stream of philosophical inquiry dealing with the basic question of how we can draw wisdom from our experience.[5]

PAST RESEARCH ON AUTOBIOGRAPHICAL MEMORY

In order to understand autobiographical memory it is important to realize that our self-schemas are supported by autobiographical recollection that is reported in the form of narrative accounts of incidents in our lives. Psychologists who study autobiographical memory note that this "life story" serves to define the individual's concept of self and communicate that concept to others.[6] To create and communicate a consistent image of the self, a narrative is necessarily selective and involves some simplification and distortion. The processes of selection, simplification, and distortion are readily observed in written autobiographies, even those composed by individuals with exceptional powers of introspection.[7]

I do not mean that all individuals have narratives of their entire lives committed to memory. I simply mean that memories of important events in our lives are retained because they are rehearsed in memory and told as stories to others.[8] Distortions occur in this rehearsal and retelling. When called upon to "tell the story" of their lives, or some important part of their lives (such as important decisions they made), people recount a sequence of these incidents, which have already been distorted by the rehearsal process.

Since autobiographical memory is reported in the form of a narrative, research on how people remember and reconstruct stories will help us understand the effects of identity on memory. There is a long tradition of research demonstrating the tendency to reconstruct and modify narrative events in recollection. From his studies of recall of unfamiliar narrative material, conducted in the 1930s, Bartlett concluded that memory is *productive* as well as reproductive.[9] When attempting to recall narrative material, people often omit elements and add others as well as rearrange the sequence of events in a process he called "imaginative reconstruction."[10] This reconstruction is controlled by individuals' "efforts after meaning."[11] An ongoing stream of later work, conducted in the '30s, '40s, '50s and '70s, extended that of Bartlett and showed that distortions such as simplification, condensation, rationalization, and conventionalization occurred most often when the original narrative material was ambiguous.[12] Our life experiences are ambiguous enough to give ample opportunities for such distortions in reconstruction. Experiments by Gardner, Pickett, and Brewer have shown that when we are conscious of our social identity, we recall narrative information consistent with that identity more readily.[13]

We have all listened to someone tell a "fish story," a story that changes and grows with each retelling. I think all of our autobiographical memories undergo some self-serving distortions. To some extent, they are all fish stories. There are at least three common patterns of distortion.[14] First, we tend to see ourselves as more central to events than we actually were. Second, we take credit for good outcomes and lay blame for bad ones. Third, we underestimate the difference between our past selves and present selves. It is this last pattern of distortion that is most closely related to the maintenance of personal identity stability.

Seeing ourselves as central to events may cause us to overestimate the impact we can have on events in the future and may create what Harvard psychologist Ellen Langer has called the "illusion of control."[15] Langer and her colleagues have produced a body of research demonstrating that human beings overestimate the amount of control they have over events. Elsewhere, I showed that such distortions bias managers' recollections of their past decisions and therefore limit their ability to use past experience to improve future decisions.[16] Sadly, memory distortions simultaneously increase managers' overconfidence in the "wisdom" they have acquired from experience.

Overconfidence in biased recollections of past experience seems to produce worse decisions and performance in businesses. Steve Clapham and I conducted a study of letters to shareholders in annual reports and showed that executives who were most prone to lay blame on the environment for past failures were least effective in improving shareholder returns in the future.[17] To explain why, I want to discuss the illusion of control and the overconfidence bias in greater detail.

The illusion of control has been documented in a series of experiments by Langer and others.[18] When subject to this bias, decision-makers tend to overestimate the extent to which events are under their control. Langer's first article on this topic reported the results of six studies that showed that decision-makers in a variety of situations overestimated their skill or the impact of their skill on outcomes.[19] Larwood and Whittaker found that both management students and managers tended to overestimate their abilities and the impact these abilities would have on a marketing simulation on which they were working.[20] The illusion of control represents overconfidence in your ability to produce positive outcomes.[21]

Langer suggested that we are subject to this bias because of the way we collect information. As we constantly seek ways to control the outcomes of important events in our lives, we form hypotheses about the effects of our actions on these outcomes. We then, "tend to seek out information that supports our hypotheses while innocently ignoring disconfirming evidence".[22] Thus, we tend to pay more attention to information that supports our illusion of personal control.

Leaders with a long history of success may fall victim to the illusion of control when they evaluate acquisitions. The recent wave of consolidations, acquisitions, mergers, and alliances in computer networking, software, e-commerce, and related industries provide examples, including Disney's acquisition of Toysmart.com, which I discussed in Chapter 1.

If the past is any guide, over half of these consolidations will fail. Often these failures result from the fact that the leaders who make the acquisition underestimate the forces they cannot control and their own level of ignorance about these forces. This illusion of control is not unique to the "new economy." The same illusion was documented by Irene Duhaime and me in our study of acquisitions and divestments in "old economy" manufacturing and retail industries.[23]

The illusion of control may have been operating among venture capital firms during the 1990s. In 1999, $56 billion was invested in venture capital funds, up from $3 billion in 1990.[24] The long years of stellar returns for venture capital firms may have caused them to become less cautious about the profit potential of new ventures, funding too many competing companies with weak business plans.

People also tend to be overconfident in the accuracy of their autobiographical memories. The overconfidence bias has been demonstrated in a number of laboratory experiments,[25] as well as in business decision-making.[26] Decision-makers tend to express excessive confidence in their judgments and predictions and this tendency toward overconfidence may be greater in experts than in novices.

Individuals with more information may be more subject to overconfidence because of the way we tend to use information. Cognitive psychologists Hillel Einhorn and Robin Hogarth suggested that when we have a large amount of information on a topic, it is easier for us to recall information that supports our judgments and predictions. But it is often difficult for us to recall and use information that disconfirms our judgments and beliefs.[27] Since experts have more information in the areas of their expertise than novices, it is easier for them to think of information that supports their judgments, and for this reason they may be more subject than novices to overconfidence.

Autobiographical memory distortion may increase overconfidence in the reality of our current identity by increasing the amount of information we recall that seems to confirm this identity. While this may allow us to make major life decisions quickly and confidently, it may also restrict the range of options we consider and reduce the amount of thought we put into these very complex and important decisions.

In the preceding discussion, I suggested that autobiographical memories may be biased to create a consistent picture of the self. Major life events can cause individuals to change their self-image. Therefore, life changes can lead to the modification of autobiographical memory that makes the remembered self more consistent with the current self. Research on autobiographical memory revision and eyewitness testimony helps explain why individuals may not be aware of the changes in their memories.

Memories of narrative material tend to change as the material is recalled and retold. Memories of personal history are selectively modified through the same processes. Kotre, for example, has described the process, often observed in middle-aged individuals, by which autobiographical memories are modified in ways that make past attitudes and behavior more consistent with present views.[28] Those who have "settled in" to a career or marriage, for example, may forget dissatisfactions and desires to escape that they experienced early in the career or relationship.

Numerous experiments have shown that we revise our memories to make our beliefs seem more consistent. For example, Bem and McConnell asked college student subjects to express their opinions on a topic of interest to them (student control over a university curriculum) and, one week later, asked them to write an essay advocating the position opposite to the one they had expressed. After writing these essays, students recalled that their earlier opinions were more similar to the ones expressed in their essays than they actually were. These results were confirmed in a later experiment by Wixon and Laird.[29]

One final collection of evidence from research on eyewitness testimony directly demonstrates that memory of past events can be altered by information received later. Numerous studies conducted by Elizabeth Loftus and her colleagues have shown that memories of important matters of fact can be modified or implanted in witnesses in such a way that they are confident enough to testify to the truth of their false memories under oath. Those subjected to such memory modification seldom report awareness of the manipulation.[30]

It is difficult for many to accept the fact that we can modify our memories and have no recollection of the process of modification. Clear evidence of the active reproductive aspects of memory often comes as a surprise to autobiographers. For example, Vladimir Nabokov, author of *Lolita*, is well known for his vivid depictions of the effects of memories on the inner lives of his characters. He was also a lifelong chess enthusiast. In his autobiography, *Speak, Memory*, he expresses surprise at his own autobiographical memory distortion.

In the first version of this autobiography, when describing the Nabokovs' coat of arms (carelessly glimpsed among some familial trivia many years before), I somehow managed to twist it into the fireside wonder of two bears posing with a great *chessboard* propped between them. I have now looked it up, that blazon, and am disappointed to find that it boils down to a couple of lions—licking their chops.[31]

To those attempting to recall autobiographical memories and benefit from their past experiences, the implications of memory distortions are disturbing. Greenwald, however, argues that forgetting their own memory revisions helps individuals preserve a belief in a consistent and relatively unchanging self and still incorporate the modifications in self-definition required by new information from a changing environment.[32] The belief in a consistent self is the basis for personal identity, and it could be argued that it would be impossible for individuals to function in a socially acceptable way without it. According to this line of reasoning, such conditions as "multiple personality" and schizophrenia represent a breakdown in the consistent self-concept.

Bandura focuses on the value of "self-efficacy" (people's belief that they can control important outcomes in their lives) in dealing with difficulties.[33] Individuals with low self-efficacy are highly vulnerable to change, and negative experiences readily reinstate their disbelief in their capabilities.[34] The firm belief in a stable self may be the basis for feelings of self-efficacy. The benefits of this belief may outweigh the problems caused by the distortion of autobiographical memory if individuals can keep the possibility of memory distortion in mind and view their own memories with some skepticism.

AUTOBIOGRAPHICAL STATEMENT

It is easy to recognize distortions in the recollections of others but difficult to believe that many of our own memories are biased. Yet I will argue that recognizing our own memory distortions can improve our decisions. The best way to make this point is to determine whether my own memories show evidence of these biases. Therefore, I will use my own recollections to illustrate the distortion of autobiographical memories in the service of identity. However, because my memories are biased, I know that I may not have an "objective" view of them. Since I want to discuss autobiographical memory using my own memories as examples, I feel it is best to provide the reader with at least some of the data I will use for the discussion.

Appendix F contains autobiographical material I wrote at the age of nineteen, which will form the basis of the discussion. Original phrasing, mistakes in grammar, and other idiosyncratic material have been preserved. Since I wrote this solely for my own use, any biases or distortions in it are likely to result from information-processing heuristics rather than from an attempt to manage readers' impressions. I will analyze the statement in light of my current autobiographical memories to provide information on the three common patterns of memory distortion, focusing on the consistency bias, through which we become convinced that our lives have been leading up to our current mix of identities. I will also discuss patterns that have been identified through the study of autobiography as a literary genre.

ANALYSIS: PATTERNS OF MEMORY DISTORTION

This analysis will begin with the three patterns of distortion in autobiographical memory described by Greenwald: the centrality bias, the self-serving bias in causal analyses, and the consistency bias. I find evidence of all three in my own autobiographical statement. The statement also provides information that will allow me to expand on the conclusions from past research.

The Centrality Bias and the Illusion of Control

Greenwald suggested that in autobiographical recollection we overstate our centrality to events. To examine this proposition, I constructed a causal map from my autobiographical statement, shown in Figure 2.1.

Since I want to recommend causal mapping in decision-making in Chapter 6, I will explain the process briefly here. It involves identifying all important causes and effects in a statement and representing them as a series of nodes with causal arrows connecting them. Thus, an individual may be able to represent a complex mental map with a single diagram.[35]

In the autobiographical statement, I attributed my parents' divorce to my own birth and its effects on them. I believe this is an example of the centrality bias. It is common for children of divorced parents to express feelings of guilt over the divorce, which suggests that this may be a common manifestation of the centrality bias in autobiographical recollection.

Figure 2.1
Cognitive Map

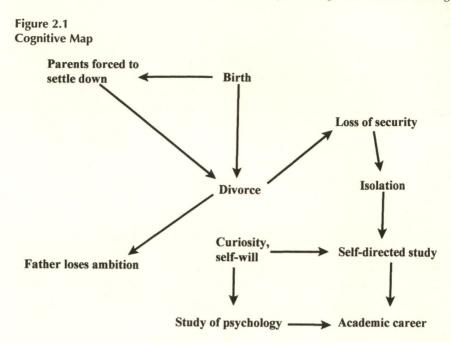

It is likely that people who overestimate their influence on past events will over-estimate their ability to influence future events. This may account for the perva-siveness of the "illusion of control" bias I discussed earlier. Those who wish to make good use of their memories in future decisions should carefully examine their beliefs about their own centrality in past events. They can remind themselves that there were multiple causes for events in which they participated and make special efforts to emphasize more complex causal models in explaining why events in their own lives turned out as they did.

Self-Serving Bias in Taking Credit and Laying Blame

We often take credit for positive outcomes in our lives and lay blame for nega-tive ones. In past research on causal attributions, taking credit for positive out-comes has been called *internal positive* attribution while laying blame on external forces for negative outcomes has been called *external negative* attribution. Accept-ing blame for negative outcomes is *internal negative* attribution while crediting ex-ternal forces for positive outcomes is *external positive* attribution. From Appendix F, the reader can verify my conclusions about my own attributions by simply not-ing the number of times I explain each positive or negative outcome by my own actions versus external forces. My own assessment is shown in Table 2.1.

The internal positives outnumber the external positives. In other words, I tended to take credit for the good outcomes in my life. This pattern has been found in studies of public statements involving executives' recollections of their companies' past performance.[36] Since my autobiography was not originally intended for public reading, this pattern of attributions cannot exist solely for the purposes of manipulating the views of others as Salancik and Meindl suggest. Rather, it is consistent with my own view that biased attributions can be the result of honest attempts to make sense of the past.[37]

It seems, however, that I did not tend to lay blame for poor outcomes in my early life. Negative outcomes are the most frequently discussed and internal negative statements equal external negatives. This is in marked contrast to the statements by executives examined in past research. In past studies, approximately two-thirds of all statements were internal positives. In other words, the most common bias was taking credit for good outcomes.[38] However, research I discussed in Chapter 1 shows that those from Asian cultures may have different patterns of attribution. In other words, both recent research and my own autobiographical memory suggest that people may show a wide range of different attribution patterns in their personal memories.

I want to expand the discussion of possible patterns of bias that can exist in autobiographical memory. I will discuss four patterns that people use to explain the progress of their lives and to construct their personal identities. These are represented in Table 2.2.

First, the most common pattern of bias found in past research is a dominance of internal positives in autobiographical statements, which reflects what I have called the "Master of My Fate" pattern. This pattern is illustrated in the autobiography of the man who saved the Chrysler Corporation (now the DaimlerChrysler Corporation) from bankruptcy two decades ago, Lee Iacocca,[39] and probably in the autobiographical memories of most successful executives. Individuals displaying this

Table 2.1
Attribution Patterns in Autobiographical Statement

	Internal	External
Positive	6	3
Negative	5	5

Table 2.2
Four Patterns of Attribution in Autobiographical Memory

	Internal	External
Positive	**Master of My Fate**	**The Lucky One**
Negative	**Mea Culpa**	**The Victim**

pattern may have difficulty understanding the limits of their own powers and may be subject to the illusion of control.

The second pattern, in which external positives dominate, corresponds to a person's belief that he or she is "The Lucky One." A small number of the autobiographies of successful people show this pattern and it is refreshing to find it. For example, in the recent book *Two Lucky People* by Rose and Milton Friedman, the Nobel laureate and his wife attribute much of their success to good fortune.[40] There is one potential problem with this attribution pattern: Individuals who feel they have been lucky may worry that they will have trouble adjusting to reversals of fortune because they lack practice in dealing with bad luck.

The third pattern, in which internal negatives dominate, is associated with guilt over past mistakes in a "Mea Culpa" mode. This pattern is perhaps the rarest in successful individuals. In fact, I was unable to find any autobiographies by business executives that fit this pattern. However, there is an example in one of the first, and still one of the best, autobiographies, the *Confessions* of Saint Augustine, written in 398 A.D. The early chapters of the *Confessions* show evidence of this attribution pattern. Augustine blamed himself for his wretched and sinful state as a young man. Such individuals may have such a low opinion of themselves that they have difficulty believing they can improve their lives in the future. Happily for Augustine, his conversion to Christianity caused a major shift in his life. Thus, in the last part of the *Confessions*, he describes himself in terms that suggest "The Lucky One."[41]

Finally, when external negatives dominate, individuals tend to see themselves as "The Victim" and may feel that their current difficulties are simply the result of past bad luck. This pattern is sometimes seen in autobiographical statements by public figures who have been disgraced. One example is the autobiography of John Z. Delorean, former executive at General Motors and, for a brief time, CEO of the Delorean Motor Company. In the late 1970s and early 1980s, when Lee Iacocca was saving the Chrysler Company, John Delorean left GM to start his own automobile company. The company was not a success and, to raise money to stave off bankruptcy, Delorean acquired a large amount of cocaine that he intended to sell. Unfortunately, he purchased the cocaine from law enforcement officers in an FBI sting operation and was subsequently arrested and tried, though not convicted.[42] Delorean's autobiography contains a great many references to those who harassed and persecuted him, including the FBI.[43]

The Victim attribution pattern is found more often among those at the opposite end of the income spectrum. An example is *The Jack-Roller: A Delinquent Boy's Own Story*, published in 1930 and perhaps the most famous of the autobiographies written under the sponsorship of "the Chicago School" of sociology. Its author blames the problems of his later life on the early influence of "a . . . no-good stepmother."[44]

Clearly, as a person's identity changes, the pattern of attributions in his or her life story will change. My own autobiographical recollections support this. Though the recollections of my nineteen-year-old self were dominated by negative outcomes, my current autobiographical recollections include many more positive outcomes.

It is obvious that a biased pattern of attributions leads to unrealistic views of self and others, which renders autobiographical memories less useful in developing guidelines for future decisions. People whose memories conform to one of the four patterns might benefit from *balancing attributions* in their recollection. That is, if a person thinks he has a tendency to lay blame on others for misfortunes, she should consciously identify ways in which he has contributed to these misfortunes. Similarly, if she sees evidence of a tendency to take credit for positive outcomes, she should identify ways in which external circumstances and other people have contributed to her successes, not to avoid seeming ungrateful but in the interests of making her memories more accurate so that she and others can benefit more from them. The explicit cultivation of gratitude is one method of achieving this. Individuals who are subject to the opposite biases, taking blame for failures but giving credit for successes to others, may balance attributions by laying blame for failure and taking credit for success, the very attributions other people develop too readily.

A final suggestion comes from my analysis of autobiographical statements by fiction writers. For example, an attributional analysis of a six-page autobiographical story by fiction writer David Duncan reveals almost no explicit attributional statements in a piece devoted almost entirely to description.[45] In contrast, autobiographical material by people like Iacocca and me is rich in attributional statements.

One technique for freeing ourselves from some of the effects of rigid causal beliefs in memories would be to recall events with a focus on description rather than attribution (e.g., recalling exactly *what* happened in a past action or decision, for example, rather than what the causal processes were). This may help us to question old assumptions about the causes of past successes or failures.

The Consistency Bias: Promoting Identity Stability through Autobiographical Memory

We tend to overestimate the similarity between our past selves and our present selves. When a particular identity is dominant, we seek to make it more "real" by revising our autobiographical memories to support the belief that it has been stable throughout our lives or that our lives have been leading up to the currently dominant identity.

In my own autobiographical statement, I reported that school and academic subjects were central to my life from an early age. This was partly because at age nineteen, I was thinking seriously about pursuing an academic work identity. I now recall that school was probably no more central to my life than it is to most young boys. I also wrote that I had felt anxiety and fear of failure at school as a boy. This was partly because at age nineteen, I felt the anxiety that comes to many who contemplate an academic career. These are both examples of the consistency bias.

The consistency bias is closely related to the hindsight bias. "Hindsight is always 20–20," as the cliché goes, and we often tell ourselves after important events have happened that we "should have known" they would. Research has shown that when we know how a decision or a series of events turned out, we overestimate how predictable the outcome was.[46] Similarly, when we look back on our lives, knowing how they "turned out so far," we tend to think we could have predicted the outcome, partly because we search our memory selectively for events that led up to our current mix of identities.

The consistency and hindsight biases lead us to overestimate of the stability of the self through time. Those subject to such biases have difficulty estimating the degree to which their current values and preferences will change over time and may therefore make unrealistic long-term plans. Many people (and businesses) planning for the future fail to consider contingency plans in case their values and identities change.

Additional insights into the consistency bias in autobiographical memory can be obtained by consulting the scholarly works on the study of autobiography as a literary genre.[47] Autobiographies are *stories* about our lives and may therefore be subject to processes like conventionalization in which details of the autobiographer's life may be distorted to fit narrative patterns common in our culture. Egan has identified several common narrative patterns in published autobiographies including "The Heroic Journey" (a pattern that probably characterizes Iacocca's 1981 autobiography), "Innocence to Experience," "Conversion" (observed in autobiographies of such diverse individuals as Roman Catholic Cardinal Newman and atheist John Stuart Mill), and "Confession."[48] Wu, in his study of sixteenth- and seventeenth-century Chinese autobiographies, found that many were based on the metaphor of a journey, suggesting that they might fit into the Heroic Journey or Innocence to Experience patterns.[49] In my judgment, my own autobiographical statement fits most comfortably into the Innocence to Experience pattern.

Recalling our lives within these narrative frameworks may make us overconfident in the predictability of our futures and may affect our decisions. For example, Lee Iacocca's Heroic Journey narrative did not allow for a quiet and uneventful retirement and this was one reason he decided to attempt, with Wall Street financier Kirk Kerkorian, a hostile takeover of the Chrysler company he had formerly "saved." By his own later admission, he "flunked retirement."[50]

Those who study autobiography as a literary genre suggest that we examine not only the statements themselves but the style in which they are written. I noted a similarity in style and approach to inquiry in the autobiographical statement, written before I had done any of my subsequent graduate work in psychology or management, and my current writing. It is tempting to say that this style of writing and thinking has been one of the stable or "real" aspects of my self-schema and that my identities have evolved around this general orientation toward exploration and inquiry; however, I may simply be falling victim to the consistency bias and overestimating the similarity between my past and present selves. If so, this example illustrates one potential consequence of this bias. It may cause us to believe that our lives have been moving toward our current mix of identities and that our current self-schema will persist into the future. We tend to believe that the core features of our self-schema remain similar over time even if the peripheral features are often changed to make them more supportive of the core features. It can be a comforting and even functional belief.

My own autobiographical statement shows an interest in inquiry and analysis of human behavior that has persisted until today. However, I associated this inquiry with academia at the time I wrote the autobiographical statement, partially because I hoped to pursue self-directed inquiry in academia for a living. I revised my memories of the importance of school and my anxiety about academic failure to make them more consistent with the academic identity.

Writing autobiographical statements at different points in your life is one way to determine which aspects of the self-schema have the greatest stability over time. Executives and others wishing to make use of this technique may wish to consult some of the serial autobiographical statements of former Chrysler CEO Lee Iacocca (1981, 1996) for examples of the biases in memory reconstruction discussed earlier.[51]

CONCLUSION

In this chapter, I have discussed autobiographical memory distortion, by which we convince ourselves that our lives have been moving inexorably toward our current set of identities. When we believe this, we are less likely to seriously consider business and life options that are inconsistent with these identities. We are also less likely to make wise use of the past. Realizing this, we may want to reduce the effects of this distortion. I have covered several approaches for doing this, and will add more in the final chapter.

An important question has to do with the accuracy and potential uses of autobiographical memories. Knowing that autobiographical memories are distorted, can we still use them to develop guidelines for future actions? Some professional students of the autobiography as a literary genre have suggested that concern for the "objective truth" of autobiographical statements is futile and misplaced and that only the "personal truth" of the author is relevant.[52] The logical conclusion of this line of thinking is that autobiography cannot provide us with reliable information about our past to guide decisions about the future.

Nothing I have read in my own autobiography or in the research on autobiographical memory justifies this extreme conclusion. Though it may be difficult for any reader to discern the truth of an autobiographical statement, it is meaningful to say that some statements are more true than others, that truer autobiographical statements provide the basis for better conclusions about the lessons that can be drawn from one person's life, and that thinking carefully about our autobiographical memories will help us develop truer autobiographical statements and ultimately to live wiser lives.

NOTES

1. G. Orwell, *1984* (New York: Harcourt, Brace & World, 1949).
2. S. Brown and K. Eisenhardt, *Competing on the Edge: Strategy as Structured Chaos* (Boston, MA: Harvard Business School Press, 1998), p. 245.
3. E. Erikson, *Young Man Luther* (New York: Norton, 1958), pp. 111–112.
4. A significant body of formal research dealing with autobiographical memory distortion lends support to this view. See, for example, A. Greenwald, "The totalitarian ego: Fabrication and revision of personal history," *American Psychologist* 35(1980): 603–618; A. Hankiss, "Ontologies of the Self: On the Mythological Rearranging of One's Life-History," in *Biography & Society: The Life-History Approach in the Social Sciences*, ed. D. Bertaux (Beverly Hills, CA: Sage, 1981).
5. I found useful discussions of this topic in a book edited by psychologist Robert Sternberg entitled *Wisdom: Its Nature, Origins, and Development* (New York: Cambridge University Press, 1990). See especially K. Kitchener and H. Brenner, "Wisdom and Reflective Judgment: Knowing the Face of Uncertainty," and D. Robinson, "Wisdom through the Ages," pp. 21–22.

6. J. Fitzgerald, "Autobiographical Memory and Conceptualizations of the Self," in *Theoretical Perspectives on Autobiographical Memory*, ed. M. Conway (London: Kulwer Academic Publishers, 1992). A. Greenwald, "The totalitarian ego: Fabrication and revision of personal history," *American Psychologist* 35(1980): 603–618. J. Kotre, *White Gloves: How We Create Ourselves through Memory* (New York: Free Press, 1995). U. Neisser, *Memory Observed: Remembering in Natural Contexts* (San Francisco: Freeman, 1982). B. Ross, *Remembering the Personal Past* (New York: Oxford Press, 1991). R. Schank, *Dynamic Memory* (Cambridge, England: Cambridge University Press, 1982). R. Schank, *Tell Me a Story: A New Look at Real and Artificial Memory* (New York: Charles Scribner's Sons, 1990). J. Singer and P. Salovey, *The Remembered Self* (New York: Free Press, 1993).

7. Literary studies of autobiography and autobiographical fiction are numerous. Pascal's *Design and Truth in Autobiography* addresses the question of distortion most directly (R. Pascal, *Design and Truth in Autobiography*, Cambridge, MA: Harvard University Press, 1960). Egan's *Patterns of Experience in Autobiography* describes the use of common cultural themes in the construction of autobiographical narratives (S. Egan, *Patterns of Experience in Autobiography*, Chapel Hill, NC: University of North Carolina Press, 1984). Coe's study of 150 childhood autobiographies (R.Coe, *When the Grass was Taller: Autobiography and the Experience of Childhood*, New Haven, CT: Yale University Press, 1984) touches on the issue of memory distortion as well, as does the analysis of Marcel Proust's *Remembrance of Things Past* by Harold Bloom (H. Bloom, *Marcel Proust's Remembrance of Things Past*, New York: Chelsea House, 1987).

8. D. McAdams, *The Stories We Live By: Personal Myths and the Making of the Self* (New York: Guilford Press, 1993).

9. F. Bartlett, *Remembering: A Study in Experimental and Social Psychology* (Cambridge, MA: Cambridge University Press, 1932).

10. Bartlett, p. 213.

11. Bartlett, p. 209.

12. C. Cofer, D. Chmiekewski, and J. Brockway, "Constructive Processes in Human Memory," in *The Structure of Human Memory*, ed. C. Cofer (San Francisco: Freeman, 1976); M. Northway, "The influence of age and social group on children's remembering," *British Journal of Psychology* 27(1936): 11–29; I. Paul, *Studies in Remembering: The Reproduction of Connected & Extended Verbal Material* (New York: International Universities Press, 1959); M. Tressalt and S. Spragg, "Changes occurring in the serial reproduction of verbally perceived materials," *Journal of Genetic Psychology* 58(1941): 255–264.

13. W. Gardner, C. Pickett, and M. Brewer, "Social exclusion and selective memory: How the need to belong influences memory for social events," *Personality and Social Psychology Bulletin* 26(2000): 486–496.

14. See Greenwald (1980) for a summary of research supporting each of these patterns.

15. E. Langer, *The Psychology of Control* (Beverly Hills, CA: Sage, 1983).

16. C. Schwenk, "The use of participant recollection in the modeling of organizational decision processes," *Academy of Management Review* 10(1985b): 496–503.

17. S. Clapham and C. Schwenk, "Self-serving attributions, managerial cognition, and firm performance," *Strategic Management Journal* 12(1991): 219–229.

18. See, for example, E. Langer, "The illusion of control," *Journal of Personality and Social Psychology* 32(1975): 311–328; E. Langer, "The psychology of chance," *Journal for the Theory of Social Behavior* 7(1978): 185–207; E. Langer, *The Psychology of Control* (Beverly Hills, CA: Sage, 1983); E. Langer and J. Roth, "The effect of sequence of outcomes in a

chance task on the illusion of control," *Journal of Personality and Social Psychology* 32(1975): 951–955; L. Larwood and W. Whittaker, "Managerial myopia: Self-serving biases in organizational planning," *Journal of Applied Psychology* 67(1977): 194–198; H. Lefcourt, "The functions of the illusion of control and freedom," *American Psychologist* 28(1973): 417–425. Langer's 1983 book *The Psychology of Control* is probably the best place to start reviewing this work.

19. E. Langer, "The illusion of control," *Journal of Personality and Social Psychology* 32(1975):311–328.

20. L. Larwood and W. Whittaker, "Managerial myopia: Self-serving biases in organizational planning," *Journal of Applied Psychology* 67(1977): 194–198.

21. Langer, E. *The Psychology of Control* (Beverly Hills, CA: Sage, 1983).

22. Langer, *The Psychology of Control*, p. 24.

23. I. Duhaime and C. Schwenk, "Conjectures on cognitive simplification processes in acquisition and divestment decision-making," *Academy of Management Review* 10(1985): 287–295.

24. See *The Economist*, May 27, 2000, pp. 71–73.

25. H. Einhorn and R. Hogarth, "Confidence in judgment: Persistence of the illusion of validity," *Psychological Review* 85(1978): 395–416; B. Fischhoff, P. Slovic, and S. Lichtenstein, "Knowing with certainty: The appropriateness of extreme confidence," *Journal of Experimental Psychology: Human Perception and Performance* 3(1977): 552–564; A. Koriat, S. Lichtenstein, and B. Fischhoff, "Reasons for confidence," *Journal of Experimental Psychology: Human Learning and Memory* 6(1980): 107–118.

26. Duhaime & Schwenk, 1985, "Conjectures on cognitive simplification processes in acquisition and divestment decision-making;" C. Schwenk, "Cognitive simplification processes in strategic decision-making," *Strategic Management Journal* 5(1984): 111–128.

27. H. Einhorn and R. Hogarth, "Confidence in judgment: Persistence of the illusion of validity," *Psychological Review* 85(1978): 395–416. See pp. 396–399.

28. Kotre, *White Gloves: How We Create Ourselves through Memory*, pp. 161–170.

29. D. Bem and H. McConnell, "Testing the self-perception explanation of dissonance phenomena: On the salience of premanipulation attitudes," *Journal of Personality and Social Psychology* 14(1970): 23–31; D. Wixon and L. Laird, "Awareness and attitude change in the forced-compliance paradigm: The importance of when," *Journal of Personality & Social Psychology* 34(1976): 376–384.

30. Loftus summarized research on the topic in a book entitled *Eyewitness Testimony*. See E. Loftus, *Eyewitness Testimony* (Boston: Harvard University Press, 1996).

31. V. Nabokov, *Speak, Memory* (New York: Putnam, 1947), p. 51.

32. A. Greenwald, "The Totalitarian Ego," p. 608.

33. A. Bandura. *Social Foundations of Thought and Action* (Englewood Cliffs, NJ: Prentice-Hall, 1986).

34. D. Wood and A. Bandura, "Social cognitive theory of organizational management," *Academy of Management Review* 13(1989): 361–368: 364–366.

35. See A. Huff, *Strategic Argument Mapping* (Cambridge: Cambridge University Press, 1990) for a more detailed explanation of the method of coding causal attributions.

36. Studies by Salancik and Meindl (G. Salancik and J. Meindl, "Corporate attributions as strategic illusions of management control," *Administrative Science Quarterly* 28(1984): 238–254) and Clapham and Schwenk (S. Clapham and C. Schwenk, "Self-serving attributions, managerial cognition, and firm performance," *Strategic Management Journal* 12(1991): 219–229) provide evidence of this bias. Further evidence is cited by these authors.

37. See the discussion of the public relations view in Salancik and Meindl (1984), "Corporate attributions as strategic illusions of management control." I have described my alternative explanation in greater detail in a study of attributions for success and failure in executives' statements to industry analysts. See the essay by Anne Huff and me in the book *Strategic Argument Mapping* (A. Huff and C. Schwenk, "Bias and Sensemaking in Good Times and Bad," in *Strategic Argument Mapping*, ed. A. Huff, Cambridge: Cambridge University Press, 1990).

38. See S. Clapham and C. Schwenk, "Self-serving attributions, managerial cognition, and firm performance," *Strategic Management Journal* 12(1991): 238–254.

39. L. Iacocca, *Iacocca* (New York: Dell, 1981).

40. M. Friedman and R. D. Friedman, *Two Lucky People: Memoirs* (Chicago: University of Chicago Press, 1999).

41. Augustine, *Confessions*, ed. R. Coffin (Baltimore, MD: Penguin, 1961).

42. For an account of Delorean's efforts to save the Delorean Motor Company, see "Biases in investor decision-making: The case of John Delorean" by Professor Thomas Bateman and me in *The Mid-American Journal of Business*, 1986, pp. 5–11.

43. See J. Delorean and T. Schwarz, *Delorean* (Grand Rapids, MI: Zondervan Books, 1985).

44. C. Shaw, *The Jack-Roller: A Delinquent Boy's Own Story* (Chicago: University of Chicago Press, 1930).

45. D. Duncan, *River Teeth* (New York: Bantam, 1996), pp. 223–228.

46. For a discussion of some of this research, see D. Kahneman, P. Slovic, and A. Tversky, *Judgment under Uncertainty: Heuristics and Biases* (Cambridge: Cambridge University Press, 1982).

47. See, for example, Coe's study of 150 childhood autobiographies, *When the Grass Was Taller* (R. Coe, *When the Grass Was Taller: Autobiography and the Experience of Childhood*, New Haven: Yale University Press, 1984).

48. S. Egan, *Patterns of Experience in Autobiography* (Chapel Hill, NC: University of North Carolina Press, 1984).

49. Pei-Yi Wu, *The Confucian's Progress: Autobiographical Writings in Traditional China* (Princeton, NJ: Princeton University Press, 1990).

50. L. Iacocca, "How I flunked retirement," *Esquire* (1996): 17–23. June.

51. Iacocca, ibid., 1996, and *Iacocca*, 1981.

52. See P. Eakin, *American Autobiography: Retrospect and Prospect* (Madison, WI: University of Wisconsin Press, 1991); M. Kadar, *Essays in Life Writing* (Toronto: University of Toronto Press, 1992); and J. Olney, *Metaphors of Self* (Princeton, NJ: Princeton University Press, 1972) for discussions of this perspective and how it is reflected in techniques like serial autobiography.

APPENDIX F:
AUTOBIOGRAPHICAL STATEMENT

Father and mother had been drifting and wandering from place to place, and job to job for nine years or so. Then dad wanted to come to Oregon. The restlessness of both my parents (especially dad) is here apparent. Once they got to Oregon I was born. At that age, memory is just developing. I tend to think it was my birth that forced them to settle down. Dad began to work and drive himself with a new purpose and started his own business. However, this purpose was not without its harmful side effects. He put on weight, neglected mother and (perhaps) he sought to build me into something worthy of striving for.

I did most of the things a young boy does. I played all I could. School was built up for me so I looked forward to it. I worked well and was an all right kid but I know I was shy. I must have liked the idea of school. I was always a fair to good but never inspired student. My goal was to please teachers and thereby Dad. I expected fair to good grades though I was never really sure what the teachers wanted from me and that made for anxiety.

I did well all through school. I was quite sensitive to criticism. Dad helped and pushed me at this time. I became dedicated to school and to becoming what he wanted me to be.

One day when I was ten, dad called me into the room and told me that Mom wanted to leave him. The next day my best friend of the past two years moved. The two events combined could have been quite a trauma. I wonder why it wasn't.

Later I met my mother's new husband. I never liked him much but I have learned to tolerate him. The divorce must have really disoriented Dad (since he said it did). He seemed to lose all ambition and did a lot of crazy things.

During this time I devoted time to reading and studying things I liked rather than assigned subjects. It seems that this tendency has diminished as I've gotten older and more realistic. However, even now I sometimes feel guilty that I still study a great deal independently and this detracts from my school study time. I realize that independent study can be useful but I fear mine is directed by my whims. I read Treasure Island and Sherlock Holmes, collected comics, and dreamed of being a superhero or a master criminal like Professor Moriarity. I imagined myself as isolated from others and in some way superior or special. All in all, I was painfully shy, wanted badly to do what others wanted so they would like me, and was very sensitive to praise and criticism.

In my sophomore year, two things happened. First, I began to study psychology. Secondly, I began to think more independently. This I regard as the earliest stirring of self-will. I became very interested in understanding how people work and what motivates them. I lost interest in the easy type of life I had wanted when younger. That is, a small place in business at an easy job where I could have plenty of time for fantasy. My interest in psychology was growing and my desire to do well in everything was also growing.

My senior year was marked by a good deal of seeming happiness, an exploration of a number of new feelings, experiences, etc., and almost constant reminders of my own worth from people close to me. On the other hand, I also had doubts, anxiety, uncertainty, etc.

I was in a lot of activities and was well known but did as little as possible in each. My goal was not to be good at anything but rather to have others think I was. I wanted to be loved and successful badly and perhaps this was the reason I was constantly concerned with my superiority or inferiority to others.

As my senior year progressed my curiosity about the mind increased. I realize that my interests were very diverse and the subjects I studied were ones which caught my attention at the moment. I do not recall most of what I studied because I was not studying in an integrated way. I was not studying but rather exploring.

During my freshman year in college, I worked very little at school. Chaos was the dominant thing in my life. I worked on independent study projects in psychology with my advisor Dr. Anderson. I began to feel that I wanted an academic career.

This sort of autobiography has several uses: First, it is important to remember that a person's conceptions and ideas about life change as he develops. However, if they are not written down they flee from memory. If they are recorded, they can be looked back on later and developed. In this way a more profound communication of feelings between yourself and others can be achieved. Second, there is a way in which the past can bind you. It involves getting your present self (perceptions, thoughts, desires) confused with your past image of yourself. Now, by actually getting into one of these autobiographies, you get an understanding of the process by which these past images are constructed. This can actually help you to escape from this problem. Third, if events are recorded objectively, you can build more effective techniques for dealing with problems by recalling your past mistakes. I must remember this autobiography is at least partly an imaginative construction based on what I want to remember from the past.

3

Promoting Identity
Distinctiveness:
Selves Defined Through
Polarizing Conflict

This thing of darkness I acknowledge mine.
— Shakespeare, *The Tempest*,[1] act 5, scene 1

Chapters 1 and 2 described how the self-schema forms and how identity is sustained by autobiographical memory reconstruction. I will now discuss how identity is defined and differentiated in social conflicts and how, through this process, different groups of individuals come to incompatible views on crucial decisions. This chapter will also serve as a transition between individual schemas, discussed in Chapter 1, and organizational knowledge structures, which will be covered in Chapter 4. Identity provides the link between individual thought processes and organizational decisions.

In the preceding quote from *The Tempest*, Prospero admits that the monster Caliban is his servant. When people engage in polarizing conflict, they describe their opponents as monsters because it reinforces their own identities. In a sense, they create monsters to serve their own interests.

Social identity theory, discussed in Chapter 2, suggests that we define our identities by identifying those who belong to our social group and those who are outsiders. As we interact with other in-group members, we develop shared perceptions, shared symbols, and shared heuristics for processing information. These develop into distinctive worldviews with their own definitions of terms and shared references.

Those who hold different worldviews are divided by their use of language. When groups with differing views attempt to engage in dialogue, they initially speak past each other without fully understanding why. It is difficult for strongly identified group members to communicate with other groups because of the differences in worldviews and the use of language. These difficulties are compounded by the stereotyping of out-groups or opponents.

Group members define their identities partly through defining their opponents. Sociologist Manuel Castells, in *The Power of Identity*, argues that identity-based social groups can be defined partly by identifying their adversaries. He demonstrates the value of identifying adversaries in his excellent analysis of groups as diverse as the Zapatistas in southern Mexico, Japan's homicidal Aum Shinrikyo cult, and a variety of environmental groups based in America but having international membership.[2]

Unfortunately, when we clearly define our adversaries, we are tempted to stereotype them. Stereotyped views plus differences in the use of key terms cause opponents to misunderstand each other. As a result, individuals and organizations can make tactical blunders, miscalculating how competitors will respond to their actions. They also miss opportunities for collaboration, negotiation, and the sharing of resources. Books like *Negotiating Rationally*[3] and *The Essentials of Negotiation*[4] discuss research on reasons why people, businesses, and societies become involved in these conflicts and excessively identified with one side. Not surprisingly, I believe that personal identity holds the key to polarizing conflict.

Many publicly debated issues show evidence of polarizing conflict. In Chapter 1, I mentioned several of them. The following section will discuss opposing views of marijuana use in the workplace and describe the ways in which the identities of combatants in this debate affect their views of data and arguments on each side.

After discussing how we define our own identities in conflicts, I explore the ways we define (or stereotype) our opponents. The work of Berger and Luckman[5] on stereotyping of out-groups will provide the context for this discussion. Aho[6] expanded on the work of Berger and Luckman and provided examples to illustrate five activities involved in stereotyping: naming, legitimation, mythmaking, sedimentation, and ritual. A recent environmental dispute will be used to illustrate the ways partisans on each side construct inaccurate views of each other through the use of these activities.

Polarizing conflict, like autobiographical memory distortion, serves to define and enhance our self-schemas but it also produces problems. The problems caused by polarizing conflict include the polarized use of common terms, the overexploitation of common resources, and escalating commitment. In the last half of the chapter, I will discuss these difficulties.

DEFINING OUR IDENTITIES IN POLARIZING CONFLICTS

In Chapter 1, I suggested that constructing an identity within the self-schema involves constructing an internally consistent and self-contained worldview that supports the self. Part of this process involves identifying those who do not share your identity or who represent a threat to your worldview.[7] Your own worldview is defined through this process and you become committed to it.

To illustrate the connections between identities and worldviews, I will discuss the public debate on the question of drug use, focusing on one aspect of this question with which I have recently been involved.[8] The debate concerns whether companies should attempt to eradicate marijuana use from the workplace and whether the federal government should expend public funds to assist companies in achieving this objective.

The term "public debate" is, perhaps, an inaccurate description of the discussion of marijuana use as it is currently conducted in political campaigns and media news reports. Like many public policy questions, those related to cannabis have become highly polarized. Most of those speaking publicly on issues such as pre-employment testing for marijuana and the marijuana-free workplace advocate one of two diametrically opposed positions on the harm caused by the substance and the appropriate governmental action with regard to it.

By identifying the assumptions of the adherents of these two positions, we can better understand their identities. It is important to remember that supporters of both positions believe they are promoting positive values. For committed advocates in both camps, the issues in the marijuana debate are moral issues and they view their perspective as occupying the moral high ground.

Since partisans on each side have their own rhetoric and often use language that conveys meanings to opponents different from what they intend, I will attempt to use neutral language in describing the assumptions of each side. I will call the two positions the Individual Liberty position and the Responsible Living position. Those who take the Individual Liberty position are in favor of less regulation of marijuana because they see themselves as making a reasonable effort to balance the needs of society with the need for individual freedom. Those who take the Responsible Living position are in favor of more regulation and see themselves as passionate defenders of the interests of those who are harmed by the drug.

Supporters of the Responsible Living position maintain that our culture puts too much emphasis on satisfying personal needs and wants. This emphasis can lead to a kind of hedonism and the single-minded pursuit of instant gratification. They feel that recreational use of drugs, including marijuana, is a manifestation of this excess, so drug use should be discouraged. If it were possible to eliminate drug use by persuasion and rational argument, they would prefer to handle the drug problem this way. However, since people are constantly bombarded by advertising and messages promoting instant wish gratification, reasoned argument is often not sufficient to deter them from engaging in behaviors they may regret later. Thus, legal prohibitions may be necessary to help people behave the way they themselves would want to behave after sober reflection.

Respect for the law is an important part of this worldview. While proponents of this view admit that some laws may be immoral and such laws should be opposed and perhaps even broken, they do *not* see the use of marijuana as an act of conscience but rather one of hedonism. They feel that if marijuana users wish to be free to smoke, they should work to change the law but obey it until it is changed.

Further, they argue that if employers are lax about drug use, it creates a climate in which those who are ambivalent about marijuana use are more likely to succumb to the temptation, much like permitting smoking on the job makes it more difficult for employees to quit. They claim that marijuana use may mask other problems on the job. If, for example, employees feel they need to reduce stress, the stress itself may be an indication that certain aspects of the job need to be changed.

For members of this faction, marijuana use on the job is a serious enough problem to justify attempts to create a drug-free workplace. The lack of clear and consistent support from research for the claim that marijuana reduces performance does not dissuade them. The fact that researchers have not yet demonstrated the harmful effects of marijuana on performance does not provide a sufficiently strong argument to counteract the argument that marijuana use is excessively hedonistic and illegal. They feel that the burden of proof should be on the opponents of pre-employment testing to provide a stronger case. Unless it can be proven that marijuana does not increase on-the-job accidents, employers should be responsible for discouraging its use in the interests of their employees and customers.

On the other hand, those who support the Individual Liberty position feel that creating a marijuana-free workplace is unnecessary and that preemployment testing creates problems of its own. They argue that since research has not proven marijuana has negative effects, there are no compelling reasons to outlaw it and to eliminate it from the workplace. Further, they do not see marijuana use as part of the commercial culture that inundates us but rather as something that helps reduce the power of self-indulgent commercialism.

Regarding the importance of obeying the law, members of this faction point to the amount of harm laws prohibiting the use of marijuana have done and say that these laws are disobeyed *because* they are unjust. This shows that both sides hold different causal models. Individual Liberty partisans assign more causal significance to the law itself than do the Responsible Living advocates and feel that the law itself has caused much of the harm attributed to marijuana use. Since preemployment marijuana testing is part of the legalistic approach to dealing with marijuana use, partisans on this side see it as a waste of money and an unnecessary threat to personal liberty.

Typically, partisans on each side state their views and pay little attention to the views of the other side. When partisans become overidentified with their views, their self-concepts and identities are threatened by the opposing side. Within such partisan contexts, it is easy to see why facts are manipulated and misinterpreted.

Those on each side judge data on the basis of their usefulness to their cause. Both unconscious psychological biases and more calculating political motives encourage committed activists to reject data that do not support their views.

Partisans committed to the Responsible Living position feel strongly that we have a moral obligation to prevent the use of intoxicants. They feel there are compelling ethical reasons for the federal government to do everything possible to eliminate drug abuse, in addition to the economic benefits that might result from decreasing use of illicit substances. However, for Responsible Living advocates, it is not necessary to prove that marijuana has a negative impact on job performance in order to justify efforts to make workplaces drug-free, in part because the purely financial consequences of drug use are not as important as the moral and ethical effects. Consequently, they demand that employers do everything possible to deter drug use unless and until their opponents offer conclusive evidence that such policies do not increase sobriety.

On the other hand, for those committed to the Individual Liberty position on drug policy, the lack of conclusive proof that marijuana reduces worker safety and productivity has dramatically different implications. Opposing any unnecessary limits on personal lifestyle choices, partisans in this camp would prefer to place the burden of proof regarding the value of a drug-free workplace on its advocates. This group feels that policy makers should be required to show that existing laws are not already too intrusive. Strong economic evidence that preemployment drug testing and other workplace antidrug measures are cost-effective would be necessary to convince committed Individual Liberty partisans that preemployment drug testing and other such practices are justified. These advocates would further argue that those favoring interference with private, informed decisions by adults should be required to prove that the policies they support are the least constraining alternatives available.

I have developed simplified cognitive maps of the proponents on each side using the same basic approach I used in drawing the cognitive map of my autobiographical statement in Chapter 2. These are included in Figure 3.1.

The research on autobiographical memory discussed in Chapter 2 suggests that people identified with each side of this debate will distort their memories of events relevant to the debate to make them more consistent with their current identities. Moreover, those who are most strongly identified with each side would have the most distorted autobiographical memories. I was unable to find data to verify this prediction in my study of marijuana in the workplace, but I did find one possible illustration of autobiographical memory distortion by politicians who are strong supporters of the war on drugs.

Some years ago, a number of national political figures made public confessions that they had used marijuana in their youth. These statements were interesting in their similarity. The marijuana use typically occurred "in a party situation," it was

Figure 3.1
Cognitive Maps in the Debate on Workplace Marijuana Testing

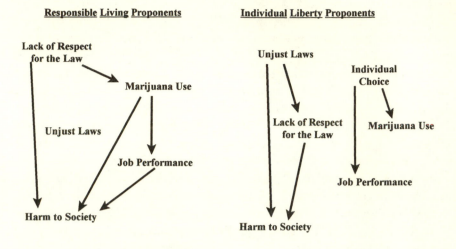

a single youthful indiscretion, and every one of the statements expressed "deep regret" that some individuals felt almost immediately after they inhaled. Former President Clinton admits he smoked marijuana but claims he did not inhale.

I believe that at least some of these confessions show evidence of autobiographical memory distortion in the service of these politicians' identities as drug warriors. I suspect that some of them may have used marijuana more than once, in contexts other than "party situations," and may have felt little or no regret at the time. Further, I do not see how former President Clinton's memory can be accurate. I have never known anyone to smoke marijuana without inhaling it.

How would such distortions in memory affect partisans' views of their own position in a debate? They should increase advocates' belief that they have held their present views for a long time and that their identities are involved in the position they support. If I, as a proponent of the Responsible Living position, incorrectly believe that I never condoned marijuana use but merely used it in response to peer pressure at a party, I am less likely to question my assumptions about drug policy.

In the introduction to this book, I listed several public policy issues on which individuals hold extreme and incompatible views. In this section of the chapter, I have attempted to describe two reasonable and compelling sets of beliefs on just *one* of these. How can we make reasonable and informed decisions on issues like the control of marijuana use when there are such divergent views on the nature of the problem? The first step is to recognize that partisan public debate is not a productive way to address this issue. The second step is for those interested in the issue to take a close look at the research to see what it does and does not say about marijuana and job performance.

Unfortunately, the process of public debate tends to make the participants increasingly entrenched in their positions. Simultaneously, autobiographical memory distortion leads to stereotyping that tends to reduce their understanding of the views and assumptions of their opponents. We can learn a great deal about the self-image of these individuals by observing how they describe their opponents. To provide an illustration and explanation of this process of stereotyping opponents, I will turn to my next example of identity-based conflict.

DEFINING OUR OPPONENTS IN POLARIZING CONFLICTS

When we categorize others into in-groups and out-groups, we construct prototypes to represent the typical features of group members and outsiders. These prototypes help us to define ourselves and others.[9] Berger and Luckman[10] and Aho[11] have shown how group identities are defined through the identification of "out-groups," those who do not share the group's worldview. This process almost always involves some stereotyping of the out-groups. The five aspects of this stereotyping are: naming, legitimation, mythmaking, sedimentation, and ritual.

For an opposing group to be defined, it must be named or labeled. In-group members define their opponents with terms like "environmental extremist" and "multinational corporate dupe." The labels are then legitimated through demonstrations of their validity. One way to do this is to cite examples of out-group members who fit the stereotype. Mythmaking refers to the development of biographical or historical accounts that explain why it is inevitable, necessary, and predictable that the members of the opposing group behave as they do. Sedimentation occurs when shared myths are communicated throughout the group. Finally, public discussions can become rituals that reinforce the stereotypes.

Aho provides examples of these five activities in a number of public debates on social issues, including the activities of the Ku Klux Klan and the genetic basis of IQ.[12] Rather than use one of Aho's examples to illustrate how identities are defined through polarized conflict, however, I will use a recent conflict surrounding the development of a gold mine in Montana. In the mid-1990s, the Phelps-Dodge Corporation and a smaller mining company named Canyon Resources announced their intention to use a process called cyanide heap leaching to extract gold from ore-bearing rock on a site near the Big Blackfoot River in Montana (made famous by the story and film *A River Runs Through It*). A group called the Clark Fork Coalition opposed the project and fought it in the courts and in the media. After a period of intensifying conflict, Phelps-Dodge withdrew from the project and the voters of Montana passed an initiative banning the use of cyanide in gold mining in 1998. Subsequently, Canyon Resources experienced a dramatic decline in its stock price and adopted a "poison pill" takeover defense. They experienced an $800,000 loss in the first three months of the year 2000.

There were two clearly identifiable opposing camps in this debate, those in favor of developing the mine and those against it. Those most strongly committed to each side expressed views commonly heard in debates about developing (or exploiting) natural resources. I will use quotes from articles published in *The Economist*[13] and the *Engineering & Mining Journal*[14] to represent the views of those favoring development and from articles in *Cascadia Times*[15] and *Sierra Magazine*[16] for those against development. I will focus on the ways partisans characterize their opponents.

As in the marijuana debate, both sides saw the issues in the debate as moral and both sides felt they occupied the high ground. Those favoring the development of natural resources saw themselves as making reasonable efforts to balance the needs of the environment with the needs for economic development and jobs. Those in favor of preserving the environment saw themselves as passionate defenders of the natural world that they love. These were essential aspects of the identities of those on both sides of the debate.

Regarding the activity of naming, those in favor of development refer to their opponents as "extremists," "lovers of big government," and "doomsters." All of these terms suggest the opponents are unreasonable. Those in favor of environmental preservation refer to their opponents as "neo-colonialists," "corporate criminals," and "purveyors of corporate greed," names that suggest a lack of love for the environment and an inappropriate concern for the financial aspects of the issue.

For the antidevelopment side, the ultimate enemy is Big (multinational) Business, which is characterized this way, "Like all good capitalists, they feel, like the trout with whom I was about to tangle, a need to aggrandize their shocking bulk."[17] For the prodevelopment side, the ultimate enemy is Big Government. They see behind the "Green Crusade" the desire of politicians to augment their own power to constrain human liberty, not merely at the national level but through the creation of a centralized body charged with global governance, which will cause national sovereignty to gradually whither away. According to Maxey, "The Club of Rome puts readers on notice that several 'global environmental crises' actually provide a basis for world/global governance that will entail the dissolution of independent nations and a supranational realignment of power."[18] The Green Crusade is a "quest for power through Global Governance."[19]

Readers will recognize the stereotyping on both sides. One of the costs of this stereotyping is that neither camp has an accurate view of its adversary.

Once the opponent has been named and stereotyped, the stereotypes must be legitimated. Books like *The Case Against the Global Economy*,[20] *Healing a Wounded World: Economics, Ecology, and Health for a Sustainable Life*,[21] *Global Meltdown: Immigration, Multiculturalism, and National Breakdown in the New World Disorder*,[22] and *Betrayal of Science and Reason*,[23] provide information to legitimize the names used against those who are in favor of development. Books like *The Vision of the Anointed*,[24] *Eco-Sanity*,[25] and *The Ultimate Resource*[26] provide information to legitimize names used against those who defend the environment.

Mythmaking occurs when proponents of each perspective discuss their speculations about the reasons their opponents take their positions. Often, these uncharitable speculations involve the personal gain opponents expect from advocating their positions. Discussions among supporters of each position serve to communicate their views, thereby ensuring sedimentation. Finally, rallies and other public actions undertaken to block or promote the development of the mine were the rituals by which the proponents of each perspective reinforced their views.

To illustrate the ways opponents are viewed, several examples of statements by advocates on each side will be presented. Looking first at the ways the prodevelopment side portrays its perceived opponents, in the book *Eco-Sanity* environmentalists are portrayed as promoters of the "crisis of the month club." In *The Vision of the Anointed*, Paul Ehrlich, a scientist prominent in the environmental movement, is described as a "Teflon prophet," who is "preeminent for having been wrong by the widest margins, on the most varied subjects—and for maintaining his reputation untarnished through it all."[27]

On the other side, in the book *Betrayal of Science and Reason*, co-authored by Paul and Anne Ehrlich, Julian Simon, the author of *The Ultimate Resource*, is described as a "brownlash spokesperson," who makes "socially dangerous and scientifically ridiculous" assertions.[28] We can learn something about the self-image of the combatants by observing how they describe those on the other side. By calling our opponents irrational and dangerous, we enhance our own identity as rational and morally upright.

The mythmaking process proceeds through the specification of tactics used by the enemy. For example, one of those strongly opposing development stated:

[Mining corporations] descend like predatory gods from outside the life of a place, force all residents, human and non-, to live by their laws of short-term supply and demand, and depart the instant their profit margins wane. . . . Cyanide miners are eager to maim us for the simple reason that they have no intention of inhabiting our region, and our long-term suffering will be their short-term profit.

Corporate prospecting is a process in which the staking of claims is blithely incidental compared to the work of purchasing politicians, smothering and bullying the opposition, gutting environmental safeguards, dominating the media, burying past travesties, and reinvesting corporate gold profits in lawyers' fees, lobbyists' salaries, and huge slush funds to handle the catastrophes that inevitably accompany this technology.[29]

Those favoring development, on the other hand, argue that "environmental extremists" operate by polarizing individuals and working with journalists who oversimplify issues to exploit fear and apprehension and create hysteria in readers and viewers that will overwhelm their better judgment. According to Maxey,

No less a political figure than U.S. Vice President Al Gore has entered the lists along with other sustainability gurus. . . . He selects an analogy linking man's destructive role in the degradation of the earth to the destructive role of the Kristallnacht ("night of broken glass") perpetrated by Nazis in Germany.[30]

History is selectively used by each side to provide support for their myths. Prodevelopment people point to wrong predictions made by their opponents in the past in order to cast doubt on their predictions about future environmental problems. For example, the *Economist*[31] pointed out that the Club of Rome and others estimated in the early 1970s that world oil reserves amounted to 550 billion barrels. Since that time, the world has used 600 billion barrels and unexploited reserves are currently estimated at 900 billion barrels. The Club of Rome made similarly wrong predictions about natural gas, silver, tin, uranium, aluminum, copper, lead, and zinc. In every case, it said finite reserves were approaching exhaustion and that prices would rise steeply.

The *Economist* used this fact to cast doubt on current predictions regarding environmental threats made by the Club of Rome in the group's recent book *Beyond the Limits*. The article also describes a bet made between "a much-feted environmentalist called Paul Ehrlich" and the economist Julian Simon in 1980. Ehrlich bet that the price of a variety of minerals would rise over the next decade as they became more scarce, while Simon bet that the price would fall as new reserves were discovered and as technological innovations reduced the need for the minerals. Simon won. This example is cited in support of the *Economist*'s stereotype of environmentalists as proudly ignorant of and hostile to economics.[32] Simon himself has accused environmentalists of ignorance of economics in such books as *The Ultimate Resource*.

Those opposed to development often emphasize the past errors made by companies to cast doubt on their current actions. For example, Koberstein, in *Cascadia Times*, cites past environmental damage by mining companies to support the conclusion that they cannot be trusted today.

Selective use of history to support the mythology of both sides in such conflicts serves to reinforce the identity and worldview of each side. However, it makes each side less willing to honestly face the internal contradictions and problems in their own views. Those who favor development often have difficulty dealing with genuine examples of market failure while those who oppose it sometimes have difficulty with the fact that some quality of life indicators, such as life expectancy in developed countries, have improved at the same time these countries have experienced increasing levels of "environmental exploitation and degradation." For ex-

Figure 3.2
Cognitive Maps in the Mining Debate

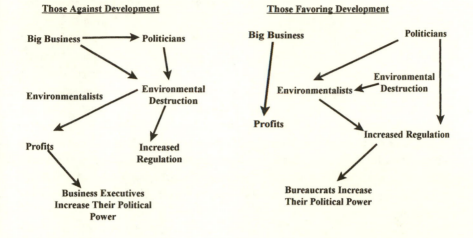

ample, in the book *Betrayal of Science and Reason*, Ehrlich makes the untrue claim that Julian Simon won his bet because the decline in metals prices from 1980 to 1990 was temporary and limited to a small number of metals.[33]

I have attempted to clarify both sides in the debate by developing simplified cognitive maps from the arguments presented by proponents. These are shown in Figure 3.2. The maps of both sides contain similar elements, but the causal relationships between these elements are very different. However, these maps do not show the fundamental differences in the ways these elements are defined by proponents on each side. Terms like "profits" and "environmental destruction" have radically different meanings to those who are identified with different sides.

In the next section, I will discuss the polarizing use of terms in our "common language" and how this reinforces our identities while simultaneously dividing us from those who use these terms differently.

SELVES, LANGUAGE, AND COMMUNICATION

As I noted at the beginning of this chapter, those who hold different worldviews are often divided by their use of language. I found the work of Cohen[34] helpful in understanding how words develop different meanings for different groups. He studied the way individuals in a small English village interpreted a shared vocabulary and demonstrated that this vocabulary concealed basic differences in beliefs. In his view, each individual "spins the common verbal currency into individually distinctive 'loops' of meaning which constitute their respective worldviews."[35]

I believe something similar happens in many polarized public debates on important issues. For example, Ehrlich recounts that Simon made a second offer to bet ecologists that "any trend pertaining to material human welfare" will improve or remain constant over the next decade. In response, Ehrlich and Stephen Schneider, a climatologist at Stanford University, offered to enter into a bet with Simon dealing with fifteen trends, including the increase in the average temperature of the earth, the level of carbon dioxide in the atmosphere, and the concentration of ozone in the lower atmosphere. Simon declined, stating that he would bet only on trends *directly* pertaining to human welfare, such as life expectancy, leisure time, or purchasing power. Ehrlich interpreted this as Simon "going back on his original challenge."[36] However, a reading of Simon's work suggests that his definition of "trends pertaining to human welfare" is consistent with his response to Ehrlich's offer, although it is inconsistent with Ehrlich's definition. Such differences in the use of terms exacerbate conflict between the two camps.

Because of differences in the understanding of terms, members of each camp make statements they consider reasonable and moderate but that sound deceitful or incomprehensible to their opponents. Since opponents understand key terms differently, they interpret information differently and have different ideas about what constitutes a "biased" view of their conflict. These claims are supported by research on perceptions of media bias by partisans.[37] Researchers presented identical samples of television network coverage of a massacre in Beirut to pro-Israeli and pro-Arab partisans, as well as to individuals who were neutral in their view of the conflict. Study participants were then asked to evaluate the fairness of these reports. Partisans, as compared to neutrals, tended to evaluate the reports as biased in favor of the opposing side. Further, partisans recalled more negative references to their side and predicted that the reports would sway neutrals in a hostile direction. These results show that the same information will be evaluated and recalled differently by those committed to different sides in a conflict.

The misinterpretation of common terms reinforces identity-building activities like mythmaking in polarized groups. These activities reduce the ability of opponents or competitors to understand each other and to predict each others' behavior. For purely tactical reasons, stereotyping one's opponent is a bad idea. Military and business strategists from the ancient Chinese general Sun Tzu to Harvard management professor Michael Porter have warned of the dangers of misunderstanding your enemy.

Strong identification with a point of view and stereotyping of competitors can also have tragic consequences for the exploitation of natural resources. In the next section, I will discuss the ways in which we abuse our shared physical and social resources when we identify too closely with one side.

SELVES AND THE TRAGEDY OF THE COMMONS

In an influential 1968 paper, economist Garrett Hardin[38] discussed a phenomenon he called the "tragedy of the commons," using the overgrazing of common land to illustrate the problem. When public land, that is, land held in common by an entire community, is freely available for grazing, it is rational for each individual owning grazing animals to put as many animals on the land as possible. This is because the depletion of the resource does not impose a cost on any one user, so each has an incentive to exploit it as quickly and fully as possible, before others do the same. The obvious result is overgrazing and eventual destruction of the land. This is called a "commons dilemma."

The archetypical example of the overgrazing of common land occurred in traditional English villages containing a plot of land considered "the village commons," where people were allowed to graze their animals. Although local communities in most of the world no longer have a village commons, in the modern world there are many resources like clean water, clean air, ocean fisheries, and publicly owned forests that we all hold in common. These resources are all subject to commons dilemmas, and as the population grows, they are more likely to be overexploited.

Following the work of Hardin and a number of other economists and political scientists, an interdisciplinary field of study has developed called "public choice." Researchers working in the public choice area have used laboratory experiments as well as observation of various communities and cultures to try to understand how commons dilemmas, which are ubiquitous in human societies, have affected people's past and present behavior.

Political scientists Vincent and Eleanor Ostrom are among those who see the "tragedy of the commons" as central to world economics and governance. Ostrom's 1990 book, *Governing the Commons*[39] reported her findings regarding the way common pool resources had been managed by those who used them (appropriators). She identified six conditions that allowed these resources to be managed successfully in order to avoid over-exploitation (the tragedy of the commons). I will summarize briefly these conditions:

1. Appropriators all know that they will be harmed if they do not adopt rules for effectively managing the resource.
2. Most appropriators will be affected in similar ways by rule changes (in other words, the rule changes are fair and equitable).
3. Most appropriators see the resource as very valuable.
4. It is relatively easy for appropriators to get information about how the resource is being used and to enforce the rules of fair use.
5. Appropriators trust each other and share norms of reciprocity (in other words, they are willing to treat others fairly in exchange for being treated fairly).
6. The group appropriating from the resource is relatively small and stable.[40]

Of Ostrom's six points, the fifth may be the most important. If norms of reciprocity and trust exist, it is more likely that appropriators will be able to agree about the value of the resource and understand that they will be harmed if effective rules for its use are not developed. Such norms will also help appropriators jointly develop fair and equitable rules for using the resource and to enforce these rules. Such cooperation will allow sustainable use of resources even when the groups using them are large, as is the case with clean air and water as well as many other important resources.

Some psychologists[41] have argued for the cultivation of a strong group identity as a means of promoting cooperation in dealing with commons dilemmas. However, while a strong group identity may promote cooperation to achieve a common end, it may also have negative consequences. Many debates on the use of natural resources and other important social issues show that strong group identification can promote conflict between groups that have fundamentally different views on managing common resources. I think the cultivation of mindful identification is a better way of dealing with commons dilemmas.

Strong identification with a group or with an organization leads to acceptance of its values and makes it more difficult to come to agreement with those outside the group on common norms. Once individuals develop identity fixation, they tend to believe that their opponents' identities are fixed as well. This leads to the belief that overcoming others is the only way to achieve their goals. This, in turn, leads to what the seventeenth-century English philosopher Thomas Hobbes, in the *Leviathan*, called "the war of all against all." Those attempting to maintain fixed identities must not only oppose their enemies but also those within their own group or organization who question the group's worldview. Eventually, these processes will result in groupthink and entrapment in escalating conflicts.

SELVES, GROUPTHINK, AND THE ESCALATION OF CONFLICT

At the group level, the process of groupthink furthers this selective perception and defensive interpretation.[42] Turner and Pratkanis have argued that groupthink is part of a social identity maintenance process that occurs when groups face external threats.[43]

Groupthink is something most people have observed in their working lives. Groups that work together sometimes become very cohesive and committed to each other over time. When faced with a threat, they close ranks or turn inward. They come to believe that the group is always in the right, that the group is powerful and even invulnerable, and that dissenters should be suppressed. Over time, these symptoms of groupthink become more severe and people cease to express dissenting views and attempt to protect the group from information that challenges its assumptions. According to Janis,[44] stereotyping of rivals is a part of the groupthink process.

Examples of groupthink are distressingly common. It seems likely that both sides in the environmental debate I discussed suffer from it. A recent movie, *The Insider*, deals with the case of a whistle-blower in the tobacco industry who initially attempts to express his reservations about the company's product. He encounters the sorts of pressures dissenters often experience when groupthink is involved. Although this individual worked for Brown and Williamson, it is likely he would have suffered the same fate at any of the major tobacco companies. Tobacco executives correctly feel they are threatened by the "antitobacco" forces, and this external threat tends to promote groupthink.

According to psychologists Elmes and Gemmill, groupthink can develop into "group mindlessness." They state: "The rigid frame of reference that characterizes group mindlessness operates as a social defense against anxiety over complexity and turbulence both inside and outside the group."[45] They argue that in mindless groups, dissenters function as "out-persons" or scapegoats, whose presence and dissenting comments allow the group to reinforce its unquestioned perceptions and assumptions.[46]

Pendell,[47] in her study of decision-making in small groups, found that when a member attempts to question other group members' opinions and solutions to problems, they often classify this member as deviant. Comments by deviant members tend to be discounted. As group members continue with defensive identification, as the survival of the group becomes their paramount concern, they become more committed to their assumptions and more detached from reality.

The process of overidentification, identity fixation, and self-schema impoverishment can also lead to entrapment in escalating conflicts. History contains many examples of escalating commitment in conflicts—from the Trojan War through the Vietnam War through the half dozen "regional armed conflicts" currently costing lives around the globe—and entrapment in interpersonal conflict has been the subject of a good deal of previous research.[48]

Many competitive decisions involve an initial commitment of resources (time, effort, money, etc.) followed by initial failure and a need for additional commitment that may save the venture. Decision-makers must determine whether to commit the extra resources and risk "throwing good money (or effort) after bad." Examples provided by Irene Duhaime and me[49] and by Barry Staw[50] show that individuals, businesses, and countries sometimes continue to commit large resources to failing competitive strategies despite continued negative feedback. Escalating commitment can pose serious difficulties in negotiations. In their book *Negotiating Rationally*, professors Bazerman and Neal provide specific examples of escalation in negotiation and ways to reduce it.[51]

In retrospect, one wonders how this "escalating commitment" to these ill-fated ventures could have continued. A number of studies have dealt with this question. In a seminal laboratory study, with the evocative title "Knee deep in the big muddy," Staw[52] used a business case in which study participants played the role of a corporate financial officer who was asked to allocate research and development funds to one of two operating divisions of a company. Subjects were then given feedback on their initial decision (either positive or negative, indicating success or failure) and asked to make a further allocation of R&D funds.

Staw found that subjects in his experiment allocated more funds after failure than after success when they were personally responsible for the initial allocation. This seems to indicate that subjects become identified with or ego-involved in the decision and attempt to defend their initial choice (and, hence, their identity) by further commitments.

Conlon and Wolf,[53] using a different experimental decision task, collected information on the problem-solving strategy of subjects. They found that subjects using a calculating strategy responded differently to information on the likelihood of the cause of the initial failure persisting into the future than did subjects who used a noncalculating strategy. Calculators did not retain as much commitment as noncalculators in the face of information indicating a long-term cause of failure. This suggested that the way decision-makers frame and approach a decision may determine the likelihood that they will escalate commitment.

Another line of research deals with psychological entrapment, a process that is essentially the same as escalating commitment. In a 1979 laboratory study, Brockner, Shaw, and Rubin[54] showed that subjects invested more when they had to make an explicit decision to terminate a series of investments than when the series was self-terminating. They also invested less if they set a limit on their investment and told another person they had done so before the experiment began.

In an experiment in a similar vein, Brockner, Rubin, and Lang[55] found that so-cial anxiety and the presence of an audience also lead to greater entrapment. Brockner, Fine, Hamilton, Thomas, and Turetsky[56] showed that the presence of an audience and information about costs are more important at some points in the entrapment process than others. Specifically, they found that cost information affected entrapment more strongly when the information was introduced early in the process. The perceived presence of an audience affected entrapment when the audience was introduced late in the process. The audience apparently intensifies identity defensiveness, supporting the notion that identity is tied to the judgments of others.

In summary, the research on groupthink, escalation and entrapment is helpful in understanding how identity relates to polarizing conflict. The groupthink research helps explain how strongly identified group members develop narrowed vision. The entrapment research has shown how public commitment and peer (or audience) pressure can lead us to invest our identities in conflicts and has provided support for the claim that strong identification with a particular social identity can lead to escalating commitment in conflicts.

CONCLUSION

In this chapter, I have outlined how identity fixation, which is intensified by autobiographical memory distortion, can be solidified through polarizing conflicts. Through the activities of naming, legitimation, mythmaking, sedimentation, and ritual, inaccurate views of opponents are perpetuated. These processes can lead to groupthink and escalation, making it difficult to resolve dilemmas about how to use common resources.

Recognizing the problems associated with polarizing conflict, John Chambers, CEO of Cisco Systems, makes a special effort to avoid demonizing competitors or federal regulators. In a June 2000, *Wall Street Journal* article he said, "I learned the hard way at IBM and Wang Laboratories that competition is good for you. . . . You don't view competitors as the bad guys. They are actually the good guys."[57] Competitors, rivals, and even regulators can be seen as "good guys" who help us rethink our assumptions about ourselves, our goals, and our strategies for achieving them. Cisco and Intel have long been receptive to the concerns of antitrust regulators, in contrast to Microsoft. Further, while Microsoft used aggressive language and demonized rivals in its internal e-mails, providing regulators with ammunition in the antitrust prosecution, Cisco employees are discouraged from doing this. This helps the company avoid unproductive conflicts with competitors and it facilitates cooperation.

The value of competition and a diversity of approaches to solving problems is illustrated by the recent mapping of the human genome. The Human Genome Project, a consortium of public sector organizations and businesses, began to sequence the human genome in the mid-1990s. At that time, those involved estimated that it would take at least ten years to complete the work. In 1998, geneticist Craig Venter learned of a quicker mapping method and suggested a collaboration. When the directors of the Human Genome Project determined that his goals were incompatible with theirs, they refused. He then formed Celera Genomics Group and began the process of mapping the human genome at incredible speed. Venter's actions stimulated executives at the Human Genome Project to intensify their own efforts. The result of this competition was that, on June 26, 2000, representatives of both the Human Genome Project and Celera announced that they had completed a "rough draft" of the gene sequence, at least five years ahead of schedule, which will speed the development of a new generation of medications and treatments for a great many diseases and disabilities.[58] Competition and conflict are potentially productive. Polarizing conflict is not.

If the participants in a conflict repeatedly cover the same ground and do not progress toward a deeper understanding of each others' worldviews, or if the participants give evidence that they are not taking the dialogue seriously, it would be appropriate to take steps to avoid polarization. I will discuss these steps in detail in Chapter 5, but first, in Chapter 4, I want to discuss the ways that identity fixation and self-schema impoverishment damage *organizations'* ability to adapt to change.

NOTES

1. See "The Tempest," in *The Oxford Shakespeare*, ed. S. Orgel (Oxford: Oxford University Press, 1987), p. 202.

2. See M. Castells, *The Power of Identity* (Oxford: Blackwell Publishers, 1997).

3. M. Bazerman and M. Neale, *Negotiating Rationally* (New York: Free Press, 1993).

4. R. Lewicki and D. Saunders, *Essentials of Negotiation* (New York: Irwin, 1996).

5. P. Berger and T. Luckman, *The Social Construction of Reality: A Treatise on the Sociology of Knowledge* (Garden City, NY: Doubleday, 1967).

6. J. Aho, *This Thing of Darkness: A Sociology of the Enemy* (Seattle, WA: University of Washington Press, 1994).

7. Aho, *This Thing of Darkness*, pp. 26–33.

8. See C. Schwenk and S. Rhodes, *Marijuana and the Workplace: Interpreting Research on Complex Social Issues* (Westport, CT: Greenwood Press, 1999), for a more detailed discussion of this issue.

9. M. Hogg and D. Terry. "Social identity and self-categorization processes in organizational contexts," *Academy of Management Review* 25(2000): 121–140. See pp. 122–124.

10. Berger and Luckman, *The Social Construction of Reality*, pp. 84–85.

11. Aho, *This Thing of Darkness*.

12. Ibid.

13. *The Economist*, December 20, 1997, "Environmental scares."

14. M. Maxey, "Mining ethical issues: The new prohibitionists," *Engineering and Mining Journal*, October (1997): 34–40.

15. P. Koberstein, "Mountains of treasure, rivers of sorrow," *Cascadia Times*, June (1997): 6–8.

16. D. Duncan, "The war for Norman's river," *Sierra Magazine*, 83, #3 (May/June)(1998): 44–57.

17. Ibid., p. 50.

18. Maxey, "Mining ethical issues," p. 35.

19. Ibid., p. 40.

20. J. Mander and E. Goldsmith, *The Case Against the Global Economy* (San Francisco, CA: Sierra Club Books, 1996).

21. J. Smith, G. Lyons, and P. Sauer-Thompson, *Healing a Wounded World: Economics, Ecology, and Health for a Sustainable Life* (Westport, CT: Praeger, 1997).

22. J. Smith, G. Lyons, and E. Moore. *Global Meltdown: Immigration, Multiculturalism, and National Breakdown in the New World Disorder* (Westport, CT: Praeger, 1998).

23. P. Ehrlich and A. Ehrlich, *Betrayal of Science and Reason* (Washington, DC: Island Press, 1996).

24. T. Sowell, *The Vision of the Anointed: Self-Congratulation as a Basis for Social Policy* (New York: Basic Books, 1995).

25. J. Bast, P. Hill, and R. Rue, *Eco-Sanity: A Common-Sense Guide to Environmentalism* (Lanham, MD: Madison Books, 1994).

26. J. Simon, *The Ultimate Resource* (Princeton, NJ: Princeton University Press, 1996).

27. Sowell, *The Vision of the Anointed*, p. 67.

28. Simon, *The Ultimate Resource*, p. 103.

29. Duncan, "The war for Norman's River," p. 53.

30. Maxey, "Mining ethical issues," p. 34.

31. *The Economist*, 1997, "Environmental scares," p. 19.

32. Ibid.

33. Ehrlich and Ehrlich, *The Betrayal of Science and Reason*, pp. 100–101.

34. A. Cohen, *Self Consciousness: An Alternative Anthropology of Identity* (London: Routledge, 1994).

35. Ibid., p. 116.

36. Ehrlich and Ehrlich, *Betrayal of Science and Reason*, pp. 101–103.

37. R. Vallone, L. Ross, and M. Lepper, "The hostile media phenomenon: Biased perception and perceptions of media bias in coverage of the Beirut massacre," *Journal of Personality and Social Psychology* 49 (1985): 577–585.

38. G. Hardin, "The tragedy of the commons," *Science* 162(1968): 1243–1248.

39. E. Ostrom, *Governing the Commons: The Evolution of Institutions for Collective Action* (Cambridge, England: Cambridge University Press, 1990).

40. Ibid., p. 211.

41. See R. Dawes, A. van de Kragt, and J. Orbell, "Not me or thee but we: The importance of group identity in eliciting cooperation in dilemma situations," *Acta Psychologica* 68(1988): 83–97.

42. The psychologist Irving Janis first developed the concept of groupthink. See I. Janis. *Groupthink: Psychological Studies of Policy Decisions and Fiascoes* (second edition) (Boston: Houghton-Mifflin, 1982); I. Janis, *Crucial Decisions: Leadership in Policymaking and Crisis Management* (New York: Free Press, 1989); I. Janis and L. Mann, *Decision-Making* (New York: Free Press, 1997).

43. M. Turner and A. Pratkanis, "A social identity maintenance model of groupthink," *Organizational Behavior and Human Decision Processes* 73(1998): 210–235.

44. Janis, *Groupthink*.

45. M. Elmes and G. Gemmill, "The psychodynamics of mindlessness and dissent in small groups," *Small Group Research* 21(1990): 28–44, p. 33.

46. Ibid., p. 39.

47. S. Pendell, "Deviance and conflict in small group decision-making," *Small Group Research* 21(1990): 393–403.

48. A piece by Joel Brockner (J. Brockner, "The escalation of commitment to a failing course of action: Toward theoretical progress," *Academy of Management Review* 17(1992): 39–61) summarizes the research up to that time and applies it to management.

49. I. Duhaime and C. Schwenk, "Conjectures on cognitive simplification processes in acquisition and divestment decision-making," *Academy of Management Review* 10(1985): 287–295.

50. B. Staw, "The escalation of commitment to a course of action," *Academy of Management Review* 6(1981): 577–587.

51. Bazerman and Neale, *Negotiating Rationally*.

52. B. Staw, "Knee deep in the big muddy: A study of escalating commitment to a chosen course of action," *Organizational Behavior and Human Performance* 16(1976): 27–44.

53. E. Conlon and G. Wolf, "The moderating effects of strategy, visibility, and involvement on allocation behavior: An extension of Staw's escalation paradigm," *Organizational Behavior and Human Performance* 26(1980): 172–192.

54. J. Brockner, M. Shaw and J. Rubin, "Factors affecting withdrawal from an escalating conflict: Quitting before it's too late," *Journal of Experimental Social Psychology* 15(1979): 492–503.

55. J. Brockner, J. Rubin, and E. Lang, "Face-saving and entrapment," *Journal of Experimental Social Psychology* 17(1981): 68–79.

56. J. Brockner, J. Fine, T. Hamilton, B. Thomas, and B. Turetsky, "Factors affecting entrapment in escalating conflicts: The importance of timing," *Journal of Research in Personality* 16(1982): 247–266.

57. *Wall Street Journal*, June 1, 2000, p. B1.

58. See *Wall Street Journal*, June 26, 2000: B2 and *Wall Street Journal*, June 27, 2000: A3.

4

Organizational Identities,
Knowledge Structures,
and Decisions

> In the behavior of organized human groups we often find a unity and coor-
> dination of behavior so striking that it has led many social thinkers to draw an
> analogy between the group and the individual, and even to postulate a "group
> mind." The mechanism whereby this coordination is achieved is not easily
> perceived.
>
> —Herbert Simon, *Administrative Behavior*, 1945[1]

In Chapter 3, I discussed some of the ways individual identities affect group and
organizational behavior but said little about the links between individual and organizational thinking and learning. In this chapter, I will describe the way the self-
schema is related to organizational knowledge structures and the conditions under
which impoverished knowledge structures are most harmful.

ORGANIZATIONAL STAKEHOLDERS, IDENTITIES,
AND KNOWLEDGE STRUCTURES

While we know that organizations don't have minds and thoughts in the same
way that individuals do, the concept of organizational knowledge structures provides a way of understanding organizational decisions and actions. The term "organizational knowledge structure" refers to the collection of data, organizational
routines and standard operating procedures, manuals, and other formal organizational mechanisms for providing information to guide the behavior of members in
performing their organizational tasks and making decisions. It also includes the
knowledge incorporated into each organizational member's self-schema and the

knowledge incorporated into the self-schemas of those who interact with the organization (including its customers, those who provide resources, and those in government who might regulate the organization). This is a rather broad definition, but I want to emphasize that there are a great many sources of knowledge in organizations and a great many elements in the organizational knowledge structure, as there are in the individual self-schema.

How do the individual-level processes of identification and self-schema impoverishment affect organizations? We can answer this question by using the concept of *organizational identity*. As with individuals, in organizations the term "identity" describes what seems central, enduring, and distinctive about an organization in the minds of those who interact with it.[2]

An "organizational stakeholder" is someone who is involved with the organization in some way and who has a "stake" in it, including its employees, shareholders, consumers, and governments.[3] The organization has a different identity in the eyes of each of its stakeholders. Since organizations have multiple stakeholders (as individuals have multiple people and groups who define their identities), it follows that they have multiple identities that can conflict with each other.[4]

For example, hospitals and other health service providers have multiple identities including the acute care identity, the for-profit business identity, the health maintenance identity, and so on. The health maintenance and for-profit identities are sometimes in conflict with each other. If organizations are not able to resolve this conflict, they may resort to illegal activity to "manage" it. Recently, the federal government filed suit against four of the largest U.S. nursing home operators for fraud. Prosecutors charged that the nursing homes owned by these companies overbilled for services in an effort to improve profits and serve their identities as profit-making ventures. Columbia/HCA Healthcare recently agreed to pay $745 million to the federal government to resolve Medicare-fraud charges, including overbilling of laboratory claims and irregularities in its handling of home health care.[5] With businesses, as with individuals, failing to resolve the demands of competing identities can be costly.

A diagram of the organizational knowledge structure appears in Figure 4.1. This diagram is similar in many ways to Figure 1.1 in describing the self-schema. In the organizational knowledge structure, different stakeholders provide different perspectives on decisions in the same way that different identities provide different perspectives on decisions facing individuals.

I am *not* saying there are no differences between individual schemas and organizational knowledge structures. However, as the cognitive scientist Herbert Simon says, both individuals and organizations are adaptive systems. Therefore, some design features should be common to both.[6] I am attempting to identify those common design features.

Figure 4.1
The Organizational Knowledge Structure

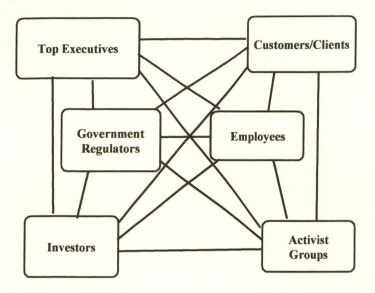

Take as an example a company like Cisco Systems, which is participating in the technology-driven "new economy." The company's shareholders see it as an investment opportunity, despite the recent disappointing performance of its stock. For government regulators, it might have a very different identity. They might see it as a potential monopoly. Top management, another stakeholder group, might see the company as a source of career advancement. Each stakeholder group is a part of the knowledge structure. When Cisco's top executives attempt to solve a problem, they can access the organizational knowledge structure by consulting organizational databases, talking with colleagues in different departments or divisions in the organization, and possibly by consulting external stakeholders.

The topic of knowledge management and transfer in organizations has become more important to both researchers and those who must lead businesses. Interest on the part of researchers is shown by a recent special issue of the journal *Organizational Behavior and Human Decision Processes*.[7] In the introduction, Argote, Ingram, Levine, and Moreland[8] argue that firms that are more effective at knowledge transfer can bring more experience and data to bear on current problems and are, therefore, more successful.

Former Microsoft Chairman Bill Gates, in the book *Business @ the Speed of Thought*,[9] devotes an entire chapter to knowledge management and introduces a concept he calls "corporate IQ." Corporate IQ, according to Gates, is not just the number of smart people you have, but how well these people can draw on each others' knowledge to solve business problems. Leaders who can access their organizations' knowledge structures more effectively can increase their corporate IQ.

This model of organizational knowledge structures also helps me to understand the concept of "corporate conscience" and morality. Legal scholars and others interested in deterring corporate crime have long puzzled over ways to encourage ethical behavior in corporations, which are essentially legal entities lacking the capacity for conscience. In the late 1700s, Edward, First Baron Thurlow, Lord Chancellor of England, said, "Did you ever expect a corporation to have a conscience, when it has no soul to be damned and no body to be kicked?"[10]

However, I argued in Chapter 1 that the "voice of conscience" in individuals is often the voice of one or more of their peripheral identities. By paying attention to these peripheral identities, individuals can make more ethical decisions. I think the same is true for organizational knowledge structures and stakeholders. Peripheral stakeholders, by raising objections to a decision, can act as the "conscience" of a business. Businesses can make more ethical decisions if their leaders listen to marginalized stakeholders' views.

For example, in the case study described in Chapter 3 dealing with the gold mine on the Big Blackfoot River, Phelps-Dodge and Canyon Resources could have made more ethical (and more profitable) decisions by listening to the Clark Fork Coalition. This case also gives insights into how to be a more effective stakeholder by attempting to understand the perspectives of OTHER stakeholders. If shareholders and environmentalists had been able to communicate more effectively, they might have realized they had common interests and attempted to work together.

The concept of organizational *image* is helpful in understanding how knowledge structures change. Top managers try to maintain a favorable image in the eyes of members and others. Often the image is not entirely consistent with the organization's identity as it is conceived by stakeholders and this causes tension in the organization. The interaction between image and identity may modify the organization's identity in the minds of stakeholders.[11] Thus, organizations' identities are *not* stable and enduring. Their knowledge structures change, as do individual self-schemas.

Members who want to believe their organization's identity is stable might distort their memories of past events to promote the illusion of stability.[12] They will also use the same labels for aspects of the organization's identity that are changing. As Dennis Gioia and his colleagues have observed, the stability is in the labels, not in the identities.[13] For example, some business schools that are undergoing identity changes continue to use labels like "world-class research institution" to describe themselves even though their definition of research and its role is very different now from what it was a decade ago.

A more vivid example is provided by the use of Kentucky Colonel Harlan Sanders as a spokesperson for Kentucky Fried Chicken (now KFC). For decades, television ads have featured "The Colonel" proudly describing his "secret recipe." As the company expanded internationally, the Colonel became an American cultural icon abroad. In a series of ads in the late 1990s, however, he was transformed from a gravel-voiced, portly old gentleman into an active, spry cartoon character with the voice of actor Randy Quaid. The label, "the Colonel," remained the same, but the reality underlying that label changed.

Multiple identities have the same potential effects on organizations as they do on individuals.[14] Using multiple identities allows organizations to adapt more effectively to a changing world. The book retailer Barnes & Noble, for example, was once threatened by the rise of Internet booksellers like Amazon.com. In response, they developed Barnes & Noble.com, which was initially a separate operation or "internal venture" within the company. Those who worked in this internal venture developed identities that were compatible with e-commerce. At the same time, there were many in the company who identified with the traditional "bricks and mortar" business. This diversity of identities made it possible for the company to enter on-line book retailing as the demand for this service increased, and, more importantly, to *integrate* both operations to become a "clicks and mortar" business.[15]

On the other hand, multiple identities can make it difficult for organizations to develop consistent strategies. Since identities determine how members interpret the problems and opportunities posed by change, those with different identities may propose conflicting strategies and goals.

A clear organizational image and identity may help diversified businesses remain focused and successful. For example, the *Wall Street Journal*[16] reported that the Anglo-Dutch conglomerate Unilever has had slower sales growth than its rivals Procter & Gamble and Nestle, partly because it lacks focus in making and integrating acquisitions. This paucity of focus reflects an absence of a clear organizational identity. On the other hand, General Electric is one of the most famous examples of a diversified company that has succeeded because it has maintained focus and identity under its former CEO Jack Welch.[17]

Organizational leaders often encourage all stakeholders to identify with their view of the essence of the organization and the demands for success in its environment. They want to ensure that everyone is "sharing the same vision" or "marching to the same drummer" or "reading from the same hymnal." Members of organizations may comply with the efforts of their leaders to strengthen their organizational identification because they recognize that a strong shared sense of identity may be necessary for the business to survive and prosper. However, if people identify mindlessly with the leader's vision, it may reduce the organization's ability to learn and adapt to new circumstances. In Chapter 3, I showed how strong identification with a group can lead to groupthink and escalating commitment, collective decision pathologies that may cause costly errors. Similarly, excessive identification with an organization can produce biases that reduce organizational learning. To clarify this process, I will describe the ways knowledge structures adapt to change.

ORGANIZATIONAL LEARNING AND KNOWLEDGE STRUCTURES

Organizational learning, discussed in such books as *The Dance of Change* by Peter Senge and his colleagues, leads to changes in organizational knowledge structures. To understand how organizations learn from experience and develop new knowledge structures, it is helpful to consider the relationship between individuals and elements of the knowledge structure.

The self-schemas of organizational members influence the development of the organization's knowledge structure.[18] To understand how this influence operates, we must understand how individuals identify with stakeholder groups. Different stakeholder groups develop shared frames of reference, shared reconstructions of past events, and shared stories and myths.[19]

Changes in an organization's environment are perceived by stakeholders, who each interpret these changes in a slightly different way. In Chapter 3, I showed how members of opposing groups interpret information in different ways because they have different identity-based assumptions. The same is true for stakeholders of an organization. Different stakeholders will view changes differently.

Coalitions of stakeholders in an organization who hold alternative identities use political processes to advocate their own views of the implications of changes.[20] Each stakeholder coalition attempts to influence others and to gain support for its interpretation of events,[21] in much the same way that partisans in the public debates discussed in Chapter 3 attempted to build support through tactics of political influence. If disagreement between coalitions becomes too intense, the organization may experience all the unpleasant consequences of polarizing conflict, including groupthink, stereotyping of opponents, and escalating commitment.

If, however, the stakeholders are able to avoid polarizing conflicts, organizational knowledge structures will change as a result of stakeholders' debates about their differing interpretations of events. Bargaining and the use of power (or "office politics") will influence the way the organization interprets change.[22]

Once the leaders or key decision-makers of the organization sense changes in the environment, they interpret the changes as either problems, opportunities, or crises.[23] These decision-makers have a strong influence on the way the organizational knowledge structure is used because they can communicate their interpretations of events to a wide range of other stakeholders.[24] That is, they can determine which aspects of the knowledge structures are considered "central" or "core" and which are considered "peripheral" aspects.

To understand how organizational knowledge structures develop and change, we must understand the distinction between *core* features of the knowledge structure and *peripheral* features. In most organizations, the leaders have defined a core set of assumptions about their mission, their justification for existence, and their basic objectives. Such seminal works as Chester Barnard's *Functions of the Executive* (1938),[25] Richard Cyert and James March's *A Behavioral Theory of the Firm* (1963),[26] and James Thompson's *Organizations in Action* (1967)[27] have discussed the ways organizations' core products, markets, and technologies are supported by core values or beliefs. Prahalad and Bettis[28] call these core beliefs the firm's "dominant logic." The core of the organizational knowledge structure consists of information and those perspectives of stakeholders that the leaders believe are central to defining the organization's mission and carrying out its activities.

The core provides the structure through which organizational members seek and interpret information. Top managers reinforce their view of the core in various ways, including public and private statements and symbolic actions. These actions are the means by which core knowledge structures are maintained.

To put it another way, the core of the organizational knowledge structure is what the leaders or the dominant organizational members say it is. Thus, it is redefined as new cliques or coalitions gain power in the organization. Leaders who attempt to create a "shared vision" or a "new culture" are essentially simplifying the organizational knowledge structure. They are specifying for other members what parts of the knowledge structure to use and how to interpret the information they obtain from it.

A shared vision has clear benefits. The more agreement there is about the core structure, the more agreement there will be about specific courses of action necessary to ensure survival and the more single-minded will be the strategic thrust of the firm. However, a high level of consensus may lead to rigid behavior and poor adjustment to change. When the leader's or dominant coalition's vision is too restrictive, this can lead to impoverishment of the organizational knowledge structure for the same reasons that rigid and restrictive definitions of personal identity can lead to self-schema impoverishment. According to Brown and Starkey,[29] an overdefined identity reduces the organization's ability to learn through the use of alternative interpretations of change.

The peripheral elements of the knowledge structure—those that are not considered central by organizational leaders—are linked to the core elements in different ways in different organizations. In some organizations, peripheral elements are considered irrelevant; peripheral stakeholders are not consulted and may even be actively discouraged from contributing. In others, peripheral aspects of the knowledge structure and peripheral stakeholders are consulted out of an appreciation of the potential value of diverse views in decision-making.

If an organization wants to preserve its capacity to respond to change, it should make use of the peripheral aspects of the knowledge structure as these may be the source of solutions to problems that are insoluble to those restricted to operating within the core elements of the knowledge structure, as the dominant organizational members define it. However, using these peripheral elements may be difficult and require individuals to "think outside the box" in the words of a current management catch-phrase. If I were given to catch-phrases, I might recommend that organizational members "preserve the peripheral."

Many organizations draw the distinction between core and peripheral values and competencies. When people at Microsoft, for example, want to emphasize how important a goal is, they say "that's absolutely core." Microsoft's current CEO, Steve Balmer, argues that the company must "narrow and simplify goals" and "focus on key employees" in order to deal with both technological change and government antitrust prosecution. This narrowing of focus might help to "rally the troops" but it might also reduce the company's ability to respond creatively to changing technology. If Balmer and others neglect the peripheral aspects of Microsoft's knowledge structure as they increase members' commitment to "core" goals, they may reduce the organizational knowledge they can draw on to deal with future changes.[30]

The benefits of preserving peripheral elements of organizational knowledge structures can be better understood through the use of the concepts of complexity and relatedness. *Complexity* refers to the amount of information or the number of elements within a knowledge structure. *Relatedness* refers to the links between elements in the knowledge structure, particularly the links between core and peripheral elements.

The complexity of the knowledge structure influences its ability to respond to environmental changes and new situations. More complex structures allow more diverse situations to be analyzed correctly but may make it more difficult for the firm to reach a final decision on a course of action. On the other hand, simpler structures may allow decision-makers to act quickly but at the expense of ignoring some signals of environmental change.[31] In order for organizations to solve new problems effectively, their knowledge structures need to be both complex and related.

Organizations with simple knowledge structures and rigid relationships between the elements in these structures are more likely to maintain the status quo and to avoid changing their strategies. Top management in these organizations may attempt to avoid adapting their schemas to the changing environment. Nisbett and Ross[32] suggest that when people cling to their existing views, they attempt to discredit uncongenial evidence. This is known as the "perseverance effect"[33] and as "strategic persistence."[34]

Organizations with complex knowledge structures and multiple, flexible links between the elements of the structures can incorporate more disagreement and alternative interpretations into their mission statements and strategies. Thus, these organizations can adjust their strategies to deal with changing environmental conditions, and they can incorporate new information into their knowledge structures more easily.

Organizations with complex knowledge structures and diversity of views can react more appropriately when unexpected problems occur and make better use of complex information. Therefore, this complexity and diversity should be very important in avoiding escalating commitment. Thus, organizations with enriched knowledge structures should be less subject to escalating commitment than organizations with impoverished knowledge structures.

However, the mere existence of diversity of views does not ensure that organizations will make decisions more creatively and adapt to change more effectively. As the next section will show, the negative effects of diversity may outweigh its positive effects in some cases.

DIVERSITY OF IDENTITIES AND VIEWS IN ORGANIZATIONS

Including peripheral stakeholders in organizational decisions and using their diversity to enhance the organizational knowledge structure should be useful. On the other hand, at times a widely shared corporate vision, limited input from peripheral elements of the organization, and a strong organizational core can be functional and perhaps produce superior results. Management researchers have explored the ways diversity affects business performance using a variety of research methods, and their research has produced conflicting results.

Some studies suggest that identity diversity can improve the organization's perceptions of the environment and the quality of decision-making. This, in turn, leads to better organizational performance. Diversity in top management teams can stimulate high-quality decisions and improve team performance.[35] In his book, *Cultural Diversity in Organizations*, Taylor Cox reviews research on the benefits of diverse cultural identities in business and public sector organizations.[36] Several sound empirical studies support the benefits of other kinds of diversity as well.[37] Research on diversity has not, however, provided consistent support for its benefits.[38] It seems that a corporate culture and team norms supporting diversity of identities are necessary for reducing the negative effects and enhancing the positive effects of group diversity.

Diversity alone is not sufficient for good performance. Psychologist Irving Janis, for example, argues that "vigilant problem-solving" is necessary in order for groups to benefit from diversity. The challenge is to find ways to encourage diverse teams to engage in such vigilant problem-solving.[39] This may involve encouraging debate and constructive conflict, conflict that focuses on assumptions and issues, increasing people's understanding of their opponents.

Two recent experiments comparing the effects of naturally occurring debate and conflict in diverse teams[40] and one study of the effects of decision-process variables on diverse teams[41] support the benefits of constructive conflict. Kirchmeyer and Cohen measured the level of constructive conflict in multicultural groups working on a business case. They found no significant relationship between the use of constructive conflict and the quality of the groups' final decisions, but they did find that constructive conflict led groups to identify more important assumptions. Constructive conflict also led ethnic minorities within the groups to make greater contributions to the decision.[42] Ken Smith and his colleagues studied management teams in high-technology firms and found that diverse teams were more effective than homogeneous ones *if* the members were socially integrated and communicated frequently and informally.[43] Tony Simons found that companies led by top management teams with diverse backgrounds and perceptions of the environment *and* high levels of debate were more profitable than those led by teams with either diversity or debate alone.[44]

Diversity of identities and views may have conflicting effects on the organizational knowledge structure and the quality of team decisions and performance. Diverse groups bring a greater number of perspectives to bear on problems and a greater volume of information. However, diversity also increases the difficulty of communication among members of the group and reduces group cohesion. Communication about differences of opinion may be difficult because of the differences between stakeholders' assumptions and their understanding of terms in the debate. Since this may lead to confrontations that are unpleasant and confusing, organizational members may avoid them.

Stimulating conflict may improve the decision process but hurt the fortunes of the individual who introduces the conflict since he or she may be seen as a troublemaker. Thus, individuals may avoid expressing divergent views. Leaders may also suppress conflict in the belief that it is harmful, especially if they are under pressure or feel threatened. As a result, the positive and negative effects of diversity may cancel each other out.

The net effects of diversity depend on how diverse identities are coordinated and managed within the organizational knowledge structure. A way must be found to structure the dialogue and conflict among stakeholders. Research on structured conflict techniques, which I will discuss in greater detail in Chapter 5, suggests that organizational decision-making may be improved through effective management of conflict, resulting in greater mastery of information and understanding of the decision, as well as less bolstering of one's own view in the face of conflicting evidence. Interpersonal and organizational processes may be improved, resulting in greater information exchange. Aso, political factors may be improved, leading to a greater understanding of others' points of view and incorporation of others' information into the final decision.[45]

In summary, organizations adapt successfully to change by enriching their knowledge structures and using the diversity within these enriched structures to develop creative solutions to new problems. For organizations in simple, stable environments, simple or even impoverished knowledge structures may do little harm. However, for organizations in complex and rapidly changing environments, an enriched knowledge structure may be a matter of life or death.

Enriched knowledge structures are also important in business ethics and socially responsible behavior. The diversity of perspectives within these structures allows companies to develop creative alternatives for dealing with moral dilemmas. This does not ensure ethical behavior on the part of companies but it does make it more likely.

ENRICHED KNOWLEDGE STRUCTURES
IN DIFFERENT CONTEXTS

Earlier in this chapter, I pointed out that leaders must decide how strongly to promote a clear and well-defined vision among organizational stakeholders. A clear vision has obvious benefits but it may reduce the complexity of the knowledge structure. In some circumstances a simple or even impoverished knowledge structure may do little harm, while in others it can be fatal. This statement is rather vague and it is time now to be more specific. When do the benefits of an enriched knowledge structure outweigh its costs?

Decision-making is more complex in some contexts than in others. Enriched organizational knowledge structures are more essential in more complex contexts. In this section, I will discuss the factors that make the organizational context more complex. While I will focus on businesses, all the factors I will discuss have parallels in government and voluntary organizations. These include environmental factors (such as turbulence and complexity), industry factors (rate of industry growth and technological change), and company factors (including company diversification and strategy).

Environmental Factors

An enriched knowledge structure is more important when the business environment is complex and changing rapidly than when it is simple and stable. This is the conclusion of a stream of organization theory literature beginning in 1965.[46] Organization theorist Richard Daft has described how complexity and rapid change combine to create environmental uncertainty.[47] He argues, reasonably, that companies must have flexible roles and must effectively integrate stakeholders in uncertain environments.

Those working for these organizations must deal with ambiguous information, learn new procedures quickly, and react swiftly to unexpected problems, all skills that should be related to self-schema and knowledge structure enrichment. Enriched knowledge structures enable organizations to move quickly and effectively match their companies' strategies to the changing demands of the environment. In more simple and stable environments, complex knowledge structures are less important so leaders may be able to promote a simple vision without endangering the organization's survival. The problem is that we never know when stable environments will change.

Industry Factors

Harvard industrial economist Michael Porter has developed an influential model of industry evolution from emergence through maturity and decline. He has also discussed the structural characteristics of industries at each stage of evolution. According to Porter, emerging industries are characterized by rapid growth and high levels of strategic and technological uncertainty. Uncertainty diminishes as the industry matures and eventually declines.[48] The earlier discussion of organizational knowledge structures suggests that complex structures should allow organizations to deal more effectively with uncertainty. Thus, in emerging industries, organizations with enriched knowledge structures should develop more effective strategies. Although the effects of knowledge structure complexity are also positive in mature industries, these effects may not be essential for survival.

Company Factors

Common sense suggests that as a business becomes more diverse, the job of top management becomes more complex. This assumption is consistent with a long stream of research in strategic management beginning with Harvard business historian Alfred Chandler's book, *Strategy and Structure* (1962).[49] As a company adds new products or lines of business, the number of stakeholders increases.[50] Thus, more complex knowledge structures will be required for more diverse businesses like General Electric than for single-industry businesses like Tyson Foods.

European management researchers Calori, Johnson, and Sarnin[51] provided evidence to support this point in their study of the cognitive maps of corporate chief executive officers. They found that the cognitive maps of successful CEOs of highly diversified international firms were more complex than those of CEOs of less diverse firms with only a national scope. Richard Rumelt, in his 1974 study of diversification, structure, and performance, observed that man-

agers favoring a narrow focus on a single industry were less effective in managing diversification.[52] Top executives with enriched self-schemas are less likely to
have such a narrow focus because they are more able to develop the broad and
diverse cognitive maps necessary for formulating effective strategies for diverse
businesses. While we would also expect self-schema complexity to have positive
effects in less diversified companies, these effects should be much weaker.

A company's strategy may also determine how important it is for the company
to have an enriched knowledge structure. In 1978, Raymond Miles and Charles
Snow defined two which they called the Defender and the Prospector.[53] Their
work has provided the foundation for a good deal of subsequent research.[54] According to Miles and Snow, the Prospectors' domain is continually evolving and
therefore always somewhat ambiguous. Further, the exploitation of an evolving
domain often requires use of new technology and frequent modification of the
details of company strategy.[55] Defenders, on the other hand, have a narrow and
stable domain that tends to change less often than the domain of Prospectors.[56]
Organizational knowledge structure complexity should be very important in explaining differences in performance among Prospectors but less important in
explaining differences in the performance of Defenders.

A final factor to consider is the structure of the communication network within
the organization. Recently, new communication technology, especially the Internet, has made possible new forms of coordination and organization in what is
sometimes called a "virtual organization." Ahuja and Carley define a virtual organization as, "a geographically distributed organization whose members are bound
by a long-term common interest or goal, and who communicate and coordinate
their work through information technology."[57]

Identification is an extremely important issue in virtual organizations because
their dispersion makes it difficult for members to have the sorts of interpersonal interactions that form the basis for identification and trust in traditional organizations.[58] However, it is important to remember that members can become
overidentified with virtual organizations as well as with traditional organizations.
Overidentification has potentially serious consequences for virtual organizations
because they require enriched knowledge structures to deal with complex problems.

CONCLUSION

Having completed this discussion of organizational identities and knowledge
structures, I can give the full cycle of impoverishment that includes both individual and organizational processes. This cycle is illustrated in Figure 4.2.

As mentioned at the end of Chapter 1, overidentification and identity fixation
lead to autobiographical memory distortion and self-schema impoverishment. As
groups or organizations composed of strongly identified individuals enter polarizing

Figure 4.2
The Cycle of Organizational Knowledge Structure Impoverishment

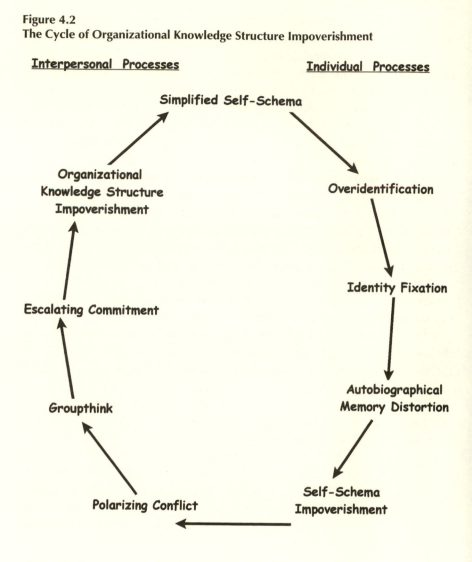

conflicts, the stereotyped views of opponents and simplified analyses of problems lead to groupthink and escalating commitment. These processes reduce the complexity of the organizational knowledge structures. Impoverished organizational knowledge structures, in turn, make it less likely that organizational members will use the full complexity of their own self-schemas in decisions.

Allowing each human being to fully develop his or her self-schema without constraint is a basic moral value. Further, it is in the best interests of organizations and society because it increases the chances that there will be a diversity of views and that among these views, there will be effective ways of adapting to changing conditions. Organizations and societies should encourage the expression of diverse individual views for both moral and practical reasons. Leaders' attempts to manipulate or enlarge their members' work identities can encourage identity fixation, which imperils the survival of organizations in rapidly changing environments.

Self-schemas and organizational knowledge structures serve important functions in our perceptual and cognitive economy. Strong personal and organizational identities can help individuals and organizations achieve difficult goals despite resistance. However, strong, mindless identification might lead to a kind of rigidity that impoverish our ability to adapt to change.

The way to avoid individual self-schema impoverishment and organizational knowledge structure impoverishment is to help people understand how to manage knowledge in both their personal and their work lives. In Chapter 5 I discuss ways organizations can enrich their knowledge structures, and in Chapter 6 ways individuals can enrich their self-schemas.

NOTES

1. H. Simon, *Administrative Behavior* (New York: Free Press, 1945), p. 124.

2. S. Albert and D. Whetten, "Organizational Identity," in *Research in Organizational Behavior*, ed. L. Cummings and B. Staw (Greenwich, CT: JAI Press, 1985), 263–295; S. Albert, B. Ashforth, and J. Dutton, "Organizational identity and identification: Charting new waters and building new bridges," *Academy of Management Review* 25(2000): 13–17.

3. For further discussion of organizational stakeholders, see R. Freeman, *Strategic Management: A Stakeholder Approach* (Boston: Pitman, 1984); and S. Scott and V. Lane, "A stakeholder approach to organizational identity," *Academy of Management Review* 25(2000): 43–62, pp. 48–56.

4. Albert and Whetten, "Organizational Identity"; S. Brickson, "The impact of identity orientation on individual and organizational outcomes in demographically diverse settings," *Academy of Management Review* 25(2000): 82–101; M. Pratt and P. Foreman, "Clarifying managerial responses to multiple organizational identities," *Academy of Management Review* 25(2000): 18–42; Scott and Lane, ibid.

5. *Wall Street Journal*, May 19, 2000, p. A3.

6. See H. Simon, *The Sciences of the Artificial* (Boston, MA: MIT Press, 1969).

7. *Organizational Behavior and Human Decision Processes*, vol. 82, no. 1 (2000).

8. L. Argote, P. Ingram, J. Levine, and R. Moreland, "Introduction: Knowledge transfer in organizations: Learning from the experience of others," *Organizational Behavior and Human Decision Processes* 82(2000): 1–8.

9. W. Gates, *Business @ the Speed of Thought* (New York: Warner Books, 1999).

10. This quote can be found in M. Metzger and C. Schwenk, "Decision making models, devil's advocacy, and the control of corporate crime," *American Business Law Journal* 28(1990): 323–277, 326. This paper also contains a more detailed discussion of the control of unethical and illegal corporate behavior.

11. D. Gioia, M. Schultz, and K. Corely, "Organizational identity, image, and adaptive instability," *Academy of Management Review* 25(2000): 63–81. M. Hatch and M. Schultz, "Scaling the Tower of Babel: Relational Differences Between Identity, Image, and Culture

in Organizations," in *The Expressive Organization,* ed. M. Schultz, M. Hatch, and M. Larsen (Oxford, England: Oxford University Press, 2000), pp. 11–35.

12. A. Brown and K. Starkey, "Organizational identity and learning: A psychodynamic perspective," *Academy of Management Review* 25(2000): 102–120.

13. Gioia et al., "Organizational identity and learning."

14. S. Albert and D. Whetten, "Organizational Identity," in *Research in Organizational Behavior,* ed. L. Cummings and B. Staw (Greenwich, CT: JAI Press, 1985), 263–295; M. Pratt and P. Foreman, "Clarifying managerial responses to multiple organizational identities," *Academy of Management Review* 25(2000): 18–42, p. 22.

15. A recent book by Pottruck and Pearce outlines the features of "clicks and mortar" businesses (D. Pottruck and T. Pearce, *Clicks & Mortar* [San Francisco: Jossey-Bass, 2000]).

16. *Wall Street Journal,* May 31, 2000, p. B1.

17. There are many books dealing with General Electric and the Jack Welch legend. For a recent example, see Robert Slater's *Jack Welch and the GE Way* (New York: McGraw-Hill, 1998).

18. D. Miller, "Stale in the saddle: CEO tenure and the match between organization and environment," *Management Science* 37(1991): 34–52; J. Walsh, "Managerial and organizational cognition: Notes from a trip down memory lane," *Organization Science* 6(1995): 280–321.

19. A great deal of work has been done on stories and myths in businesses and other organizations and how these myths affect the views and decisions of members. See, for example, J. Aho, *This Thing of Darkness: A Sociology of the Enemy* (Seattle, WA: University of Washington Press, 1994); R. Dunbar, J. Dutton, and W. Torbert, "Crossing mother: Ideological constraints on organizational improvements," *Journal of Management Studies* 19(1982): 91–108; B. Hedberg, P. Nystrom, and W. Starbuck, "Camping on seesaws? Prescriptions for a self-designing organization," *Administrative Science Quarterly* 21(1976): 41–65; A. Huff, "Industry influences on strategy reformulation," *Strategic Management Journal* 4(1983): 119–131; M. Jelinek, *Institutionalizing Innovation: A Study in Organizational Learning Systems* (New York: Praeger, 1979); M. Lyles, "Learning among joint venture sophisticated firms," *Management International Review* 28(1988): 85–98; C. Manz and H. Sims, "Vicarious learning: The influence of modeling on organizational behavior," *Academy of Management Review* 6(1981): 105–114; J. Martin, "Stories and Scripts in Organizational Settings," in *Cognitive Social Psychology,* ed. A. Hasdorf and A. Isen (New York: Elsivier-North-Holland, 1982), 225–305.

20. R. Lord and R. Foti, "Schema Theories, Information Processing, and Organizational Behavior," in *The Thinking Organization,* ed. H. Sims and D. Gioia (San Francisco: Jossey-Bass, 1986), 20–48; C. Prahalad and R. Bettis, "The dominant logic: A new linkage between diversity and performance," *Strategic Management Journal* 7(1986): 485–501; S. Taylor and J. Crocker, "Schematic Bases of Social Information Processing," in *Social Cognition,* ed. E. Higgins, C. Herman, and M. Zazza (Hillsdale, NJ: Erlbaum, 1981).

21. M. Lyles and I. Mitroff, "The impact of sociopolitical influences on strategic problem formulation," *Advances in Strategic Management* 3(1985): 69–81.

22. J. Bower, *Managing the Resource Allocation Process* (Boston, MA: Graduate School of Business, Harvard University, 1970); Lyles and Mitroff, ibid.; H. Mintzberg, *Power in and Around Organizations* (Englewood Cliffs, NJ: Prentice-Hall, 1983); J. Pfeffer, *Power in Organizations* (Marshfield, MA: Pitman, 1981).

23. J. Dutton and S. Jackson, "Categorizing strategic issues: Links to organizational action," *Academy of Management Review* 12(1987): 76–90.

24. See John Kotter (J. Kotter, *The General Managers*. New York: Free Press, 1982); and Michael Tushman et al. (M. Tushman, B. Virany, and E. Romanelli, "Effects of CEO and executive team succession on subsequent organizational performance," Columbia University Working Paper, 1989).

25. C. Barnard, *Functions of the Executive* (Cambridge, MA: Harvard University Press, 1938).

26. R. Cyert and J. March, *A Behavioral Theory of the Firm* (Englewood Cliffs, NJ: Prentice-Hall, 1963).

27. J. Thompson, *Organizations in Action* (New York: McGraw-Hill, 1967).

28. Prahalad and Bettis, 1986. "The dominant logic," *Strategic Management Journal*.

29. Brown and Starkey, 2000. "Organizational identity and learning," *Academy of Management Review*, p. 110.

30. For a more detailed discussion of this topic, see *Wall Street Journal*, June 9, 2000, p. B1.

31. J. Walsh and L. Fahey, "The role of negotiated belief structures in strategy making," *Journal of Management* 12(1986): 325–338.

32. R. Nisbett and L. Ross, *Human Inference: Strategies and Shortcomings of Social Judgment* (Englewood Cliffs, NJ: Prentice-Hall, 1980).

33. W. Fiske and S. Taylor, *Social Cognition* (Reading, MA: Addison-Wesley, 1984).

34. D. Miller, "Stale in the saddle: CEO tenure and the match between organization and environment," *Management Science* 37(1991): 34–52.

35. W. Glick, C. Miller, and G. Huber, "The Impact of Upper-Echelon Diversity on Organizational Performance," in *Organizational Change & Redesign*, ed. G. Huber and W. Glick (New York: Oxford Press, 1993); D. Hambrick and P. Mason, "Upper echelons: The organization as a reflection of its top managers," *Academy of Management Review* 9(1984): 193–206.

36. T. Cox, *Cultural Diversity in Organizations: Theory, Research, & Practice* (San Francisco: Berrett-Koehler, 1994).

37. Bourgeois collected information on the perceptions of environmental uncertainty and organizational goals of ninety-nine top-level executives in twenty firms. Consensus on perceived environmental uncertainty and goal consensus were associated with lower financial performance. Also, diversity of views was positively correlated with overall accuracy of the perception of environmental uncertainty within firms. See L. Bourgeois, "Strategic goals, perceived uncertainty, and economic performance in volatile environments," *Academy of Management Journal* 28(1985): 548–573; p. 564. DeWoot, Heyvaert, and Martou found that companies that had a heterogeneity of orientation and frequent disagreement made better decisions regarding strategic change. See P. DeWoot, H. Heyvaert, and F. Martou, "Strategic management," *International Studies of Management and Organization* 7(1977): 60–75; p. 66. Grinyer and Norburn also found that a high level of disagreement among top executives was related to high performance. See P. Grinyer and D. Norburn, "Planning for existing markets," *International Studies of Management and Organization* 7(1977): 99–122. See also K. Bantel and S. Jackson, "Top management and innovations in banking: Does the composition of the top team make a difference?" *Strategic Management Journal* 10(1989): 107–124; A. Murray, "Top management group heterogeneity and firm performance," *Strategic Management Journal* 10(1989): 125–142; C. O'Reilly and S. Flatt, "Executive team demography, organizational innovation, and firm performance" (Working paper, Berkeley, 1989).

38. Diversity has very complex effects. Most studies have examined diversity of backgrounds and diversity of views separately. Two recent studies, however, have assessed the interaction between these two types of diversity and their relationship to performance.

Neither of these studies found significant relationships between diversity, consensus, and performance. Simons measured diversity of environmental perceptions as well as educational and functional variety in a sample of electronic component manufacturing firms and found no significant relationships between any of these variables.

Using samples of firms in the electronic components and machine tool industries, Cliff West and I measured the diversity of top management teams on twelve demographic variables and the teams' consensus on goals and means of reaching goals using a method similar to that used in earlier research. Like Simons, we found no significant relationship between demographic diversity, consensus, and firm performance.

For further information on the effects of diversity, see T. Simons, "Top management team consensus, heterogeneity, and debate as contingent predictors of company performance: The complementarity of group structures and processes," *Proceedings of the Academy of Management National Meetings* (Vancouver, British Columbia, 1995); C. West and C. Schwenk, "Top management team strategic consensus, demographic homogeneity, and firm performance: A report of resounding nonfindings," *Strategic Management Journal* 17(1996): 571–576; and R. Priem, "Top management team demographic homogeneity, consensus, and firm performance in stable environments (Paper presented at the National Academy of Management meetings, Washington, D.C., 1989).

39. I. Janis, *Crucial Decisions: Leadership in Policymaking and Crisis Management* (New York: Free Press, 1989). See also C. Kirchmeyer and A. Cohen, "Multicultural groups: Their performance and reactions with constructive conflict," *Group and Organization Management* 17(1992): 153–170; D. Tjosvold, *The Conflict-positive Organization: Stimulate Diversity and Create Unity* (Reading, MA: Addison-Wesley, 1991).

40. Kirchmeyer and Cohen, ibid.; Simons, 1995, "Top management team consensus," *Proceedings of the Academy of Management National Meetings*.

41. K. Smith, K. Smith, J. Olian, H. Sims, D. O'Bannon, and J. Skully, "Top management team demography and process: The role of social integration and communication," *Administrative Science Quarterly* 39(1994): 412–438.

42. Kirchmeyer and Cohen, 1992. "Multicultural groups," *Group and Organization Management*.

43. Smith et al., 1994, "Top management team demography and process . . . ," *Administrative Science Quarterly*.

44. Simons, 1995. "Top management team consensus," *Proceedings of the Academy of Management National Meetings*.

45. These claims are supported by the following sources: S. Alper, D. Tjosvold, and K. Law, "Interdependence and controversy in group decision-making: Antecedents to effective self-managing teams," *Organizational Behavior and Human Decision Processes* 74(1998): 33–52; D. Johnson and D. Tjosvold, "Constructive controversy," in *Conflict in Organizations*, ed. D. Tjosvold and D. Johnson (New York: Irvington, 1983); R. Mason and I. Mitroff, *Challenging Strategic Planning Assumptions* (New York: Wiley, 1981); D. Tjosvold, "Implications of controversy research for management," *Journal of Management* 11(1985): 21–37.

46. F. Emery and E. Trist, "The causal texture of organizational environments," *Human Relations* 18(1965); 21–32; J. Pfeffer and G. Salancik, *The External Control of Organizations: A Resource Dependence Perspective* (New York: Harper and Row, 1978), pp. 63–68.

47. R. Daft, *Organization Theory and Design* (5th ed.) (Minneapolis/St. Paul, MN: West, 1995), pp. 83–92.

48. For more information on this model, see M. Porter, *Competitive Strategy* (New York: Free Press, Ch. 10; 1990), pp. 159–164.

49. A. Chandler, *Strategy and Structure* (Cambridge, MA: MIT Press, 1962).

50. Daft, 1995, *Organization Theory and Design*.

51. R. Calori, G. Johnson, and P. Sarnin, "CEOs' cognitive maps and the scope of the organization," *Strategic Management Journal* 15(1994): 437–457.

52. R. Rumelt, *Strategy, Structure, and Economic Performance* (Cambridge, MA: Harvard University Press, 1974), pp. 136–138.

53. R. Miles and C. Snow, *Organizational Strategy, Structure, and Process* (New York: McGraw-Hill, 1978).

54. See, for example, T. Amburgey and A. Miner, "Strategic momentum: The effects of repetitive, positional, and contextual momentum on merger activity," *Strategic Management Journal* 13(1992); 335–348; W. Barnett, H. Greve, and D. Park, "An evolutionary model of organizational performance," *Strategic Management Journal* 15(1994): 11–28.

55. Miles and Snow, 1978, *Organizational Strategy*, pp. 49–67.

56. Ibid., pp. 31–48.

57. M. Ahuja and K. Carley, "Network structure in virtual organizations," *Organization Science* 10(1999): 741–757.

58. B. Wiesenfeld, S. Raghuram, and R. Garud, "Communication pattersns as determinants of organizational identification in a virtual organization," *Journal of Computer-Mediated Communication* 3(1998): 1–20.

5

Using Conflict Productively

> What kills spontaneous fictions, what recalls the impassioned fancy from its improvisations, is the angry voice of some contrary fancy. Nature, silently making fools of us all our lives, never would bring us to our senses; but the maddest assertions of the mind may do so, when they challenge one another.
> —George Santayana, *Skepticism and Animal Faith*, 1923[1]

In previous chapters, we have seen how individual self-schemas and organizational knowledge structures become simplified and, eventually, impoverished. Yet many individuals and organizations escape from the cycle of cognitive simplification and adapt effectively to a changing world. I don't pretend to know all the secrets by which they accomplish these small miracles, but I can offer some suggestions for helping organizations make better use of their knowledge structures.

Some organizations are able to enrich their knowledge structures by using the diversity of views that exist within them. By encouraging dialogue and conflict between those holding different views, they can avoid the problems associated with simplistic knowledge structures. This chapter deals with the benefits of dialogue and structured conflict within groups and organizations.

THE MAGIC OF DIALOGUE?

Dialogue has become an increasingly important topic in recent years, as shown by the number of popular books on the topic. Titles include *Dialogue and the Art of Thinking Together*,[2] *Dialogue*,[3] and *The Magic of Dialogue*.[4] Dialogue is also an important subject in *The Fifth Discipline*, and *The Dance of Change* by Peter Senge and his colleagues. According to these authors, the term "dialogue" is often misunderstood. Isaacs defines dialogue as "a sustained collective inquiry into the processes, assumptions, and certainties that compose everyday experience"[5] and distinguishes it from "debate," "discussion," "conversation," and similar terms.

Some of these books do not show an adequate appreciation of the factors that make dialogue difficult. Isaacs, for example, provides the following initial guidelines for those engaging in dialogue:

1. Suspend assumptions and certainties
2. Observe the observer
3. Listen to your listening
4. Slow down the inquiry
5. Be aware of thought
6. Befriend polarization[6]

The quality of dialogue would certainly improve if participants followed these guidelines. However, the earlier chapters of this book show how difficult it is for individuals attempting to maintain their identities to do this. For example, Item 1 tells us to suspend assumptions. In Chapter 1, I described how certain assumptions about the self can provide the foundation for personal identity. Genuine suspension of these assumptions might undermine an individual's identity and make self-directed action more difficult. Item 6 suggests that we befriend polarization, meaning that we should seek out polarized views and explore them in dialogue. I agree, but as I demonstrated in Chapter 3, polarization is a basic process by which identity distinctiveness is maintained. Befriending polarization, which could weaken the distinctiveness of your identity, is much easier said than done. In stimulating dialogue, it is important to avoid provoking defensive reactions when challenging identity-based assumptions.

Many companies have designed formal programs for promoting dialogue and have reported some success. These firms include Shell,[7] IBM, Levi Strauss, Digital Equipment, and Hewlett-Packard.[8] Shell has been especially active in this area, promoting dialogue in conjunction with its use of multiple scenarios in strategic planning. Duke Energy, a marketer of natural gas and electricity, recently developed multiple scenarios for the future of the U.S. economy (scenarios with names like "The Big Slowdown" and "Economic Treadmill") and used these scenarios to stimulate critical thinking and dialogue about the company's strategic plans.[9] Dialogue has been a useful part of strategic planning for an uncertain future. However, to realize the full benefits of dialogue, organizations must structure the conflict resulting from the different identities and assumptions held by stakeholders.

STRUCTURED CONFLICT AND DEVIL'S ADVOCACY

Structured conflict is not a specific technique but a general approach to decision-making in organizations. Structured conflict goes by many names including devil's advocacy, dialectical inquiry, and multiple advocacy.

The term "devil's advocacy" is often used to describe structured conflict in business decisions. Everyone has seen someone "play devil's advocate," and many have their own ideas of the role a devil's advocate should play. Most people agree that the devil's advocate should introduce dissent into decision-making. This is especially important in situations where premature consensus keeps people from challenging assumptions.

There are a great many examples of devil's advocates in the business world. John Bogle, founder and former chief executive of the Vanguard Group of mutual funds, has served this function in the mutual fund industry for decades. He argues that the portfolio managers of the Fidelity Group and many other actively managed mutual funds focus too much on short-term profits, trade too often, charge excessive fees, and fail to discharge their basic fiduciary responsibilities to their investors.[10]

Devil's advocates can be effective because of a common human trait: We can see biased thinking much more readily in others than in ourselves. This may be because of the way we structure information in the self-schema and our susceptibility to the biases and attributions discussed in Chapter 2. Because we structure information relevant to our decisions in a self-serving way, we can always find reasons to justify our biases and stereotyping. However, others lack the information that supports our own self-justification. Sometimes this allows them to identify our biases more effectively than we can ourselves.

Those who have recommended devil's advocacy agree that devil's advocates introduce conflict in order to improve decision-making. However, they disagree on a number of questions, including when devil's advocates should intervene in the decision process, how the devil's advocates should introduce conflict, the types of support the devil's advocates should have, and whether or not the role should rotate among organizational members. In this section, I will describe basic devil's advocacy and its major variants. At the end of this section, I'll outline the major differences in the conceptions of the techniques used.

Simple Devil's Advocacy

Devil's advocacy as an approach to dialogue has been discussed in the management literature since the late 1960s, but recommendations for the use of devil's advocates can be traced back over two hundred years before that, to the era of Pope Benedict XIV. The term "devil's advocate" (or Promoter of the Faith) dates from the twelfth century, when the position was created by the Catholic Church as part of the process of canonizing saints. The devil's advocate was an individual appointed specifically to raise questions about whether an individual should be officially recognized as a saint. This was and is a vital issue for the Catholic Church. A wrong decision on this question could mislead the faithful and even imperil their souls.[11]

In the early 1700s, a Canon lawyer named Prospero Lambertini was appointed to the position of devil's advocate. Lambertini was later elected Pope and took the name of Benedict XIV. In 1737, he summarized his advice based on twenty years' experience as devil's advocate in a multivolume work entitled *De Servorum Dei Beatificatione et Beatorum Canonizatione* (On the Beatification of Servants of God and the Canonization of Blesseds). He recommended that the devil's advocate

1. formulate the questions necessary for interrogating witnesses
2. collect the diverse opinions expressed at meetings
3. outline in writing possible difficulties with the case
4. raise objections to the candidate[12]

Although the canonization procedure is based on a legal model, it seems that the devil's advocate does not argue a case as does a trial lawyer, attempting to *prove* that the candidate is not a saint. Instead, he raises questions that are then answered by those promoting the candidate's case.[13] In 1910, an English Catholic cleric by the name of Macken offered these words of praise for the process,

The utmost care and accuracy are observed at every stage, and, looking at the matter from the purely human point of view, it must be admitted that if there is any institution, any known method of investigation, capable of arriving at a full knowledge of the truth, the calm, deliberate procedure of the Church is eminently entitled to this distinction.[14]

More recently, in recommending the use of devil's advocates by policy makers as a way to avoid groupthink, Irving Janis[15] has suggested that, when there is a great deal of agreement between policy makers and a danger of premature consensus, the chief executive should assign one or more group members to the role of devil's advocate. This person should "present his arguments as cleverly and convincingly as he can, challenging those advocating the majority position." This person should introduce much needed controversy by raising issues in a low-key style in order to avoid unproductive conflict and promote vigilant problem solving.[16]

Others have expanded on these recommendations,[17] suggesting that the devil's advocate should elicit the assumptions underlying a given policy and help the group critically examine these assumptions. He or she should actively collect information contrary to the proposed plan or policy, remain sensitive to unpopular views, and periodically present the most reasonable possible case for alternative beliefs and plans to policy makers.

Some years ago, Anne Huff and I examined conflict in a budgetary decision involving a group of high-level public school administrators in Joliet, Illinois.[18] Administrators primarily used devil's advocacy to challenge and define three basic types of assumptions: assumptions about data, assumptions about stakeholders, and assumptions about goals and values. We observed several things about naturally occurring devil's advocacy in established groups of decision makers:

1. The devil's advocate function is widely dispersed among group members.
2. In some cases, individuals serve as their own devil's advocate, essentially arguing both sides of an issue. In other cases, individuals argue against positions they are known to support in order to ensure these positions are critically examined.
3. Within a single discussion, the testing of assumptions often does not lead to a final decision; rather, it becomes part of the data-gathering process.

Problems with Simple Devil's Advocacy

When organizations are unable or unwilling to take a devil's advocate's proposals seriously, a variety of problems can arise. A devil's advocate might become "domesticated" so that his objections are discounted and he loses his effectiveness. In many established decision-making groups, the devil's advocate's objections and cautions are discounted even before they are delivered. For example, when President Lyndon Johnson authorized the bombing of North Vietnam in the late 1960s, an aide, Bill Moyers (currently of PBS) played devil's advocate and argued against the bombing. His objections had no effect on Johnson's policy, but they did earn him the nickname "Mr. Stop-the-Bombing."[19]

In Chapter 3, I described the ways groups can turn dissenters into "scapegoats." Scapegoating and domestication are always potential dangers for devil's advocates. When they happen, they can render a devil's advocate useless.

One devil's advocate in the group that Anne Huff and I studied might have been domesticated. This person frequently played the role of devil's advocate. Other group members indicated in individual interviews that his comments were often "off base," but his input was considered useful for stimulating others in the group to define their own positions. In the budget meetings, when this person brought up an objection to a particular budget cut, other members of the group quickly attempted to demonstrate that the objection did not have merit. As a result, few of his statements were actually reflected in the final recommendations for budget cuts.

It might be that this particular devil's advocate had been neutralized. However, this person helped convince the rest of the group that they had behaved rationally and had considered a wide range of perspectives and alternatives. As the other decision-makers articulated the reasons for rejecting the devil's advocate's points, they became more committed to their existing assumptions. This suggests that devil's advocates can increase the confidence of a group even if that group is pursuing a mistaken course of action.[20]

Political scientist Aaron Schlaim observes that devil's advocates may be subject to severe pressures to conform if their superiors are unwilling to consider alternative views. He cites the example of Joachim von Ribbentrop, Hitler's foreign minister, who had an unshakable conviction that Great Britain would never go to war against Germany. He warned all members of his staff: "If it came to my notice that anyone had expressed a contrary opinion I would kill him myself in his office, and take responsibility before the Fuhrer for it."[21] Von Ribbentrop's staff was no place for devil's advocates.

Business and political leaders may discourage devil's advocates because they tend to become "carping critics," who do not offer constructive alternatives to the strategic recommendations they criticize and may be demoralizing to decision-makers.[22] For example, those involved in the Roman Catholic Church's canonization process have complained that devil's advocates sometimes became carping critics, focusing excessively on small details and prolonging the dispute process unnecessarily. Further, the disputes often became heated and extremely negative. Eventually, an official was appointed to edit the written documents summarizing the disputes because of "all the profanity and curses" used by the Church officials involved in the arguments.[23]

In 1983, the Catholic Church, under Pope John Paul II, made a number of reforms in the canonization process. Although the office of Promoter of the Faith still exists, the adversarial process of devil's advocacy has been abolished, ending a seven-hundred-year tradition. Since that time, the number of canonizations has increased dramatically. Some have expressed concerns about this. For example, Woodward argues:

My foremost concern remains the fact that, with the abolition of the Devil's Advocate and his staff, there now is no one charged with the responsibility to challenge the evidence brought forward by the candidate's postulator. Put another way, everyone involved in a canonization now has a stake in its positive outcome. This, it seems to me, leaves the Catholic faithful unprotected against the possibility that a powerful and influential group might manipulate this process which the church had struggled for centuries to perfect, for the benefit of an unworthy candidate. Without the Devil's Advocate, who can prevent such an outcome?[24]

Devil's advocates need not slow decision-making Research on fast decision-making among computer firms by Kathleen Eisenhardt showed that companies with high levels of conflict and devil's advocacy made decisions just as quickly as those with less dissent.[25] If there are problems with the devil's advocate process, the solution is to modify rather than abolish the process. Several variants of devil's advocacy have been developed that might allow organizations to improve the process and retain the benefits of structured conflict.

Multiple Advocacy

Multiple advocacy is an expanded version of simple devil's advocacy. Alexander George, a political scientist who has studied presidential decision-making, claims that multiple advocacy is superior to devil's advocacy because it includes more advocates and more options.[26] In multiple advocacy, representatives of several minority opinions and unpopular views present these to decision-makers to encourage them to question the assumptions underlying the favored policy. By comparison, simple devil's advocacy typically involves only a single critique.

A key role in this process is that of the custodian of unpopular views. The custodian attempts to ensure "That there is no major maldistribution of resources among the proponents of various views (important resources include: power, influence, competence, information, analytical resources, and bargaining and persuasion skills); that there is no involvement by the top-level decision maker(s) in the debate; and that there is adequate time for give and take."[27] Multiple advocacy, like devil's advocacy, is most useful in "novel situations in which important values are at stake but which cannot, or should not, be dealt with by selecting one of the standard responses from the organization's available repertoire."[28]

Dialectical Inquiry

Another alternative technique designed to improve simple devil's advocacy is called dialectical inquiry.[29] This technique involves creating dialectical debate as a means of examining assumptions. Often, decision-makers are clustered into groups that differ substantially in policy preferences. The groups develop alternatives to a recommended strategy or plan by identifying assumptions on which it is based and about which the group members disagree. Some companies have attempted to incorporate this kind of debate into their decisions about acquisitions by establishing a "green team" to argue for the acquisition and a "red team" to argue against it.[30]

An important part of dialectical inquiry is the explicit identification of pivotal assumptions, those that provide the foundation for the strategy and on which there is the strongest disagreement.[31] Since the time of key decision-makers is valuable, they should not waste time evaluating assumptions that are not critical to the strategy or assumptions about which there is little disagreement. After a debate about alternative plans, decision-makers discuss these assumptions and negotiate to arrive at a pool of common assumptions.

Ian Mitroff and his colleagues have had some success with structuring dialectical debates in strategic planning with the U.S. Census Bureau as well as a number of businesses. Some detail on their activities is provided in Appendix G at the end of the chapter.

Dialectical inquiry requires the development of explicit counterplans based on assumptions different from those underlying the favored plan. However, a devil's advocate does not have to develop an explicit counterplan. If a favored strategy has been identified early in the decision-making process, the techniques for constructing divergent groups and identifying pivotal assumptions may be used as a basis for constructing a critique that merely challenges the key assumptions but offers no alternative plan.

Major Differences

The discussions of alternative forms of structured conflict contain conflicting recommendations. Among researchers, there is general agreement that devil's advocates should introduce conflict by challenging previously formed assumptions and alternatives. However, there is disagreement on how this can best be done. One difference involves the point at which the devil's advocate should intervene. Herbert and Estes argue that the devil's advocate should intervene *after* a proposal has been developed and should prepare a counterplan if the situation warrants it. This view is shared by Cosier and de Rivera. However, Janis and Mann, as well as George, suggest that the devil's advocate should intervene throughout the decision process.

A second point of difference concerns whether devil's advocates should focus on critiquing the majority position or whether they should actively advocate alternative views. Cosier suggests that the devil's advocate should focus on the critique of the favored plan rather than the development of a counterplan. Jervis, Herbert and Estes, and de Rivera also recommend a focus on the critique of favored policies, but suggest that advocating alternative policies may be appropriate under some circumstances.

George and Mitroff, in their improvements on devil's advocacy, recommend that counterplans be identified. Mason and Mitroff have developed techniques for choosing members of the decision-making group to prepare counterplans, while the primary focus of George's custodian is to ensure that those representing opposing perspectives or counterplans are given the resources to effectively advocate them.

Finally, these authors differ on the question of whether a single person should perform the role of devil's advocate permanently or whether the role should rotate among group members. Janis and Mann and de Rivera imply that the role should be assumed by a single group member over a long period of time. George's custodian role is also long-term. However, the critics of devil's advocacy point out that this practice may lead to domestication of devil's advocates and a reduction in their effectiveness. Herbert and Estes suggest that the role should be rotated among organizational members as a form of management training.

Academic research on these techniques began in the 1960s and has produced several dozen studies. (See Appendix G for an overview). The field and laboratory research strongly support the effectiveness of different forms of structured conflict over the more common approaches to organizational decision-making that do not involve the introduction of conflict. Results of field research demonstrate that decision-makers who use dialectical inquiry feel it improves their decisions over the expert-based approach they had been using previously. Their analysis of data is more thorough and their understanding of the decision is more complete.

The research reviewed in Appendix G shows that all forms of structured conflict have benefits, but that the plan/critique format of simple devil's advocacy improves decision-making most consistently. Specifically, it reduces the narrowing effect of expert advice, increases the number of strategic alternatives generated, and improves decision-makers' use of ambiguous environmental information in making predictions.

Although a significant body of empirical evidence indicates that the use of devil's advocacy typically improves performance, those who have argued against the technique's effectiveness correctly point out that in some cases its use has not prevented disastrous errors, including President Lyndon Johnson's decision to escalate the bombing of North Vietnam in the late 1960s. Therefore, it is necessary to clarify the proper role of devil's advocates and establish realistic expectations for their effectiveness. It is also necessary to draw suggestions from the research for making devil's advocates as effective as possible.

SYMPATHY FOR THE DEVIL: UNDERSTANDING THE NEED FOR DEVIL'S ADVOCACY

For devil's advocates to have any impact on decisions, their role must be valued and their objections taken seriously. Without such commitment, the devil's advocate may serve merely to reassure decision-makers that they have heard both sides of an issue. Decision-makers may attempt to domesticate those playing the role of devil's advocate and, failing that, may exclude them from decision-making. If misused, devil's advocacy can reduce vigilant problem-solving and increase groupthink.

In order for decision-makers to take the devil's advocate seriously, they must be willing to admit that there are multiple ways of viewing a problem and that the assumptions underlying their own view may not be correct. The factors influencing this willingness are not well understood. However, decision-makers' tolerance of ambiguity—their ability to deal with ambiguous information from the environment—has been shown to be important.[32] Those who are tolerant of ambiguity are less likely to become defensive when the devil's advocate points out uncertainties. A second factor is the decision-makers' prior experience. Prior failure makes people more receptive to devil's advocates' comments.

The organization's knowledge structure may also determine whether devil's advocates will be helpful. In organizations with a rigid culture that is strongly defended in response to perceived external threat, the knowledge structure may be impoverished and decision-makers may find it difficult to question their assumptions as the devil's advocate suggests. However, as Janis[33] and Janis and Mann[34] point out, such organizations may need a devil's advocate more than those with enriched knowledge structures.

Time pressure may also be a factor determining how seriously the devil's advocate's advice is taken. Devil's advocates may be ignored by decision-makers facing a deadline, even though they may need a devil's advocate more under such circumstances.[35] However, as noted earlier, devil's advocacy need not slow decision-making if done properly.

One final factor that reduces the effectiveness of structured conflict is the belief that organizational members must clearly understand and share the leader's vision. The man who popularized the concept of the "learning organization," Peter Senge, for example, suggests that shared vision and a strong commitment to that vision are necessary for organizations to learn the right lessons from past failures. He also gives specific recommendations for building such a shared vision.[36]

Collins and Porras[37] argue that in building a company's strategic vision it is important to identify the company's "core ideology" and then to build the vision statement using vivid descriptions to ensure "alignment" of employees with the vision and employees' commitment to "Big, Hairy, Audacious Goals". Indeed, employees' absolute commitment to a shared vision of the future is seen by many leaders or change agents as being so important for their organizations' continued survival that it must be encouraged with rewards and sanctions.

Such behavior evokes concern in those who recall the economist Frederick von Hayek's warnings about the dangers of the enforcement of shared visions in totalitarian societies. In *The Road to Serfdom*, published in 1944,[38] he points out that the leaders in such societies place great emphasis on the need for a commonly accepted system of goals that make it possible for all action to be directed toward a single aim, rather than having activities guided by the whims and fancies of irresponsible individuals. Hayek's focus was on societies, but these warnings apply equally well to organizations.

In short, what John Stuart Mill called "true eccentricity" must be encouraged. Mill's essay "On Liberty" was written about British society in 1859, but his analysis is true of many business organizations today:

Precisely because the tyranny of opinion is such as to make eccentricity a reproach, it is desirable, in order to break through that tyranny, that people should be eccentric. Eccentricity has always abounded when and where strength of character has abounded; and the amount of eccentricity in a society has generally been proportional to the amount of genius, mental vigor, and moral courage which it contained.[39]

In our culture, the very word "eccentric" is often a polite way of describing someone who is "crazy." However, a recent study of eccentric personalities shows that eccentrics as a whole have fewer symptoms of mental disorders than the general population and that their divergent views sometimes represent a sensible challenge to prevailing social pathologies.[40] Historically, these deviant opinions have often proven sound and valuable with the passage of time.

Organizational eccentrics help preserve peripheral aspects of the knowledge structure. For this reason, they can be a valuable resource for those seeking innovative solutions.

Microsoft's entry into Internet services was originally considered an eccentric idea, outside the focus of the leader's vision for the company. Bill Gates had to be persuaded to broaden his vision by those in the company who supported this initially deviant idea, although he now strongly believes Microsoft's future lies in the Internet. A peripheral idea has become a core idea. Microsoft's experience may argue for the value of ideas initially perceived as eccentric and for greater tolerance of eccentricity than is common in most businesses today.

Without tolerance for eccentric ideas, it is unlikely that any technique for encouraging the expression of diverse views will improve decision-making in a firm. Andrew Grove of Intel makes this point when he argues that top management must open its ears to what he calls the Cassandras in the organization.[41]

SUGGESTIONS FOR USING STRUCTURED CONFLICT

Even if decision-makers are able to look critically at their assumptions, they may not receive the full benefit of structured conflict if the devil's advocate does not play the role effectively. Based on past research, I will identify some of the important questions to ask in deciding whether to use structured conflict and how to make it more productive.

What Is the Nature of the Decision?

All the field applications of devil's advocacy involve very complex and ill-structured problems. Nonetheless, some people think that the technique should be used almost routinely in organizational decision-making. However, since research has not addressed the effects of structured conflict on routine, structured problems, I cannot recommend it for such problems. The technique should be reserved for more complex, ill-structured and important decisions.

In many decisions, lower-level organizational members may have more detailed information on the data relevant to the decision than the top-level decision-makers to whom they report. In such cases, it is especially important that peripheral elements of the knowledge structure be accessed. Top managers should not play the role of devil's advocate because they may lack the expertise to do so effectively. Instead, the role should be played by members of the organization who have appropriate expertise but differing assumptions. The critique and plan can then be discussed with management. If, on the other hand, top managers have a good understanding of the data and sufficient expertise, they may play the devil's advocate role themselves.

In technical decisions, the major concern is to improve the quality of data analysis and the rationality of decision-making. In political decisions, the major concern is to represent the views or demands of groups affected by the decision. It may be that dialectical inquiry and multiple advocacy, as variants of devil's advocacy, are more effective at dealing with political decisions. By allowing representatives of affected groups to prepare counterplans, and possibly by using a custodian to ensure that they are given resources to develop the counterplan, their input may be elicited more effectively than by simple devil's advocacy.

What Is the Level of Preexisting Conflict?

When the decision is full of conflict and group members are strongly advocating different strategies, the devil's advocate should be active throughout the decision-making process.[42] She should attempt to clarify the differences in assumptions that underlie the differences in strategies.[43] Mason and Mitroff, in *Challenging Strategic Planning Assumptions*, discuss a number of procedures for identifying assumptions by examining beliefs about stakeholders and for identifying the pivotal assumptions that are the fundamental premises of each group's recommendations.[44] In their book, *Dialogue*, Ellinor and Gerard also offer some useful suggestions for identifying and questioning assumptions in order to reframe disagreement.[45] However, a devil's advocate familiar with the organization's operations may be able to identify these assumptions without the help of special techniques.

The devil's advocate in this situation may also be required to play a role similar to that of George's custodian to ensure that each group is assisted in developing its case. There should be a dialogue in which each group is allowed to present its case followed by responses from other groups and questions from those who have final responsibility for making the decision. Studies have shown that this approach is effective in clarifying assumptions.[46] If the group must reach consensus, it may be necessary to go through an assumption negotiation stage.[47] If consensus is not required, those with final responsibility for the decision should play a role similar to George's "magistrate" in order to avoid becoming prematurely committed to one position.

If the decision-making process is characterized by *too little* conflict and a preferred alternative has been identified with too little questioning of assumptions, the devil's advocate should play a different role.[48] Here the devil's advocate should initiate assumption questioning and problem reformulation by identifying critical assumptions underlying the preferred alternative and using these as the basis for a forcefully presented critique.

How Should the Devil's Advocate Criticize?

Some research suggests that the use of a critique that does not specify an alternative plan is more effective than a specific counterplan.[49] However, with adequate training, decision-makers may be able to use the plan-counterplan format as effectively as the plan-critique format. If the devil's advocate has the time and resources to develop them, both a critique and counterplan may be more effective than either alone.[50]

The devil's advocate should avoid strongly identifying with a particular position and becoming a carping critic of those who oppose it. An excessively critical devil's advocate may demoralize decision-makers, especially those who proposed the initial plan. Instead, the devil's advocate should play the role of a process consultant interested only in bringing assumptions to the surface and improving decision-making. One study showed that a carping critic form of devil's advocacy did not improve decision-making, but that a less emotional, more objective form of devil's advocacy did.[51] The objective form of devil's advocacy was also superior to the carping critic form in groups communicating through computer networks.[52] Carping critics polarize decision processes, evoking defensiveness, stereotyping of rivals, and all the other negative consequences of polarizing conflict discussed in Chapter 3.

One Devil's Advocate or Many?

It is still not clear whether it is best to have a single person play the role of devil's advocate for a series of decisions or whether this role should rotate among group members. If a single individual plays this role over a series of decisions, that person, through practice, becomes a more effective devil's advocate. On the other hand, rotation of the role may give the entire group a clearer understanding of the devil's advocate process and prevent the negative consequences that sometimes result from identifying a single individual as the devil's advocate.

If one person adopts the role, he or she should attempt to identify another individual in the group whose views on the decision diverge from the rest of the group to assist in preparing the critique. If the role shifts to a different person for each decision, the person selected should generally be someone whose assumptions about the decision differ from most of the other group members.

If leaders are attempting to enrich their organization's knowledge structure through the use of multiple devil's advocates, they might consider appointing a permanent custodian. This person would take responsibility for preserving peripheral elements of the knowledge structure and helping top managers use them in making crucial organizational decisions. As mentioned in Chapter 4, organizational databases can store some peripheral elements of the knowledge structure. However, since stakeholders themselves are also part of the knowledge structure, a custodian needs to maintain personal contacts and information sources beyond those contained in a database. People with enriched self-schemas make the most effective custodians.

CONCLUSIONS

In this chapter, I have described how diversity of views and identities can be used productively through structuring conflict in the process of dialogue. By doing this, organizations can deal with impoverishment of knowledge structures and the self-schemas of their members.

There is still a great deal we don't know about when and why devil's advocates are effective. Our understanding of structured conflict will continue to increase if managers, consultants, and academic researchers can work together to evaluate how it functions in specific cases.

Devil's advocates should be used only if decision-makers can honestly question their basic assumptions and if they have a sincere commitment to the process. Without such commitment, devil's advocates may be useless or even harmful.

Unfortunately, the mind-set in some organizations is not conducive to effective use of devil's advocacy. Devil's advocacy fails when leaders lack open-mindedness and fear dissent. Fear of dissent is sometimes mistaken for good management. Executives who insist on absolute commitment to their vision may appear to be leading effectively when they are actually suppressing diverse perspectives. Some companies may have to reduce their commitment to the leader's "strategic vision" in order to encourage the expression of the full range of members' views, some of which may conflict with the stated vision of the leader, and some of which will be decidedly eccentric.

As shown in Chapter 4, it is possible for an organization to have a clear strategic vision *and* make use of the peripheral elements of its knowledge structure, but doing so is not easy. Attempts to enforce consensus may reduce the organization's ability to effectively use the knowledge at its disposal.

NOTES

1. G. Santayana, *Skepticism and Animal Faith: Introduction to a System of Philosophy* (New York: Scribner, 1923), p. 8

2. W. Isaacs, *Dialogue and the Art of Thinking Together* (New York: Doubleday, 1999).

3. L. Ellinor and G. Gerard, *Dialogue: Rediscover the Transforming Power of Conversation* (New York: Wiley, 1998).

4. D. Yankelovich, *The Magic of Dialogue* (New York: Simon & Schuster, 1999).

5. Isaacs, 1999, *Dialogue*, p. 25.

6. Ibid., p. 33.

7. Ibid.

8. Ellinor and Gerard, 1998, *Dialogue*, pp. 233–236.

9. See *Wall Street Journal*, July 7, 2000, p. A10.

10. See, for example, his article in the *Wall Street Journal*, June 20, 2000, p. A26.

11. K. Woodward, *Making Saints: How the Catholic Church Determines Who Becomes a Saint, Who Doesn't, and Why* (New York: Touchstone, 1996), p. 68.

12. See Woodward, ibid., pp. 73–76, and P. Molinari, "The Devil's Advocate" *New Catholic Encyclopedia*, vol. 4 (New York: McGraw-Hill, 1967), pp. 829–830.

13. See Woodward for a discussion of the process, especially pp. 67–68, 76, 81–82, 91–95, and 377.

14. C. Macken, *The Canonization of Saints* (Dublin: Hill and Sons, 1910), p. 196.

15. See I. Janis, *Groupthink: Psychological Studies of Policy Decisions and Fiascoes* (second edition) (Boston: Houghton-Mifflin, 1982); I. Janis, *Crucial Decisions: Leadership in Policymaking and Crisis Management* (New York: Free Press, 1989); and I. Janis and L. Mann, *Decision-Making* (New York: Free Press, 1989).

16. Janis, 1982, *Groupthink*, p. 215.

17. See R. Cosier, "Dialectical inquiry in strategic planning: A case of premature acceptance?" *Academy of Management Review* 6(1981): 643–48; J. de Rivera, *The Psychological Dimension of Foreign Policy* (Columbus, OH: Charles E. Merrill, 1968); T. Herbert and R. Estes, "Improving executive planning by formalizing dissent: The corporate devil's advocate," *Academy of Management Review* 2(1968): 662–667; R. Jervis, "Hypotheses on misperception," *World Politics* 20(1968): 457–474; R. Jervis, *Perception and Misperception in International Politics* (Princeton, NJ: Princeton University Press, 1976).

18. C. Schwenk and A. Huff, "Argumentation in Strategic Decision-Making," in *Advances in Strategic Management*, ed. D. Lamb and P. Shrivastava (Greenwich, CT: JAI Press, 1986), 189–202.

19. For a discussion of the domestication of devil's advocates in political decision-making, see G. Reedy, *Twilight of the Presidency* (New York: World Books, 1970), p. 11 and J. Thompson, "How could Vietnam happen? An autopsy," *Atlantic Monthly*, April(1968): 47–53.

20. Schwenk and Huff, 1986, "Argumentation in Strategic Decision-Making."

21. A. Schlaim, "Failures of national intelligence estimates: The case of the Yom Kippur war," *World Politics*, April(1976): 355–378, pp. 374–375.

22. To my knowledge, this concept was first discussed by Richard Mason in 1969 (R. Mason, "A dialectical approach to strategic planning," *Management Science* 15(1969): B403–14).

23. Woodward, 1996, *Making Saints*, p. 94.

24. Ibid., p. 4.

25. See K. Eisenhardt, "Making fast strategic decisions in high-velocity environments," *Academy of Management Journal* 32(1989): 543–576, p. 562. Also, K. Eisenhardt, "Speed and strategic choice: How managers accelerate decision-making," *California Management Review* 32(1989): 39–54.

26. A. George, "The case for multiple advocacy in making foreign policy," *American Political Science Review* 66(1972): 751–785.

27. Ibid., p. 759.

28. Ibid., p. 763.

29. See Mason and Mitroff (R. Mason and I. Mitroff. *Challenging Strategic Planning Assumptions*, New York: Wiley, 1981) for a more detailed discussion of this technique and how to use it.

30. See James Brian Quinn's discussion in his book *Strategies for Change* (J. B. Quinn. *Strategies for Change: Logical Incrementalism,* Homewood, IL: Irwin, 1980)

31. Mason and Mitroff, 1981, *Challenging,* p. 49.

32. C. Schwenk, "Effects of inquiry methods and ambiguity tolerance on prediction performance," *Decision Sciences* 13(1982): 207–221.

33. Janis, 1982, *Groupthink.*

34. Janis and Mann, 1977, *Decision-Making.*

35. George, 1972, "The case for multiple advocacy," p. 759.

36. P. Senge, *The Fifth Discipline: The Art and Practice of the Learning Organization* (New York: Doubleday, 1990).

37. J. Collins and J. Porras, "Building your company's vision," *Harvard Business Review* (September/October, 1996): 10–17.

38. F. Hayek, *The Road to Serfdom* (Chicago: University of Chicago Press, 1944).

39. J. S. Mill, *On Liberty.* Albury Castell, ed. (New York: Appleton-Century-Crofts, 1859/1947), p. 67.

40. D. Weeks and K. Ward, *Eccentrics: The Scientific Investigation* (Stirling, England: Stirling University Press, 1988).

41. A. Grove, "Navigating strategic inflection points," *Business Strategy Review* 8(1997): 11–18.

42. Janis, 1982. *Groupthink;* Janis and Mann, 1977, *Decision-Making.*

43. I. Mitroff, J. Emshoff, and R. Kilmann, "Assumptional analysis: A methodology for strategic problem-solving," *Management Science* 25(1979): 583–93.

44. Mason and Mitroff, 1981, *Challenging,* pp. 43–49.

45. Ellinor and Gerard, *Dialogue,* pp. 92–95 & 349–351; pp. 199–203.

46. H. Mitroff, V. Barabba, and R. Kilmann, "The application of behavioral and philosophical technologies to strategic planning: A case study of a large federal agency," *Management Science* 23(1977): 44–58.

47. Mason and Mitroff, 1981, *Challenging,* p. 52.

48. Herbert and Estes, 1977, "Improving executive planning"; Jervis, 1968, "Hypotheses on misperceptions"; Jervis, 1976, *Perception and Misperception*; Cosier, 1981, "Dialectical inquiry in strategic planning."

49. R. Cosier, "The effects of three potential aids for making strategics on prediction accuracy," *Organizational Behavior and Human Performance,* 22(1978): 295–306; R. Cosier, "Inquiry method, goal difficulty, and context effects on performance," *Decision Sciences* 11(1980): 1–16; R. Cosier, T. Ruble, and J. Aplin, "An evaluation of the effectiveness of dialectical inquiry systems," *Management Science* 24(1978): 1483–90; C. Schwenk, "Effects of inquiry methods and ambiguity tolerance on prediction performance," *Decision Sciences* 13(1982): 207–221; C. Schwenk and R. Cosier, "Effects of the expert, devil's advocate and dialectical inquiry methods on prediction performance," *Organizational Behavior & Human Performance* 26(1980): 409–424.

50. Schwenk, 1982, "Effects of inquiry methods."

51. Schwenk and Cosier, 1980, "Effects of the expert, devil's advocate and dialectical inquiry."

52. J. Valacich and C. Schwenk, "Structuring conflict in individual, face-to-face, and computer mediated group decision-making: Carping versus objective devil's advocacy," *Decision Sciences* 26(1995b): 369–394.

APPENDIX G:
PAST RESEARCH ON
STRUCTURED CONFLICT

Although there are significant differences between simple devil's advocacy, dialectical inquiry, and multiple advocacy, the three will be discussed in this summary of past research as variants of the basic devil's advocate approach. The basic devil's advocate procedure is defined here simply as a procedure involving the use of one or more persons to raise objections to favored strategies, challenge assumptions underlying them, and possibly point out alternatives.

The research on the variants of devil's advocacy will be discussed as a basis for developing recommendations for its effective use. A number of field and laboratory experiments have been reported in the strategic management literature on dialectical inquiry (DI), which involves the development of an explicit counterplan, compared to a simplified form of devil's advocacy called the DA, which involves only the development of a critique without an explicit counterplan. This research can be of value to managers desiring direction in the effective use of devil's advocates.

Mason (1969), who developed descriptions of the techniques based on the work of Churchman (1966), suggested that the DI is more effective at exposing underlying assumptions than the DA because the DI involves the generation of constructive alternatives, whereas the devil's advocate in the DA merely plays the role of an adverse and often carping critic of the favored plan or recommendation. Thus, he suggests that the DA does not assist in the development of a new set of assumptions or a new worldview.

However, both the DA and DI approaches are, according to Mason (1969), distinctly superior to what he calls the expert (E) approach, which is seen as the most common approach to top management decision-making. In this approach, members of a planning department or consultants provide expert advice and recommendations regarding the plans the organization should follow. Mason suggests that the planning recommendations contain hidden assumptions that are frequently not communicated to management, but that may reinforce management biases. This is one of the most critical drawbacks to this approach (1969, pp. 406–407).

The DI has been used as an aid to corporate decision-making in a number of field experiments. Mason (1969) studied the effects of the DI on strategic decision-making in an abrasives manufacturing company. He obtained a strategic planning document from the company's planning department, identified its ten underlying assumptions, and constructed a counterplan based on opposite assumptions. The plan and counterplan were then presented to management in a structured debate. Mason reported that the company's managers were more satisfied with the strategy they developed as a result of using the DI. Specifically, they felt it led to a "new encompassing view" of the planning problem, to the identification of key assumptions, and to the generation of new alternatives.

In a public sector application, Mitroff, Barabba, and Kilmann (1977) used the DI on a planning problem in Washington, D.C., at the Bureau of the Census. Census Bureau employees were given a lecture on the DI. Forty-five of the employees decided to participate in the next stage of the study and were then clustered into five homogeneous groups. These groups then produced planning reports suggesting new future directions for the Bureau—reports differing significantly from one another. Next, the assumptions underlying each report were identified and debated. Finally, representatives from each group formed an executive group that produced a final integrative report. According to Mitroff et al., this report contained several interesting ideas about the Bureau of the Census' role in the year 2000 and several alternatives that the participants found innovative and exciting.

Emshoff and Finnel (1978) developed a more detailed procedure for applying the DI to strategic planning, which they called strategic assumptions analysis. This technique contains (in addition to the dialectical debate on assumptions) an *assumption negotiation* phase. This phase occurs after decision-makers have been divided into groups and the groups have generated two or more plans based on different interpretations of the organizational data base. As part of the assumption negotiation phase, members of each group are required to identify and question assumptions from the other groups that are "most perturbing to the group's policy—those assumptions which are hardest for each group to live with" (1978, p. 11). These are then discussed and negotiated in order to arrive at a common assumption pool. Thus, strategic assumptions analysis involves the generation of both counterplans and critiques.

Emshoff and Finnel examined the effects of strategic assumptions analysis in a company they called Basic Materials. A planning group at the company used the technique to revise a strategic plan they had developed. The authors concluded that strategic assumptions analysis ensured a more thorough analysis of the data and produced a revised strategy that was superior to the initial strategy (1978, p. 30).

Strategic assumptions analysis was applied by Mitroff, Emshoff, and Kilmann (1979) to a pricing decision in a drug company. Here, the managers had divided themselves into three groups, each advocating a different pricing policy. There was considerable conflict in the decision-making group from the beginning. Therefore, it was not necessary to use any special procedures to formulate divergent groups. The consultants entered the decision-making process at its beginning and focused their attention on clarifying the assumptions between groups. Through the use of strategic assumptions analysis, the three groups of managers examined their divergent assumptions and negotiated to arrive at a common assumption pool that was the basis for agreement on a final pricing policy. The authors reported that this procedure produced more and better alternatives and led to a different pricing policy than the one that would otherwise have been chosen.

Thus, the field research provides some support for the assertion that the DI is effective in helping managers deal with ill-structured problems. It deepens decision-makers' understanding of a problem, reduces the narrowing effects of expert advice, leads to the generation of new alternatives, and increases decision-makers' satisfaction with the decision. However, these conclusions are somewhat tentative since the field studies relied on managerial judgments of the effects of the DI and because they did not include control conditions.

Another line of research has dealt with the value of conflicting interpretations of data and the comparative effectiveness of the DA approach and, in more controlled settings, DI. In these experiments, the researchers did not attempt to capture the full complexity of devil's advocacy or dialectical inquiry as they were used in the field. Rather, they focused on what they felt was the central feature of the DI, the presentation to decision-makers of two conflicting interpretations of the same database through a plan and counterplan. This was compared to the DA format that involved a single interpretation of the data and a critique of this interpretation suggesting no alternative. These experiments involved the presentation of a standardized plan and critique to all DA subjects and a standardized plan and counterplan to all DI subjects.

Cosier (1978) developed E, DA, and DI treatments for a laboratory setting and measured their effects on performance at a multiple-cue probability learning (MCPL) task. The task required individuals to predict criterion values using three cues having a probabilistic relationship to the criterion. Subjects in the E Condition received a planning report from an "expert" recommending that they give most weight to one particular cue in making their predictions. This, according to Mason, represented the most common approach to organizational decision-making, the expert (E) approach. Subjects in the DA Condition received this same "expert" report plus a critique that questioned the assumptions of the first report but offered no alternative recommendations, a treatment incorporating the essential elements of the DA as described by Mason (1969). Subjects in the DI Condition were given the "expert" report plus a counterplan suggesting an alternate set of cue weights.

All subjects made twenty predictions in each of three distinct conditions. In the first condition, the cue-criterion relationship was consistent with the recommendations of the expert report. In the third condition, the relationship was consistent with the counterproposal. The second condition represented a compromise between the proposal and the counterproposal. Cosier found that in the third condition, the DA subjects made significantly more accurate predictions than the E or DI subjects. Thus, the results of this study tended to favor the DA.

Later laboratory studies by Cosier, Ruble, and Aplin (1978), Cosier (1980), and Schwenk and Cosier (1980) using a similar experimental design have generally shown that compared to the simpler E approach, the DA and the DI improve the ability of subjects to discover the relationship between cues and a criterion and employ that relationship in making predictions. However, the DA appeared to be more effective than the DI.

Schwenk (1982) examined the effects of decision-makers' ambiguity tolerance and a combined critique and counterplan (DA/DI) treatment on performance at the MCPL task. He found that for decision-makers high in ambiguity tolerance, the DA/DI led to better prediction performance than an E, DA, or DI treatment alone. However, only the superiority of the DA/DI to the E was statistically significant, while the superiority of the DA/DI to the DI was marginally significant. Schwenk (1984a), using the MCPL task and student subjects, showed that the DI treatment was more effective than the DA for subjects who were highly involved in the decision-making task, while the DA was more effective for subjects lower in commitment to the task. Schweiger and Finger (1984) found no significant differences between subjects given the DA or DI treatment in an MCPL task—a finding that is difficult to reconcile with the results of nearly all other MCPL studies.

The DA and DI have also been examined using case analysis tasks and simulations. Schwenk and Thomas (1983a) showed that the DA/DI treatment improved the cost effectiveness of solutions and reduced the tendency to collect too much information in a group of managers working on a business case. Schwenk (1984b) investigated the effects of the DA and DI as well as the medium through which they were presented on decision-makers' generation of alternatives and final choice of a recommendation. He found that the DA treatment, presented in written rather than oral form, led to the generation of more strategic alternatives than the DI or E approaches presented in written form. Also, the DA reduced the effects of an expert report on decision-makers' final recommendations more than did the DI. However, both the DA and DI were perceived by subjects to be more valuable than the E.

Cosier and Rechner (1985) showed that a DA treatment was more useful than a DI treatment for student subjects making decisions in a business simulation. However, the DA was not found to be more effective than the DI with a group of experienced managers using the same simulation.

Schweiger, Sandberg, and Ragan (1986) showed that both DA and DI treatments increased the quality of assumptions and recommendations when compared to a consensus approach in a laboratory experiment involving a case analysis task and groups of MBAs. In this experiment, the DI was superior to the DA in terms of the quality of assumptions surfacing. However, subjects given the consensus treatment expressed more satisfaction and desire to continue working with their groups as well as greater acceptance of their groups' decisions. This suggests that there may be some negative consequences of the conflict generated by the DA and DI.

Murrell, Stewart, and Engle (1993) showed that the effects of devil's advocacy depend on the type of task the group is performing. When the task involves determining which of the group members has the best understanding of a problem, devil's advocacy is helpful. However, when the task involves group members simply discussing the problem and coming to a group judgment, devil's advocacy may actually be harmful, perhaps because it forces group members to confront one another.

Stone, Sivitanides, and Margo (1994) found that the cognitive complexity of the group influenced the effects of devil's advocacy. Devil's advocacy groups with low-complexity members produced lower-quality recommendations and participated less equally in decision-making than both high- and low-complexity groups that used the dialectical inquiry technique.

Alper, Tjosvold, and Law (1998) studied groups with both cooperative and competitive goals working on complex problems. They found that groups with cooperative goals were better able to use techniques of constructive controversy than groups with competitive goals.

Some time ago, I conducted a meta-analysis of all previous experiments on DA (Schwenk 1990). Based on the aggregated results of sixteen experiments involving over 1,500 subjects, it was concluded that formal DA does produce higher-quality decisions than the expert approach. More recent research in computer-mediated environments suggests that this technique may also be useful when problem-solving is done in groups communicating electronically rather than face to face (Valacich and Schwenk 1995a, b).

Though past research supports the value of structured conflict, many questions remain to be addressed. Katzenstein (1996) has identified a number of theoretical issues, including the structuring of arguments and the training of subjects, that should be considered by those working in this area in the future.

6

Using Identities Productively

To study the self is to transcend the self. To transcend the self is to be enlightened by all beings.
      —Dogen Zenji, thirteenth-century Buddhist patriarch[1]

In this chapter, I will discuss individual-level techniques for using identities to think more clearly about important issues and to reach better decisions about them. In the preceding chapters, I have attempted to identify the reasons why many important issues are so difficult to address and have laid the groundwork for the recommendations I will make in this chapter.

I will now return to the individual level and describe techniques for enriching self-schemas, and for enabling individuals to obtain the benefits of their self-schemas and social identities while simultaneously maintaining the flexibility necessary to incorporate information that challenges these identities and to deal with those who have differing views. I will discuss five basic approaches for enabling individuals to enrich their self-schemas and use them more effectively in making important decisions: mapping the self-schema in decision-making, mindful identification, autobiographical reflection, structured internal conflict, and constructing dialogues.

MAPPING THE SELF-SCHEMA IN DECISIONS

Individuals who are strongly identified with their organizations may not fully access their self-schemas in decision-making because they draw exclusively on their work identities. Focusing on only one identity reduces the cognitive effort and time required to make a decision, so it is appropriate for the frequent small decisions we face each day. When we habitually use only a small part of the entire self-schema, however, it may be difficult to access all of it for important decisions.

Techniques exist for helping people use their cognitive maps more effectively in decision-making, and these techniques can be adapted to assist in the effective use of the self-schema.[2] I gave an example of such a map developed from my own autobiography in Chapter 2. Recent research has shown that drawing your cognitive map before making an important decision can help you take a less biased view of the problem. Hodgkinson, Brown, Maule, Glaister, and Pearman,[3] for example, had undergraduate students work on a business decision and draw their cognitive maps. To do this, the students identified the important variables in their decision and drew network diagrams showing the causal relations between these variables. Half of the students drew their cognitive maps *before* making their decision, the other half drew their maps *after* the decision. Half of all students were given the information framed in a positive way; in other words, the information was presented in such a way as to encourage risk-taking. The other half received information encouraging risk-aversion in the decision. Those who articulated their cognitive maps before making the decision were less affected by the way the problem was framed than those who drew their maps after making the decision.

This research suggests that our cognitive maps and schemas (including self-schemas) are not always completely evoked in all decisions. In everyday decisions, considering all aspects of the self-schema may be too time-consuming to be worth the effort. However, in especially important decisions, our habit of focusing on only one or a few identities can cause us to take too narrow a view of the problem.

Drawing a map of the self-schema can help in crucial decisions, whether they are business decisions or life decisions. Karl Weick has argued that the way you make sense of change is grounded in the way you define your identity. The more identities you have access to, the more different meanings you can extract from any situation.[4]

Mapping the self-schema can help people access more of their identities than they would otherwise, thus clarifying the implications of the self-schema for important decisions. The example I provided in Chapter 1 may be helpful in developing diagrams of the major identities in the self-schema and the linkages between them.

MINDFUL IDENTIFICATION

In Chapter 1, I discussed mindless identification with group and organizational roles. I will now develop the distinction between mindful identification and mindless identification. Work on mindfulness[5] and the contrast between mindful and mindless action[6] provides the basis for the definition of mindful identification.

Ellen Langer argues that mindfulness is a habitual state of mind in which old schemas are continually reexamined and redefined. She defines mindlessness as the rigid reliance on old categories, while mindfulness involves the continual creation of new ones.[7] Mindfulness includes openness to multiple points of view[8] and a focus on process rather than outcome.[9] In her own words,

When we are mindful, we implicitly or explicitly (1) view a situation from several perspectives, (2) see information presented in the situation as novel, (3) attend to the context in which we are perceiving the information, and eventually, (4) create new categories.[10]

Mindfulness is a central part of Buddhist meditation and Langer's discussion can be extended using Buddhist sources.[11] Suzuki, for example, discusses mindfulness in the context of what he calls Beginner's Mind. He contrasts this state of mind with Expert's Mind by saying that "in the beginner's mind there are many possibilities, but in the expert's mind there are few."[12]

Experts have very detailed and complex schemas within their domain of expertise. Experts in the game of chess, for example, possess schemas that specify how to respond to almost any board positions. Beginners, on the other hand, are *aschematic* and must consciously think through each move. Experts' schemas embody assumptions about chess strategy that reduce the number of possible moves they consider thereby instantly eliminating foolish moves that beginners waste time pondering. In complex social decisions, however, the "rules" are not as fixed or clearly understood as they are in chess. In life decisions, options that seem foolish at one time may seem brilliant at another time because the "rules of the game" have changed. In crucial decisions, therefore, it is dangerous to exclude options based on outmoded assumptions.

Beginner's Mind is a kind of intellectual humility in which individuals attempt to question the assumptions embodied in their schemas. The most difficult and potentially most rewarding applications of Beginner's Mind involve the self-schema. The Theravada Buddhist tradition includes specific techniques for developing mindfulness.[13] These techniques can be used to critically examine the self-schema and can help in what Langer calls the creation of new categories.[14]

Mindful use of the self-schema involves careful observation of the ways identities affect daily activity and decision-making, similar to what Brown and Starkey call critical self-reflexivity.[15] Since we are often not fully conscious of our multiple identities, observation of our behavior (mindful use of the self-schema) may make us more aware of our assumptions about ourselves and thus allow our self-schemas to become more explicit. This, in turn, will ensure that they will be more easily recalled during introspection.

Mindfulness may help to counteract reification of identities and self-schema impoverishment by drawing our attention to the complexity of our self-schemas.

On the other hand, unreflective or mindless action and decision-making may worsen self-schema impoverishment since they involve automatically enacting the same identity in response to similar decision situations.

Different decisions may evoke different identities and different elements of the self-schema. Mindful action and mindful decision-making will make individuals more aware of these different identities and the potential conflict between them. This conflict might help to correct some of the decisional biases that can result from the a narrow range of identities. Individuals in organizations who practice mindful identification are less subject to autobiographical memory distortion, group mindlessness, suppression of dissent, and escalating commitment than those who fall victim to mindless identification. However, mindful individuals who take seriously the implications of conflicting identities might experience more internal conflict than those who automatically adopt a single identity as a basis for each decision and action. Even productive conflict can be unpleasant. Appendix H contains further material on mindfulness and techniques for cultivating it.

AUTOBIOGRAPHICAL REFLECTION

In Chapter 3, I outlined the ways autobiographical recollections support an individual's current dominant identity and described some common biases in the way people explain events in their lives. Here, I want to discuss some exercises for dealing with autobiographical distortions. The benefits of these exercises can be summarized as follows: If your memories are biased, the lessons you draw from them will also be biased. If, for example, you feel your life has been leading up to your current dominant identity (the consistency bias), you may be biased against views and decisions that threaten your identity. If your work identity is dominant, the consistency bias will influence the way you make decisions that affect your organization's identity. The exercises may expand the range of options we consider in making crucial decisions about work and life.

We often base our identities on beliefs about the causes of past events in our lives; beliefs that can be biased. In Chapter 2, I discussed attributional analysis and provided an example using my own autobiographical reflections. Attributional analysis can be used to identify possible biases in the way we explain important life events or decisions. For example, a person who believes others are responsible for the difficulties in his life may adopt the identity of The Victim.

We can correct attributional biases by attempting to "balance" attributions. If we tend to take too much credit for good outcomes, for example, we can deliberately identify other people and other events that were responsible for these good outcomes. By contrast, if we accept too much blame for negative outcomes, we can remind ourselves of the external factors that contributed to these outcomes.

Under the influence of the consistency bias, it is easy to believe that our past and future selves have the same basic values, but this assumption often proves to be false. Writing autobiographies at different points in our lives and reviewing them can help us to appreciate how much change has occurred. When planning for the future, it may be wise to think of our present and future selves as different people who may have different identities and different values.

Through retrospective reconstruction, we come to believe that the past has led inevitably to our current self-concept, and this may make us less willing to question the assumptions underlying our dominant identity. Important personal and business decisions involve our self-concept. If we are unwilling to question it, we may be rigid and defensive in our decision-making.

To correct this bias, we can attempt to recall incidents in our past that did *not* lead to our present condition, that were *not* consistent with our present self-concept. For example, if you remember yourself as having been a winner throughout your life, and this makes you unwilling to admit failure, you may purposely recall past defeats and disappointments in order to remind yourself that you have survived failure in the past. This sort of directed recollection might help you to avoid escalating commitment to a doomed venture.

STRUCTURED INTERNAL CONFLICT

The principles of structured conflict discussed in Chapter 5 can also be applied at the individual level. Through the use of structured conflict, organizations can benefit from the diversity of views among their members. The same is true of individuals. Individuals, like organizations, contain multiple identities that can be used to better understand and solve problems.

Most people have had the experience of "debating within themselves" and "being of two minds" about a decision. Often, they will make a decision at one time, when "in one frame of mind," and reconsider it later "in a different frame of mind." This reconsideration often takes the form of an internal mental dialogue that mimics the dialogues we have when we discuss decisions with others.

We commonly find this kind of internal debate and vacillation unpleasant, because it provokes anxiety and because we are disturbed by the fact that we do not have clear preferences coming from a single dominant identity. In response to this unpleasantness, we sometimes attempt to simplify the decision by choosing one identity or perspective as the "right" one and then making the decision that is consistent with this perspective. Reducing internal conflict may be appropriate for small decisions in which the choice matters little. For important decisions, however, prematurely reducing internal conflict may cut off creative alternatives.

Efforts to make productive use of internal conflict may intensify uncertainty but, as the research on devil's advocacy shows, it can improve decisions. Instead of attempting to escape internal conflict, we need to pay close attention to the alternative arguments that come to mind and attempt to identify the alternative assumptions and identities they represent.

Chapter 5 included several recommendations for using structured conflict effectively. They are briefly summarized here as a basis for suggestions on using structured internal conflict:

1. The use of structured conflict should be reserved for the most important and ill-structured decisions.
2. If preexisting conflict is low, the devil's advocate should focus on stimulating assumption questioning. However, if preexisting conflict is high, the devil's advocate should focus on structuring conflict.
3. The devil's advocate may sometimes need to play the role of custodian to ensure that those voicing dissenting opinions are given assistance and resources to develop their views effectively.
4. Dissenters must avoid becoming carping critics.
5. Most importantly, those using structured conflict must take the process seriously. They must avoid becoming prematurely committed to a point of view or a decision and using dissenters merely to reassure them that they have "considered all sides."

I will now briefly discuss how the rules for using structured conflict can be modified to help individuals nurture the conflict between opposing identities within their own self-schemas. The guidelines for structured internal conflict are modifications of those listed above. Therefore, they are numbered to correspond to the numbering of the rules given above.

1. Individuals should not waste time using structured internal conflict for the small decisions in life. This sort of thinking requires time and effort and should be reserved for important decisions.
2. If individuals do not feel conflicted about an important decision, they should consider carefully whether the course of action they have decided upon is consistent with the values inherent in all of their multiple identities. This may raise conflicts that will help rethink the course of action. If, on the other hand, they already feel conflicted about a decision, they should focus on *structuring* this conflict. They should clearly identify the conflicting values and the identities in which these values are grounded.
3. Individuals may find that some of the conflicts they feel are grounded in values and identities that they tend to discount or ignore. They should make a special effort to focus on these values and identities and to develop the arguments that flow from them in the same way that a custodian helps dissident members of a group develop their arguments.
4. As mentioned earlier, some people tend to become carping critics of their own tendency to vacillate between alternatives. They verbally abuse themselves for not being decisive about important issues. However, given the complexity of the self-schema, indecision about important work and life issues is inevitable. Therefore, when using structured

internal conflict, individuals should welcome indecision and use their own internal conflict to bring their assumptions to the surface.

5. People must take structured internal conflict seriously for the process to be effective. If they use the techniques recommended here merely to reassure themselves that they have considered all sides, all they will get from devil's advocacy is overconfidence in a biased decision.

CONSTRUCTING DIALOGUES

The final technique for enriching the self-schema is constructing dialogues. This involves mentally rehearsing a discussion between people with opposing views and articulating their differences. It is difficult for most people to imagine how individuals with strong opposing beliefs might construct their arguments and responses to one another. However, attempting to do so often increases one's understanding of the issues that divide people.

In a sense, this technique is an extension of structured internal conflict. In constructing dialogues, however, we develop discussions between representatives of different points of view instead of structuring the disagreements between different identities within our own self-schema.

To imagine how individuals on each side of a conflict would respond to each other, it is necessary to alternately articulate each of the opposing perspectives. The exercise can suggest solutions to conflicts that may not be apparent to the participants. Therefore, it may be of benefit to anyone involved in conflicts, especially devil's advocates and their custodians in business decision-making.

There are many examples of dialogues in life and fiction to provide guidance in developing your own. Films like *Twelve Angry Men* and *My Dinner with André* show that dialogue can make a movie exciting even if it has no action or special effects. Plato's dialogues provide models that continue to shape people's ideas about how to discuss crucial decisions. They might be useful as models if used with caution.[16] You can play these dialogues out in your head, but sometimes it is helpful to write them down for the same reason that it is sometimes useful to draw cognitive maps; having something on paper can aid your memory and clarify your thinking.[17]

Identifying alternative perspectives in a decision may not be entirely straightforward. Mitroff and Lindstone[18] suggest one way of identifying alternative views by focusing on three basic perspectives: The Technical Perspective, based on a view that a particular decision is basically a technical matter amenable to logical and scientific analysis; the Organizational Perspective, from which decisions are seen as governed by organizational constraints; and the Personal Perspective, in which the decision is seen as a matter of power, influence, and prestige.

In an earlier book, I provided another way to define distinct views by dividing the research on business decision-making into three perspectives: the Rational

Choice Perspective, the Organizational Perspective, and the Political Perspective.[19] Those who hold the Rational Choice Perspective assume that their goal is to make the most rational decision and that errors result from biases that reduce rationality. Others, who adopt the Organizational Perspective, feel that decisions should reflect organizational goals, culture, and identity, even if such decisions do not meet the standard of "objective rationality." Errors occur when decisions are not consistent with the organizational identity. Finally, those who look at decisions from a Political Perspective assume that decisions are the result of political processes and that errors result from a failure to deal with interest groups and coalitions in organizations.

These differences in perspectives can lead to profound differences in preferences and decision styles. In constructing a dialogue, it may be useful to consider whether the characters in the dialogue hold any of these alternative perspectives.

Constructing dialogues is not only, or even primarily, a technique for resolving conflicts. It is mainly an approach for expanding an individual's understanding of diverse views. By making the competing perspectives clear, constructing dialogues can enrich an individual's own self-schema. The following are some suggestions and rules of thumb that may be helpful in developing a dialogue.

1. Examine statements by those advocating conflicting points of view and identify assertions that seem least plausible and most open to dispute; those assertions that are most likely to be challenged by partisans on the other side. Ask yourself what opponents would find most objectionable or offensive in these statements.

2. Attempt to determine what the advocates would have to believe in order to make their statements plausible or logically compelling. Cognitive mapping can help in this process and allow you to construct representations of the schemas or ideologies that underlie differences.

3. Learn the key terms in the debate and what they mean to both sides. Often these terms are defined differently by each side and the users are not aware of the differences. This makes it more likely that they will be "divided by their use of language." In environmental debates, terms such as "risk" and "safety" often mean different things to the partisans on each side.

4. Identify the most important, visible advocates on each side and the most influential sources of information cited by partisans. If you get a chance to talk to committed advocates on either side, ask who they listen to or admire and what they read to help them define their positions and obtain information about the issue. This will be useful in identifying opinion leaders and important assumptions shaping the debate.

5. Different beliefs often lead to different predictions about the future. Try to identify the predictions partisans on each side would make and how they would test these predictions.

6. Learn how partisans describe the views of their opponents. How do they explain the "errors" their opponents have made in reasoning?

To clarify these suggestions, I will describe how I applied them in studying the environmental debate discussed in Chapter 3, involving the proposed gold mine on the Big Blackfoot River in Montana.

1. In examining the two opposing positions I identified several statements by proponents on each side that would be open to dispute. These included the statement by an opponent of development that "Corporate miners are willing to maim us for the simple reason that they do not inhabit our community, region, or state, and our suffering happens to be their profit." On the other side, a proponent of development made the claim that environmentalists are seeking "global governance that will entail the dissolution of independent nations and a supranational realignment of power."

   Advocates on each side of the debate would probably be angered by such statements from their opponents. As noted in Chapter 3, such anger indicates that the points being discussed are important to each side and worthy of further investigation.

2. In my study of the environmental debate, I attempted to determine what the opponents of development would have to believe about people who work for mining corporations in order to feel that they are willing to maim those outside their community. I also tried to specify what the prodevelopment people would have to believe about environmentalists to conclude that they are attempting to promote global government.

3. I identified a great many terms that had different meanings to the partisans on each side. These include, "risk," "safety," "profitability," "sustainability," and even basic words like "pollution," "freedom," and "the environment." You must pay close attention to the way these terms are used to detect subtle differences in meaning. Although these differences are small, they sometimes prevented partisans from making sense of the statements of opponents. For example, if a mining company engineer makes the statement that a given technology is "safe," it will sound disingenuous to an environmentalist, who assumes that the word "safe" means that the level of risk is zero.

4. In the environmental debate, I identified Paul Ehrlich and Julian Simon as important, visible partisans. When advocates on each side read what these people have written, they often feel they are reading clear and forceful statements of views they themselves hold, although few agree with everything Ehrlich and Simon say.

5. The predictions regarding the prices of certain metals that led to the bet between Julian Simon and Paul Ehrlich were handled in the opposite way from what I would recommend. Instead of leading members to question their views, the outcome of the predictions led each group to become further entrenched in their own views.

6. In Chapter 3, I discussed partisans' descriptions of their opponents in the environmental debate and concluded that these descriptions were unflattering. The prodevelopment side claimed their opponents cared nothing about jobs for the region while the antidevelopment side said their opponents cared nothing for the environment. Imagining dialogues between partisans helped me understand that both sides were attempting to achieve something of real value. However, the process of polarizing conflict made it difficult for either side to understand the value of their opponent's goals.

An example of a written dialogue is found in Appendix I. This dialogue deals with conflicting views of the nature of the self, so it allows us to return to topics discussed in Chapter 1 using a different format.

SUMMARY OF TECHNIQUES FOR ENRICHING
THE SELF-SCHEMA

Table 6.1 gives a summary of the techniques recommended in this chapter. The left-hand column lists specific problems and the next two columns list exercises and techniques for dealing with each. Each technique is useful for dealing with multiple problems. For example, autobiographical reflection can reduce both autobiographical memory distortions and identity fixation.

In this chapter, I have argued that examining our own memories, assumptions, and self-schemas honestly and carefully is important in making productive use of

Table 6.1
Techniques for Self-Schema Enrichment

Specific Problems	Technique	Specific Practices
Under use of the self-schema	Self-schema mapping	Cognitive mapping Memory aids

Overidentification
Identity fixation
	Mindful identification	Creation of new categories
		Theravada and Zen
		   mindfulness practices
		Alternate identities in
		   decision-making

Autobiographical distortion	Autobiographical reflection	Balancing attributions
		Past and future selves as
		   different people
		Serial autobiographies
		Focus on memories
		   inconsistent with current
		   self-concept
		Reinterpreting memories
		Focus on choice points

Unquestioned assumptions Illusion of control Escalation	Structured internal conflict	Simple devil's advocacy Multiple advocacy Dialectical inquiry Strategic assumption analysis

Inability to appreciate
   alternate points of view
	Constructing dialogues	Identification of positions,
		   assumptions, data and
		   proponents
		Partisans' descriptions of
		   opponents
		Use of fictive techniques

our identities. This kind of self-assessment allows us to make crucial life decisions in a way that balances the needs of multiple identities and keeps the self-schema flexible enough to adapt to change.

CONCLUSIONS AND QUESTIONS: IDENTITY, DIVERSITY, AND DIALOGUE IN BUSINESS AND LIFE DECISIONS

In the introduction to the book, I noted that many people feel the pace of change today is unprecedented. Although there have been many times in the past when change has been drastic and rapid, the change occurring in the modern world challenges our basis assumptions about ourselves. Divisive issues separate us and often lead us to stereotype our opponents, creating polarized conflicts. These conflicts engage our deepest sense of who we are; they shape our identities.

Global change has raised questions of social and personal identity, questions that have been eloquently described in several recent books. For example, in *The Saturated Self: Dilemmas of Identity in Contemporary Life*,[20] psychologist Kenneth Gergen observed that new communications technology has dramatically increased the number of institutions and individuals with which we interact. As a result, this technology has increased the number of different social identities we must assume and, therefore, the potential conflict between identities. Further, as globalization makes us more aware of other cultures, our faith in our own cultural norms and values is threatened.

British sociologist Anthony Giddens, in his book, *Modernity and Self-Identity: Self and Society in the Late Modern Age*,[21] observes that individuals today are besieged by competing social demands and identities. Making sense of these competing demands and constructing a coherent self is difficult and stressful because we no longer share a strong belief in traditional institutions and values.

The Protean Self: Human Resilience in an Age of Fragmentation by Robert Lifton[22] echos Giddens's and Gergen's points. According to the author, modern selves tend to be fragmented and changeable. In extreme cases, individuals change from one identity to another (or "reinvent" themselves) as social situations demand, with little continuity between the successive selves they enact.

I agree with these authors that deciding between the demands of different identities can be confusing and stressful, but I believe they do not pay adequate attention to the potential benefits of multiple identities. As I have emphasized throughout this book, even though multiple identities may make it more difficult to decide what to do in our work or personal lives, they give us multiple ways to understand and solve novel problems. They enrich our self-schemas.

I have argued that our "selves" and the "organizations we identify with" are cognitive constructions. I have also explained why self-schema and knowledge structure enrichment may be vital to the survival of individuals and organizations coping with change. By understanding that our selves are not fixed but changeable, it may be possible to use multiple identities in productive ways.

They key to using multiple identities wisely is mindful integration of identities in decision-making. Although there are no hard and fast rules for determining which identity should predominate in any particular decision, individuals can choose between the demands of different identities on a case-by-case basis without formal rules. Without assuming that any one of their identities is more "real" than others, they may be able to balance their identities' conflicting perspectives and evaluation criteria.

There may be a limit to the number of identities a person can incorporate in his or her self-schema. Integration of identities requires careful reflection and thought about how each identity relates to the others. This reflection takes time and each identity that is added must be integrated with existing identities. As new identities are added, the effort required for integration increases. Individuals may have to decide on a discrete number of identities they will commit to and they may have to abandon identities if they feel "saturated" or "overloaded."

Needless to say, I have not given an exhaustive list of techniques for enrichment, but I hope the organizational and individual approaches I have discussed will be useful in developing your own methods of self and organizational enrichment. Developing and using these techniques can lead to better decisions for individuals, groups, and organizations.

Individual and organizational decisions are shaped by individual and organizational identities. By reflecting mindfully on their identities, those making crucial decisions can view them from multiple perspectives. Decisions will not merely reinforce existing identities and assumptions but will help individuals question assumptions and modify identities.

Figure 6.1 provides a visual summary of the structure of the self-schema and the organizational knowledge structure. The diagram represents both the self-schema with multiple identities and the organizational knowledge structure with multiple stakeholders. As stated earlier, I am not attempting to minimize the differences between individual and organizational identities. However, self-schemas and knowledge structures do share structural features. In enriched structures, no single identity or stakeholder group dominates the others and there are multiple linkages between them.

In chapter 4, I described self-schema and organizational knowledge structure impoverishment as a vicious circle but the steps in the impoverishment process do not always occur in this order. Self-schema impoverishment, for example, does not always lead to polarizing conflict. The two may occur simultaneously. Further, there may be feedback loops between activities that reinforce the whole cycle. For example, self-schema impoverishment will reinforce identity fixation even if the

Figure 6.1
The Structure of Individual and Organizational Identities

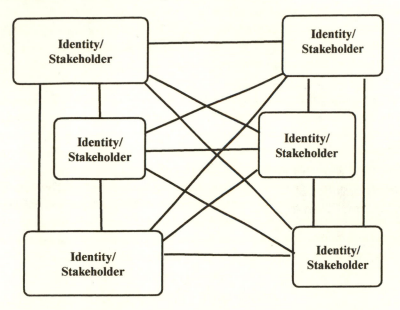

individual is not involved in polarizing conflict. Finally, synergies between individual and organizational enrichment techniques are applied at different points in the cycle.

However, thinking of impoverishment as a vicious circle is useful in describing ways of escaping it and improving decisions. We can use either individual or organizational approaches to reverse the process and create a positive feedback cycle that leads to enrichment. I have represented such a positive cycle in Figure 6.2.

There are two points at which we can intervene to halt the mutually reinforcing processes of individual and organizational impoverishment. First, we can directly improve organizational knowledge using structured conflict techniques, drawing on the peripheral views in the organization to enrich management's understanding of particular decisions. This will make it less likely that individuals identified with the organization oversimplify their own self-schemas.

Alternately, we can intervene using the techniques described in Chapter 6 to enrich self-schemas. This will reduce identity fixation and memory distortions, thus reducing the likelihood of self-schema impoverishment. If *our* organizations engage in polarizing conflict, *we* may be able to help transform this conflict into joint problem-solving, reducing groupthink and escalating commitment.

Some have argued that, if we have an enriched self-schema with multiple identities none of which dominates the others, we will develop a confused sense of self

Figure 6.2
The Cycle of Knowledge Enrichment

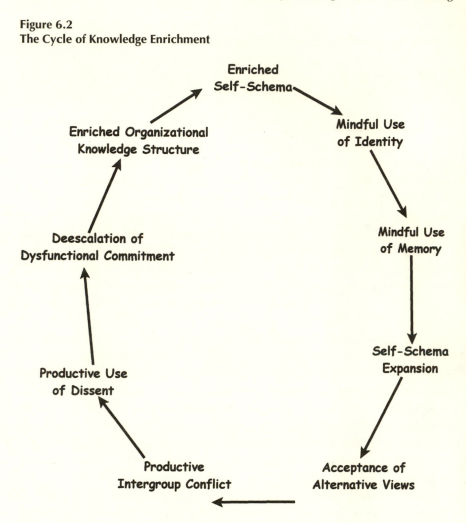

that will make real moral conviction impossible and weaken our ability to resist the destruction of commonly held values and resources. Will self-schema enrichment lead to a situation in which, in the words of William Butler Yeats, "The best lack all conviction, while the worst are full of passionate intensity?"[23]

Some have claimed that a stronger belief in the reality of our identities and the moral responsibilities they imply would have helped us resist the evils of Hitler, Stalin, and others who have plagued the twentieth century.[24] Similarly, partisans on both sides of the environmental debate and the debate on marijuana in the workplace often behave as if mindfully examining the assumptions that underlie their identities is merely the first step toward capitulation.

Perhaps the best way to address this concern is to examine the behavior of those who have enriched self-schemas. If their behavior shows they are subject to this fault, the costs of enrichment may outweigh its benefits. My own experience suggests that they will be less likely to commit themselves rashly but can have very strong commitment to courses of action if they decide such commitment is warranted.

Self-schema enrichment increases an individual's willingness to listen to devil's advocates and to enter into dialogues with opponents. Such dialogues can lead to mutual questioning of assumptions and help in the development of what was referred to in Chapter 3 as norms of reciprocity and trust. Once such norms exist, it is possible that institutional arrangements and rules can be constructed that will allow people to use common resources without destroying them.

In the introduction, I discussed the changing world and the value of enriched self-schemas and organizational knowledge structures in dealing with change. Strong visionary leaders may promote intense identification with their organizations and their strategies for ensuring survival and success. If they succeed, the shared vision may help organizational members pull together to achieve common objectives. However, encouraging identity fixation is not only morally wrong; it is also a bad use of human resources. In the long run, the knowledge structure is impoverished, the "corporate IQ" declines, and the wisdom available within the organization diminishes. Such organizations are less likely to adapt effectively to change.

Intervention at either the organizational or the individual level can disrupt the process by which the organization and the individual impoverish each other. I hope the concepts I have discussed in this book will enable individuals and organizations to use their own diversity to explore new ways to adapt to the changing world.

NOTES

1. Dogen Zenji, "Genjokoan," in *Shobogenzo*, trans. K. Nishayam (Tokyo, Japan: Nakayama Shobo, 1975), p. 1. An alternative translation can be found in K. Tanahashi (trans.), *Moon in a Dewdrop* (San Francisco, CA: North Point Press, 1985), p. 70.

2. Colin Eden and his colleagues, for example, have developed methods for helping people articulate their cognitive maps during the decision-making process. See C. Eden and F. Ackerman, *Making Strategy: The Journey of Strategic Management* (London: Sage, 1998); C. Eden and J. Spender, *Managerial and Organizational Cognition: Theory, Methods, and Research* (London: Sage, 1998).

3. G. Hodgkinson, N. Brown, A. Maule, K. Glaister, and A. Pearman, "Breaking the frame: An analysis of strategic cognition and decision-making under uncertainty," *Strategic Management Journal* 20(1999): 977–985.

4. K. Weick. *Sensemaking in Organizations* (Thousand Oaks, CA: Sage, 1995), pp. 18–24.

5. E. Langer, *Mindfulness* (Reading, MA: Addison-Wesley, 1989); E. Langer. *The Power of Mindful Learning* (Reading, MA: Addison-Wesley, 1997).

6. E. Langer, A. Blank, and B. Chanowitz, "The mindlessness of ostensibly thoughtful action," *Journal of Personality and Social Psychology* 36(197): 635–642.

7. Langer, 1989, *Mindfulness*, p. 63.

8. Ibid., p. 70.

9. Ibid., p. 75.

10. Ibid., p. 78.

11. Two schools of Buddhism that stress meditation are the Theravada and Zen schools. Useful works in the Theravada tradition include B. Buddhadasa, *Mindfulness with Breathing* (Bangkok, Thailand: Pholpun Printing, 1988); T. Hanh, *The Sutra on the Full Awareness of Breathing* (Berkeley, CA: Parallax Press, 1988); and M. Walsh, *Thus Have I Heard: The Long Discourses of the Buddha* (London: Wisdom Publications, 1987). Useful Zen sources include P. Kapleau, *The Three Pillars of Zen: Teaching, Practice, and Enlightenment* (Boston: Beacon Press, 1965) and S. Suzuki, *Zen Mind, Beginner's Mind* (New York: Weatherhill, 1970).

12. See Suzuki, *Zen Mind, Beginner's Mind,* p. 21.

13. Some of these are contained in the *Mahasatipatthana Sutta* or the *Discourse On the Four Foundations of Mindfulness* (see Walsh, 1987, ibid., 335–350). These techniques involve mindful awareness of the phenomena that are often identified with the self (including the body, feelings, and mind). Such a practice naturally reveals that there is no fixed self evident in any of these phenomena. The *Anapanasati Sutta* or the *Discourse on the Full Awareness of Breathing* expands upon this approach by tying mindfulness practice to the contemplation of breathing (see Buddhadasa, 1987, ibid.; Hanh, 1988, ibid.).

14. Langer, 1989, *Mindfulness.*

15. A. Brown and K. Starkey, "Organizational identity and learning: A psychodynamic perspective," *Academy of Management Review* 25(2000): 102–120; see pp. 110–111.

16. In using Plato's dialogues as models, keep three points in mind. First, in the dialogues I have read, Socrates nearly always wins. It is not necessary for your own imaginary dialogues to have a winner. Second, most Platonic dialogues include a summary section where arguments are concluded and things are neatly wrapped up. Real dialogues are messier than this.

Third, some of the dialogues give evidence of a kind of mean-spirited taunting that is unproductive in real dialogue. In the *Euthyphro*, for example, Socrates questions a young man who is about to have his own father prosecuted for blasphemy, a crime punishable by death at that time in Athens. When he is unable to make the young man see reason, Socrates, in frustration, taunts him as he walks away to begin the legal proceedings against his father. These dialogues are great partly because they reflect the human dimension in intellectual disputes and this dialogue reflects Socrates' perfectly human response to frustration. In constructing imaginary dialogues, you must decide how much the characters will give vent to their frustration and defensiveness, just as you must decide how much you will give vent to these feelings in real-life dialogues.

17. Techniques of fiction writing can be used to make the characters and circumstances of the dialogue believable and to introduce some drama into the discussion, since genuinely important issues are often discussed with emotion and drama. In choosing characters in the imaginary dialogue, select those you feel will be the best representatives of each point of view and who can argue their cases forcefully. Creating vivid characters to represent each view helps you appreciate the emotion associated with the debate. In putting the dialogue

together, you should assume that both sides will listen attentively to each other, but it is not necessary to assume that they will understand each other.

18. I. Mitroff and H. Lindstone, *The Unbounded Mind* (New York: Oxford University Press, 1993).

19. C. Schwenk, *The Essence of Strategic Decision Making* (Lexington, MA: D.C. Heath, 1988).

20. K. Gergen, *The Saturated Self: Dilemmas of Identity in Contemporary Life* (New York: Basic Books, 1991).

21. A. Giddens, *Modernity and Self-Identity: Self and Society in the Late Modern Age* (Stanford, CA: Stanford University Press, 1991).

22. R. Lifton, *The Protean Self: Human Resilience in an Age of Fragmentation* (Chicago, IL: University of Chicago Press, 1999).

23. This is from the poem "The Second Coming," written in 1919, at the end of World War I. See W. Yeats, "The Second Coming," in M. Abrams, ed., *The Norton Anthology of English Literature*, Vol. 2 (New York: W.W. Norton, 1986), p. 1948.

> Turning and turning in the widening gyre
> The falcon cannot hear the falconer;
> Things fall apart; the center cannot hold;
> Mere anarchy is loosed upon the world,
> The blood-dimmed tide is loosed; and everywhere
> The ceremony of innocence is drowned;
> The best lack all conviction, while the worst
> Are full of passionate intensity.
> Surely some revelation is at hand;
> Surely the Second Coming is at hand.

24. Mortimer Adler and others have made this claim. Historian Patrick Diggins provides a summary of arguments on both sides. See P. Diggins, *The Promise of Pragmatism: Modernism and the Crisis of Knowledge and Authority* (Chicago: University of Chicago Press, 1991), pp. 386–406.

APPENDIX H:
MINDFULNESS ON THE JOB

[From Ellen Langer, *Mindfulness*, New York: Addison-Wesley, 1989, pp. 133–152.]

The ability to shift contexts may be just as valuable to a manager or on the assembly line as it is to an artist or physicist. Fatigue, conflict, and burnout can all result from being mired in old categories, trapped by old mindsets. In fact, virtually all the advantages of mindfulness described in the earlier chapters can be found in the workplace. For employer and employee alike, mindfulness may increase flexibility, productivity, innovation, leadership ability, and satisfaction. Since most of us, almost all day, almost all week, are either traveling to work, working, worrying about work, or planning the work ahead, the applications of mindfulness to the work setting are particularly useful.

An old Vedic proverb admonishes, "Avert the danger not yet arisen." To catch the early warnings of trouble, we must be alert to new information, to subtle deviations from the way things typically go. In the office study described in Chapter 2, a memo was circulated that said only, "Return this memo immediately." Most of those who received it did not notice its absurdity. Because it was in most respects similar to memos they saw every day, they mindlessly returned it. From this we can see how larger problems can result from initially small, unnoticed changes. When mindful, people tend to notice such problems before they become serious and dangerously costly. Whether it is a slight shift on a dial in a nuclear energy plant, or the first hint of what Theodore Levitt of the Harvard Business School calls the "shadow of obsolescence,"[1] the early signs of change are warnings and, to the mindful, opportunities.

The workplace is full of unexpected stumbling blocks that can get in the way of productivity. To a mindful manager or employee, these become building blocks. They don't impede progress because they are seen as part of an ongoing process, rather than disastrous deviations from past procedure. Take a situation in which instead of the usual four people "required" to do a job, only three turn up, or one in which a piece of equipment routinely used in production is down for the week. If the employees in that department are locked in old mindsets, the work will come to a screeching halt. A mindful employee, oriented to the present, might reassess the job as one for three people, or for whatever equipment was at hand. Deviations from some habitual way of working are less problematic if there is tolerance for uncertainty and no rigidly set method in the first place. The "deviations" then become simply elements of the present situation.

SECOND WIND

As we saw with the Coolidge Effect described in Chapter 3, fatigue and satiation do not necessarily occur at fixed points. To a large extent, mental and physical exhaustion may be determined by premature cognitive commitments; in other words, unquestioned expectations dictate when our energy will run out.

As far back as 1928, psychologist Anita Karsten studied situations that at first feel good, but with repetition become neutral or uncomfortable.[2] She put subjects in "semi-free situations" in which they were given tasks to do but were instructed that they could stop working whenever they were tired. They were told to do the work as long as they enjoyed it. Tasks were of two types: continuous activities such as drawing, and tasks that come to a quick end but are repeated, such as reading a short poem again and again. (Tasks like chess that are long but come to an end were not used.)

For each type of task, the subjects worked until they grew weary. The investigator then changed the context. For instance, after the subjects had drawn until exhausted, the investigator asked them to turn the page over and re-draw the last picture they had drawn, to show the experimenter how fast they could draw it. The "totally exhausted" subjects had no difficulty repeating the drawing in the new context. Another subject was given the task of writing *ababab*... until he had had enough. He went on until he was mentally and physically exhausted. His hand felt numb, as though it couldn't move to make even one more mark. At that moment the investigator asked him to sign his name and address for a different purpose. He did so quite easily. He was not feigning exhaustion. Rather, the change of context brought renewed energy.

When Karsten had subjects read poems aloud, after a while they became hoarse. When they complained to her how they hated the task, however, the hoarseness disappeared. Similarly, another subject, who claimed to be so fatigued that she could no longer lift her arm to make even one more hatch mark, was then seen casually lifting her arm to fix her hair.

New energy in a new context is known to most people as a "second wind." We see examples of it daily. Take a harried young scholar who has been working all day writing a book, while also taking care of his rambunctious two-year-old daughter. By the time his wife comes home to help, he is too exhausted to move. But just then a call comes from a friend asking if he would like to play basketball. He leaps up and dashes off to play for four hours.

In each of these cases, a mindset of fatigue was lifted by a shift in context initiated by someone else—the investigator or a friend. Mindful individuals use the phenomenon of second wind to their own advantage in a more deliberate way. Staggering different kinds of paperwork, changing to a different work setting, and taking a break to jog or make a phone call are all ways to tap latent energy by shaking free of the mindset of exhaustion. (Mindfulness in itself is exhilarating, never tiring.) A self-starting, autonomous employee can do it for herself; a mindful manager can make it happen for others. The challenge for management is to introduce context changes within the required work load.

Another kind of mindset that can lead to fatigue is the way we define a task. When we begin any undertaking, we have a mental picture of its beginning, middle, and end. In the beginning we tend to be energetic and mindful. In the middle phase, we may perform the task mindlessly or mindfully. If we are performing it mindfully, we are involved in creating new distinctions while we do it. We do not have a sense of ourselves as separate from the task. The task may seem effortless as long as we are involved in process and distinctions are being created. If we do the task mindlessly, we rely on distinctions already made. As the task nears its end, we typically become focused on outcome and also expect fatigue to occur. We now notice the task as separate from ourselves as we evaluate the outcome. When we near the end of activities that we expect to be tiring, fatigue arrives. This mental picture of the end of a task is a self-imposed context and makes fatigue almost inevitable. Changing contexts *before* reaching this point may prevent fatigue. A simple change of activity will not necessarily bring this about, however. The change must be *experienced* as a new context. If a new physical exercise, for example, is still seen as exercise, the expectation of fatigue in that context may remain.

In an interesting study psychologists Janice Kelly and Joseph McGrath had subjects perform various tasks either under severe time constraints or with plenty of time. If the first task had to be completed in a hurry, there was plenty of time for the second and vice versa. Subjects apparently made a premature cognitive commitment to the requirements of the first task. When no longer under time pressure, subjects became unnecessarily fatigued, performing as though still under the clock.[3]

INNOVATION

Changing of contexts, as we've seen in earlier chapters, generates imagination and creativity as well as new energy. When applied to problem solving, it is often called reframing. A young musician recently told me of his long-standing inability to finish the songs he composed. This had bothered him deeply, and he felt like a failure as a composer until he reframed his "problem." Rather than seeing himself as incapable of finishing a song, he realized what a great gift he had for composing new themes. He then teamed up with someone who is great with musical detail and together they are highly prolific.

Changing contexts is only one path to innovation. Creating new categories, exploring multiple perspectives, and focusing on process all increase the possibility that a novel approach to a problem will be discovered. A tolerance for uncertainty on the part of management is also encouraging. If a manager can risk deviation from routine ways of doing things, creative employees can thrive and contribute. If not compelled only to make a product better and better, they may find ways to make a different, better product.

The imaginative use of "outsiders" can encourage each of the types of mindfulness just mentioned.[4] A man or two in an all-female company, a teenage board member, or a blind retiree can bring in new ideas. Independent consultants can fill the same role. Creating the position of outsider in a company, regardless of the characteristics of the person hired to fill it, can keep important questions flowing. Just as a traveler to a foreign culture notices what people indigenous to that culture take for granted, an outsider in a company may notice when the corporate natives are following what may now be irrational traditions or destructive myths. When routines of work are not familiar, they cannot be taken for granted and mindfulness is stimulated.

In *Getting to Yes*, Roger Fisher and William Urey suggest ways that negotiators can generate within their own minds the kind of perspectives brought by outsiders from different disciplines: "If you are negotiating a business contract, invent options that might occur to a banker, an inventor, a labor leader, a speculator in real estate, a stockbroker, an economist, a tax expert, or a socialist."[5] This openness to multiple perspectives—an essential ingredient in mindfulness—supports a policy of workers switching responsibilities, or switching career midstream. If the switch is within a field, rather than across fields, the benefits of a fresh perspective can outweigh the problems of having to learn a new technical jargon. For example, if an art historian became a vision psychologist, or vice versa, each might have something different to bring to the question, "How is a three-dimensional object rendered in two dimensions?" Distance from the mindsets of an industry is vital in designing products. Take a company that makes wheelchairs. Now that the elderly population is increasing, so should their business. Some people come to need wheelchairs the way others come to need eyeglasses. But unlike eyeglasses, wheelchairs have looked the same for years. There is no reason, other than habit, that wheelchairs must look so medical and ominous. Designers are now beginning to see wheelchairs as racing cars, as recreational vehicles, as colorful, comfortable, and zippy ways to get about. Eight years ago, in a nursing home where I consulted, we had residents decorate their own wheelchairs to make them more appealing and/or functional. The very word *wheelchair* seemed to take on a different flavor after this project. Just recently, I came across advertisements for the "Wildcat," the "Palmer 3," and the "Turbo"—three sleek new designs that seem to redefine what being in a wheelchair means.

As pointed out earlier, innovation can be dampened by too narrow an image of the task. People who make wheelchairs could see themselves in the transportation business or the recreation business in order to break out of the mindsets associated with handicaps and hospitals. Theodore Levitt, whose famous phrase "marketing myopia" could be translated into "mindless marketing," came up with a delightfully poignant example of obsolescent mindsets: the buggy whip industry. While one could argue that no amount of product innovation could have saved this business, a new self definition might have: "Even if it had only defined its business as providing a stimulant or catalyst to an energy source, it might have survived by becoming a manufacturer of, say, fanbelts or air cleaners."[6]

Narrow definitions of competition go hand-in-hand with narrow mindsets about a product. Small banks, for instance, see themselves in competition with other small banks, in the role of collectors and lenders of money to and from their communities. A bank like Citibank, which saw its function as an "information processing activity," was able to compete much more powerfully. In the same way, the maker of Royal or Remington or Smith Corona typewriters would not have found their real competition by looking at one another. Over in another corner, a division of IBM was gearing up to knock them out of the running with the Selectric typewriter. This was a totally new concept for producing words on paper, later to be supplanted by the personal computer and word processors in all their forms.

One way to escape narrow definitions is to consider the actor/observer difference. A student made me aware of a good example of this in government. At the end of every fiscal period, agencies and researchers given government monies rush to spend whatever money that remains in their budgets rather than return unspent money to the government. They've used what they needed and now waste the rest. From a taxpayer's perspective, this seems irrational. Why squander the money rather than return it to be used by others? The reason is that if the agencies do not spend the money, their budgets for the next fiscal year will be reduced—"They didn't need it last year so they probably don't need it this year either," frugal officials would say. And so agency after agency wastes money to keep future budgets healthy. The clever solution that my former student, Otto Brodtrick, suggested, based on his auditing experience for a Canadian government agency, took into account the point of view of those receiving the funds. If each year an agency's budget were guaranteed to be what it would have been had it spent all the money given, plus half of what it did not spend, both individual agency and government would prosper. For instance, if the agency were given $10,000 and spent only $8,000, it would get $10,000 the next year plus half of what it saved ($1,000), for a total of $11,000. The following year, if, of the $11,000 it spent only $10,000, it would get $11,500 the next year. Both sides would end up winning. Future budgets would be healthy and current spending would be sensible. The agency or researcher would be pleased to return rather than waste money not needed in the present because of the guarantee of more money in the future.

THE POWER OF UNCERTAINTY FOR MANAGERS

Employee behavior, mindless or innovative, is not likely to be independent of a manager's style. Of all the qualities in a manager conducive to innovation and initiative, a degree of uncertainty may be the most powerful. If a manager is confident but uncertain—confident that the job will get done but without being certain of exactly the best way of doing it—employees are likely to have more room to be creative, alert, and selfstarting. When working for confident but uncertain leaders, we are less likely to feign knowledge or hide mistakes, practices that can be costly to a company. Instead, we are likely to think, "If he's not sure, I guess I don't have to be right 100 percent of the time," and risk taking becomes less risky. Employees are more likely to suggest process and product changes that could be beneficial. Admission of uncertainty leads to a search for more information, and with more information there may be more options.

Debra Heffernan, a doctoral student at Harvard, and I conducted research that looked at the power of uncertainty in an organizational setting.[7] We evaluated the degree of certainty of managers in the organization by asking them, among other questions, how many of the decisions they make each day have absolute correct answers. We also assessed their general level of confidence. Questionnaires were given to employees to assess their work relationships with the managers. We found that those managers who were confident but relatively uncertain were evaluated by their employees as more likely to allow independent judgment and a general freedom of action.

Because people perceived as bright and knowledgeable tend to become managers, the sense that the boss knows *the* answer is pervasive and asking questions is potentially intimidating to employees. If managers make clear that they see certainty as foolhardy, it is easier to ask questions based on one's own uncertainty. Questions provide a good deal of information for managers. Moreover, if managers seek out information from employees to answer these questions, both will probably become more mindful and innovative.

Ironically, although work may often be accomplished mindlessly, with a sense of certainty, play is almost always mindful. People take risks and involve themselves in their play. Imagine making play feel routine; it would not be playful. In play, there is no reason not to take some risks. In fact, without risk, the pleasures of mastery would disappear. Imagine mindlessly skiing or horseback riding; imagine going to the theater to see the same old play without searching for a new twist; imagine doing crossword puzzles already done, to which you remember all the answers. We tend to be more adventurous at play because it feels safe. We stop evaluating ourselves. Play may be taken seriously, but it is the play and not ourselves that we are taking seriously—or else it is not really play at all. It would seem, then, that to encourage mindfulness at work, we should make the office a place where ideas may be played with, where questions are encouraged, and where "an unlucky toss of the dice" does not mean getting fired.

Many managers, however, become anxious when faced with a question for which there are no easy answers. When challenged with a question about the rationale for a policy, they reach for the ready-made replies that we all learned in childhood: "Do it because I told you to." In organizations, a very familiar mindset is evident in the reply: "What if we let everybody do that?" Many innovative ideas have probably been squelched by that phrase. If only a few want to do something (whatever the "it" is), what difference does it make? If everyone in fact wants to do it, perhaps it should be done. At a nursing home where I consulted, an elderly woman wanted to make a peanut butter sandwich in the kitchenette instead of going to the dining room for dinner. The director said, "What if everyone wanted to do that?" If everyone did, the nursing home might save a lot of money on food. At the very least, it would have been useful information for the chef. Should deviant procedures that occur only once in a while be tolerated? Should unanimous desires for change lead to a new policy? Such questions may be important for any organization. Answers like, "What if everyone wanted to?" or "We've never done it that way before," turn an opportunity for innovation into a dead end. In the academic world, where certainty and scientific proof are much prized, the need to acknowledge uncertainty is valued but still often fiercely resisted. One day I arrived late for the meeting of a committee formed to award a teaching prize, only to find my colleagues upset, confronted with an "impossible" moral dilemma. The problem they faced was that there were five nominees for the prize and only three to five letters of recommendation for each. How could we make a sensible decision based on so little evidence? The question at first seemed reasonable. However, the rather unkind way the committee came down on the person in charge of gathering the nomination materials made me think twice about it. They pointed a finger at her as though she had violated some absolute unwritten rule. With three to five letters the award would be "arbitrary." There should be more information; everyone agreed. But what does "more information" mean? What would be conclusive evidence of teaching skill? Should the letters be from students who currently are taking the course, or those who just finished it? If they were taught well enough maybe the lesson should still influence them after the course is over; perhaps the letter should be from people who took the course two years ago. Or should it be five years ago? Should the letters be from the good students, the poor students, or all the students? One could make a reasonable argument for each. Or should letters be from students at all? Colleagues know what goes into teaching in the first place. What about some combination such as half of each, two faculty to every one student asked, and so on?

When I tuned back in to the meeting, I suggested that since the decision about how many and what kind of recommendations could never be based on "enough information," we should go ahead and award a prize this year and for future years make an arbitrary but explicit rule of thumb to follow. Instead of an endless search for certainty and mountains of paper, an arbitrary rule allows any committee, in academia or a corporation, to get on with a decision. By remembering that this rule was simply an agreement, the construction of one committee, however, one is more willing to change it when circumstances change without having to attack those who came up with it. Rules are best to guide, not to dictate.

Besides a quality of confident uncertainty, there is another quality of leadership that is well known but harder to define. Charisma in leaders has a magical aura, which may account for the belief that leaders are *born* and not made. In a recent investigation conducted with John Sviokla of the Harvard Business School, I tried to explore an aspect of charisma that may be linked to the power in uncertainty and mindfulness.[8]

We first looked at charisma in a theatrical setting. Actors who were performing in plays around the Harvard campus, such as *The Importance of Being Earnest, Miss Julie, The Merchant of Venice,* were randomly assigned to two groups. Those in one group were instructed to perform their parts in as novel a way as possible, varying it within the realm of the character. Those in the other group were asked to perform their parts as consistently with the script as possible. After the play, the members of the audience, unaware of our instructions to the actors, were handed a brief questionnaire to rate the actors' charisma. Those actors instructed to perform in a novel way were rated as more charismatic.

To investigate this phenomenon further, in another setting, we gave encyclopedia salespeople instructions similar to those we gave the actors. One group was instructed to approach each new prospect as if he or she were their very first customer. Though they stuck to the "script," they subtly adapted their approach as needed. The other group was told to be as consistent in their approach as possible: "The more consistent you are, the higher your sales will be." The first group of salespeople was seen as significantly more charismatic than the second. Curiously, they were also seen by customers as more knowledgeable about their product, even though this knowledge did not vary among the salespeople. They approached each customer in a more flexible manner, and their pitch had more impact. A certain open-mindedness would seem to enhance powers of persuasion as well as charisma.

BURNOUT AND CONTROL

Burnout, a problem in a wide variety of workplaces from emergency rooms to corporations, is compounded by mindlessness. Rigid mindsets, narrow perspectives, the trap of old categories, and an outcome orientation all make burnout more likely. Conversely, as we have seen, changing contexts and mindsets, or focusing on process, can be energy-begetting. Many of us know the energizing effects of a new job. There is an excitement in learning new things, mapping out a new territory. As the job becomes familiar, however, enthusiasm and energy wane. Burnout sets in when two conditions prevail: Certainties start to characterize the workday, and demands of the job make workers lose a sense of control. If, in addition, an organization is characterized by rigid rules, problems that arise feel insurmountable because creative problem-solving seems too risky. When bureaucratic work settings are of the "we've always done it this way" mentality, burnout is no stranger.

In medical settings, where errors may cost lives, these conditions are especially characteristic. Debra Heffernan and I tried to combat burnout in Stevens Hall Nursing Home in North Andover, Massachusetts.[9] We introduced the staff to ideas of uncertainty and control so as to make them more mindful. We demonstrated that the "facts" they used to guide their caregiving were really probabilities and not certainties. We had meeting after meeting in which we questioned how they could be so sure of the rationale behind their policies. We paid particular attention to those mindsets that may induce dependency in the residents and rob them of control. For example, a blind elderly resident wanted to smoke. This was burdensome to the staff, who felt he must be accompanied to prevent him from burning down the establishment. Their solution had been to allow him to smoke only two cigarettes a day. But how could they be sure that he needed help? Another patient's disease made it hard for her to brush her hair. When a member of the staff brushed it for her, he or she was unwittingly implying that she could not do it for herself. One of the more dramatic cases was a woman who couldn't remember to go to the dining room. The staff felt they had to escort her so that she wouldn't starve. These cumulative and seemingly relentless responsibilities, seen as essential, contributed to feelings of burnout.

Once the staff understood that their justification for these solutions were much weaker than they had thought, they were able to find other ways of solving the problems. By returning some control to the residents, they made their own jobs easier. For example, they came to realize that there was no firm reason to believe that a blind man couldn't learn to smoke safely. In fact, he already knew where and how to smoke without danger. They just had to give him a chance. The woman who had trouble brushing her hair was happier doing it herself as long as she approached the task in very small, incremental steps. And no one starved. Her hunger helped the forgetful woman remember where the dining room was. Seeing that problems may be solvable without relying on old rules made the staff feel more in control; seeking solutions made them more mindful. Records comparing the period before our intervention and a similar period of time afterward showed that staff turnover was reduced by a third. Less feeling of burnout meant less reason to leave. These results, though not experimentally derived, suggest that burnout is not inevitable. In a recent experimental investigation conducted at Lewis Bay Head Injury Facility, we offered the nurses and other caregivers a similar kind of mindfulness training. With the resultant change of outlook, and a renewed sense that new solutions were possible, the staff in this demanding and potentially depressing situation showed a significant increase in morale and job satisfaction.

This kind of "care for the caregiver," restoring a feeling of control and options, may become more and more important in hospitals. Nursing shortages, pressures resulting from cost containment, legal constraints, and technical complexity all contribute to increased stress on staff. In a report from a committee at the Harvard Medical School set up to study fatigue in residency training, the reduced length of stay for hospitalized patients ("quick-in and quick-out") was seen as a cause of increased exhaustion among residents. When patients are discharged prematurely, and evaluated by other doctors before they are admitted, the resident loses a sense of control over the case, seeing his or her role as purely mechanical. A lack of mindful involvement in the patient's recovery is clearly implicated in this kind of burnout. In fact, the faculty recommendations included ways of restoring the "cognitive and intellectual function in the management of the patient," that is, mindfulness.

Since the world of work confronts us with the same puzzles that face us in the rest of our lives, these observations about the effects of mindfulness on the job could become a book in themselves. It is probably also clear to readers familiar with business and management that the more progressive thinkers in this field have long been aware of the dangers of fixed mindsets and outcome orientation and the advantages of multiple perspectives and shifting context, but under other labels. In the 1920s, Mary Parker Follett, a pioneer in management studies, anticipated certain of these ideas, emphasizing especially the value of a shift in mindsets. Follett's warnings about an obsession with outcome are pertinent for any manager today: "A system built round a purpose is dead before it is born. Purpose unfolds and reflects the means."[10] Certainty tends to develop with continued success. There is a tendency to continue doing whatever has worked, ironically making successful businesses more vulnerable to petrified mindsets. I spent part of a recent sabbatical at the Harvard Business School, where colleagues helped me streamline some of the ideas in this chapter. Some of us even made a game out of considering desk plaques for executives:

Mindlessness is the application of yesterday's business solutions to today's problems.

Mindfulness is attunement to today's demands to avoid tomorrow's difficulties.

NOTES

1. T. Levitt, "Marketing myopia," *The Harvard Business Review* 38, no. 4 (1960): 45–56, reprinted in 53, no. 5 (1975): 26–174.

2. A. Karsten (1928), "Mental Satiation," in *Field Theory in Human Science*, ed. J. De Rivea (New York: Gardner Press, 1976).

3. J. R. Kelly and J. E. McGrath, "Effects of time limits of task types on task performance and intrreaction of four-person groups," *Journal of Personality and Social Psychology* 49 (1985): 395–407.

4. Rosabeth Moss Kanter and Howard Stevenson, both of Harvard Business School, write about a version of this idea in business: R. Kanter, *The Change Masters: Innovation for*

Productivity in the American Corporation (New York: Simon & Schuster, 1983); H. Stevenson and W. Sahlman, "How small companies should handle advisers," *Harvard Business Review* 88, no. 2 (1988): 28–34. Also, Irving Janis describes a version of this idea in the political arena: I. Janis, *Victims of Groupthink* (Boston: Houghton Mifflin, 1972).

5. R. Fisher and W. Urey, *Getting to Yes* (Boston: Houghton Mifflin, 1981).

6. T. Levitt, "Marketing myopia."

7. E. Langer and D. Heffernan, "Mindful managing: Confident but uncertain managers," Harvard University, 1988.

8. E. Langer and J. Sviukla, "Charisma from a Mindfulness Perspective," Harvard University, 1988.

9. E. Langer, D. Heffernan, and M. Kiester, "Reducing burnout in an institutional setting: An experimental investigation," Harvard University, 1988.

10. M. P. Follet, *Dynamic Administration: The Collected Papers of Mary Parker Follett* (Bath, England: Bath Management, 1941), quoted in P. Graham, *Dynamic Management: The Follett Way* (London: Professional Publishing, 1987).

APPENDIX I:
AN EXAMPLE OF A DIALOGUE

Earlier in this chapter I provided recommendations for those constructing dialogues as a means of helping to understand the details of conflicting points of view. However, this process is best illustrated by an example. This is not the *only* way to construct a dialogue. Since I am interested in alternative views of the self, I have constructed a dialogue between representatives of two extreme views: The Thirteenth Dalai Lama (the predecessor of the current Dalai Lama) and Sherlock Holmes, a representative of the Victorian-era views on the self that William James criticized. The following dialogue provides another approach to summarizing some of the most important concepts dealt with in this book.

THE ADVENTURE OF THE THIRTEENTH DALAI LAMA

To Sherlock Holmes, he was always "that curious little Asian boy, with a head like an egg, calm eyes, thick lips, and a mind beyond my comprehension." Though I have reviewed my notes on this singular case many times over the years and though the case is of obvious interest to admirers of the world's foremost consulting detective, I have hesitated to publish it. It will not, I fear, enhance his reputation. It will, however, provide indispensable information on the limits of a deductive intelligence of the first water. I decided, in the end, to leave instructions that the case not be published until the end of the next century. If, as I hope, my friend's reputation has grown during that time, and the science of reasoning has advanced beyond its current primitive level, this case may aid those who pursue this science into the next century.

Though my stories about Holmes's exploits have a relatively wide readership, it would perhaps be immodest of me to assume the reader is familiar enough with my chronicles to recall my earlier report on Holmes's visit with the Dalai Lama Thupten Gyatso, the thirteenth of that line. In my story "The Adventure of the Empty House," I described Holmes's escape from Professor Moriarity and subsequent years of travel. Indeed, it was Holmes's own reading of this tale that led him to recount some of the details of his visit, details so strange that I must remind the reader of Holmes's meticulous attention to factual detail. We may take it as true that the events occurred exactly as he reported them.

I learned the details of the bizarre and disturbing meeting between the "God King of Tibet" and the world's foremost practical reasoner as Holmes and I sat in the flat at 221b Baker Street. I was, at the time, living nearby with my second wife who had not yet passed away, and I made it a practice to breakfast with my old friend as often as possible. I recall it was the beginning of one of those gray, rainy winter days for which London is justly famous. Mrs. Hudson had cleared away the breakfast dishes and I sat gazing abstractedly at the rain and soot particles creeping down the panes of glass. Holmes filled his pipe with a pungent Latakia tobacco and proceeded to fill the room with clouds of smoke as he produced a copy of *The Strand* magazine.

"Really Watson, I must speak with you about this latest effort of yours. Once again you have obscured the science of deduction with your emphasis on the sensational details of the crime. Further, you have provided little of practical value to those wishing to learn my methods."

I had long been familiar with my friend's habit of smoking noxious tobacco when he wished to bait me into an argument. Therefore, I simply replied calmly, "It would be instructive if you could give me a few specific examples, Holmes. Shall I bring pen and foolscap and jot them down?"

"Your sarcasm does you credit, Watson," he said with a laugh. "But certainly you could have devoted less time to your description of the terrors of the Reichenbach Falls and more to a description of the Japanese art of Baritsu, which enabled me turn the tables on the late Professor. Even more importantly, why did you not provide your readers with some details about the chat I had with the Dalai Lama?"

"Regarding your first point, I did not feel the details of Japanese wrestling were of interest to the general reader. Regarding your second point, I could not provide information to my readers that you have never provided to me," I said with a calm which seemed to provoke his ire.

"Poppycock! Do you mean to say I never told you a word about that little Mongol boy?"

Holmes's words added to the discomfort I was feeling in my leg. Damp weather always seemed to intensify the pain from the bullet I still carry as a souvenir of my time in Afghanistan in Her Majesty's Army. I rose from the chair and began to pace the room in agitation.

"I know my mind is not the equal of yours," I said. "But do you really believe I would have failed to recognize the importance of such information or that I would have simply forgotten the details of your meeting with a man who is a god in his own country but about whom virtually nothing is known in the civilized world?"

I snatched the copy of *The Strand* from his hand. "I will," I said, "read you every word you told me about the meeting. It begins after the bit about Moriarity's death, where you explain why you decided to confide in your brother Mycroft and not me." I found the appropriate page of the story and read:

"*. . . The trial of the Moriarity gang left two of its most dangerous members, my own most vindictive enemies, at liberty. I traveled for two years in Tibet, therefore, and amused myself by visiting Lhasa and spending some days with the head Llama.*"

With this, I closed the magazine. My irritation increased considerably when I saw that the editors of the magazine had not corrected the spelling of "Lama" as

I had clearly instructed on the galley proofs, thereby giving the impression that Holmes had spent time with a South American animal rather than a Tibetan wise man.

It is a rare thing to see Holmes perplexed. "I must beg your pardon, my dear friend. It is clear I never told you about it. What a regrettable lapse! I cannot think why I forgot to tell you about this adventure. My brain is usually not so muddled. Still, better late than never. We can pass a pleasant hour away from this land of rains in the Land of Snows."

Holmes's intense manner was at odds with his casual speech. Further, he was not a man to have "forgotten" something as important as this.

"First of all, I must explain why it was absolutely necessary to contact my brother Mycroft. I had to hide in the most remote spot on earth. Tibet was the logical deduction. No European is allowed in the country and some who have attempted to enter have been expelled by force of arms. The Tibetans, like Mycroft, value their privacy. Moriarity's gang would never search for me there because they would conclude it is simply impossible that I should be there. Mycroft, however, has something of a reputation in certain circles for arranging the impossible."

I had the pleasure of meeting Holmes's brother Mycroft in connection with the depressing affair of the Greek interpreter and the theft of the plans for the Bruce Paddington submarine. My own experience confirmed Holmes's almost unbelievable assertion that Mycroft's mind was superior to his own.

"I am sure I mentioned that Mycroft works as a civil servant in the British Government," Holmes said with a mischievous smile.

"You also mentioned that during certain international crises it is accurate to say that he IS the British Government," I reminded him.

"Quite so. My brother has always had the most remarkable memory; he seems to know every detail of every important policy decision taken within the last century. He also has acquaintances in the most out-of-the-way places who owe him favors. Certain members of the East India Company and the British Raj were particularly eager to repay past favors by helping his brother establish a new identity and fade from sight. They provided me with a new identity, that of the Norwegian explorer Lief Sigerson, and the necessary papers to make that identity believable. They also bore the considerable expense of outfitting an expedition in Darjeeling, on condition that I never publish any account of my travels, which might make things difficult for the Tibetan officials who approved my entry against the explicit policy of the Tibetan government.

"From Darjeeling, I made the eighteen-mile trip by cart-road to the Teesta River valley. The most uncomfortable part of the trip was the next sixty miles to the Tibetan frontier. I found the leeches particularly troublesome. It is rather dreary to sit down at the end of a long day's trek and remove from your legs those bloated creatures who have been feeding on your life blood.

"We followed a pony-track through Kalimpong, gradually climbing along the river to Rangpo, and then passed through Sikkim on the way to the Jalep La, our pass through the mountains. I shall not soon forget the views I saw there. The vastness and strangeness of the terrain and the absence of a period of twilight between evening and night contributed to my own feeling of isolation. I was the only European in our small expedition, alone in a group of yellow faces and incomprehensible tongues, traveling under an assumed name, with the whole civilized world thinking I was dead."

Knowing Holmes as I did, I could well imagine how he must have felt. I suddenly realized that he had regretted not telling me he was still alive but had only now found the means to express his regret. For perhaps the only time in my life, I correctly deduced what Holmes was about to say.

"Watson, it is difficult for a man like me to admit an error in judgment but it is a capital error to deny such a mistake when it does occur. My failure to communicate with you during the last three years was an error in judgment. Do I have your forgiveness for it?"

"My dear fellow, think nothing of it," I said. I knew Holmes would recall the many times in our friendship when he had used these exact words to dismiss a mistaken deduction or an error in judgment on my part.

"Very good then. We shall say no more about it. Let us return to the Tibetan frontier. Having crossed the Jalep La, we were still over two hundred miles (and several mountain passes) from Lhasa. The story of this journey is not without its points of interest, but let me skip it for now. Upon arriving in Lhasa I sought out the Head Lama to present him with the traditional white scarf and an unopened letter Mycroft had given me with instructions to present it to the Head Lama. Mycroft said it was from 'a person of some importance who could provide a sterling character reference for me.'

"It took some time to arrange the meeting with an individual who claimed to be the 'Head Lama.' I arrived at the Potala, the Dalai Lama's palace, at the appointed hour on a bitterly cold morning. The exterior of the palace is splendid but the interior is surprisingly dark. I was shown to a small bare room where I found an old man in monk's robes. With his breath smoking in the icy air he asked me, in surprisingly good English, if I would like a cup of tea. Though Tibetan tea is nearly undrinkable because it contains the butter of the stinking yaks, it warms one wonderfully.

"As it happened, my host turned out not to be the Dalai Lama who was, of course, a boy of fifteen living in seclusion at the time. At first he merely said he was a friend of the Dalai Lama. When I protested that I had instructions to give my letter directly to the Head Lama, he explained that he actually outranked the Dalai Lama in spiritual maters though he was subordinate to him in purely temporal affairs. I decided that it would be wise to give him the letter. Upon reading the letter he smiled with a subtlety which I had seen on the faces of many of the residents of the Potala.

"'Mr. Sigerson, we are members of a very isolated and backward race. Can you please explain to me, who is Queen Victoria?' he said with perfect innocence, playing along with Mycroft's joke on me. Naturally, I was surprised though I had suspected that she might be the author of the letter.

"'She is the beloved monarch of the greatest empire since Rome,' I replied.

"'In her letter she says you are a very fine chap and that you have helped her government on several occasions. Is this true?'

"'I have rendered some small service to Her Majesty on more than one occasion.'

"'She asks that we give you sanctuary and says that you have very special talents that may be of use to us. What are these talents, Mr. Sigerson?'

"Though I did not wish to give myself away I did wish to give him some general idea of my talents in case they should be needed in this out-of-the-way spot. I chose an indirect answer.

"'In addition to being an explorer I am also a scientist of sorts. My specialization is the science of deduction. Through the practiced application of the principles of this science I can draw conclusions and solve a variety of little puzzles in all sorts of areas that escape others. Indeed, the results can be quite startling at times. By way of demonstration, I will tell you the few details I have been able to deduce about you and what is on your mind at the moment. First, though I have not met you before this hour, I can deduce the obvious facts that you are an extremely busy and competent professional man who has risen from a humble background because of natural talent. Early in your life you nearly ruined your health through intense study, but approximately twenty years ago you went through a profound personal experience that transformed you both physically and spiritually. You have a level of personal discipline that is remarkable even among these monks. You also have a very large problem upon which you wish to ask my help and a small personal problem which you had not intended to bring up. I do not know whether I can help you with your larger problem but I know that it involves the Dalai Lama himself. You will be pleasantly surprised to learn I can help you with the small personal problem.'

"You know my methods, Watson. I always watch to see how the client reacts to these disclosures. The Lama sat for one full minute with no change of expression or movement, with his gaze intently fixed on mine. Then the lines of his brown weathered face shattered and reformed into the smile of a child of two."

"'Help me with my small problem, then we shall perhaps discuss the large problem,' he said with a laugh and a clap of his hands.

"'Very well. Your small personal problem at the moment is that you have a very severe migraine headache. A physician friend of mine, Dr. Watson, has helped me recognize the symptoms well enough. I am sure he would say your case is as severe as any he has seen. I believe you would be heeding your own doctor's advice and resting in bed if you did not have a very good reason for meeting with me. Further, the quiet but efficient search your attendants have been conducting since I arrived attests to the fact that they are attempting to find a small object that will, in some way unknown to me, cure your condition. Your own extraordinary level of self-discipline is shown by the fact that you can even carry on this conversation in the face of what, to most people, would be intolerable pain. The fact that the small object has not yet been found allows me to illustrate one of the principles of my deductive science: When we eliminate the impossible, whatever remains, however unlikely, must be the truth. Since the object has not been found elsewhere, it follows that it must be on your person. In your pain and eagerness to meet with me, you did not conduct a thorough search of your own clothing. If your Holiness will stand and loosen his robes, I believe the object will fall to the floor.'

"Almost before I had finished speaking, he sprang up and threw his robes wide, sending a small jade figurine flying across the floor. His attendant snatched it up excitedly and handed it to him, grinning and jabbering in his incomprehensible language as he pointed toward me and bowed deeply, placing his palms on the floor. Meanwhile, the Lama's face scarcely changed, but I could see that the pain seemed to leave him almost instantly when he touched the small image of a woman in robes holding a bowl.

"'I presume I have Mr. Sherlock Holmes to thank for this clever and compassionate act,' he said, giving me the first of a series of surprises which must have delighted him. I believe that I stared at him for a full minute before I said simply, 'Yes.' Despite his obvious intelligence and alien manner of speech, the man had a simple truthfulness which encouraged one to reciprocate.

"With the obvious air of a man with no time to waste on trifles, he did not ask me to tell him HOW I knew of his past and of his large and small problems but instead moved directly to the main business.

"'Mr Holmes, you are quite right on all particulars of which you spoke. I know enough of the English to know that they like to "come right to the nub" and not "beat about the bush" so I will tell you that we do seek your help on a problem involving the training of our current Dalai Lama.'

"'I see you have mastered the skill of reading another's thoughts to an unusual degree. It is a useful skill and will be essential in your work with our young Dalai Lama. I am pleased you have been sent to help us.'

"'No one sent me sir,' I replied. 'I came of my own accord.'

"'True enough Mr. Holmes, true enough,'" he replied. 'Allow me to change the subject and ask you to explain again to me please the "Science of Deduction?"'

"'Simply put, your Holiness, it is the science of drawing particular conclusions from general principles.'

"'And you used these principles to deduce that I was in pain and eager to find my healing amulet?'

"'Yes. It is obvious to me when a man is attempting to control pain, though you seem to be more adept at it than anyone with the possible exception of certain Yogis of my acquaintance. Further, your quick expectant glances at your attendants showed you expected them to find something to relieve your pain.'

"'How utterly amazing, Mr. Holmes. You say that it is "obvious" to you when another person is attempting to control pain?'

"'Of course, through his tensed muscles, his facial grimaces, and so on.'

"'But how do you know that facial grimaces mean someone is in pain?' Was he trying to be obtuse?

"'From common human experience,' I said with some impatience.

"'So your conclusion was based not on deduction from a set of givens but on your access to common human experience?'

"'Of course, common human experience provides the general principles from which we deduce particulars.'

"'Does it indeed, Mr. Holmes? Would not the German philosopher Immanuel Kant, whose ideas have reached even this backward country, disagree with you? Even your fellow Englishman John Stuart Mill questions whether experience provides the grounds for the sort of general principles you describe. I believe he uses the word INDUCTION rather than deduction to describe the process of practical reasoning at which you seem to be so adept.'

"'Sir, you have me at a disadvantage. I know only enough of Kant and German Idealism to know it is useless to me in my work. I know little more of the work of Mr. Mill. If I am, as you say, an expert, does it not follow that I should be the best authority on the nature of this reasoning process?'

"'No, Mr. Holmes, it does not. A man may know how to use a tool without really understanding it. Let me illustrate. Do you play chess?'

"'Not very well, but in this sport my country leads the world. The name of Harold Staunton will live forever in the history of the game.'

"'Some men play chess very well but cannot tell you how they decide on any particular move. Similarly, some men are very good military commanders or administrators but cannot tell you exactly how they reached some of their best decisions. However, some who are not great thinkers but who know their own minds through careful training may observe some truths which escape the notice of the most expert practitioners. May I ask you, please, to fix this point in your mind as we discuss the ways you may help our Dalai Lama.'

"At this point he paused, but I waved him on with some impatience. For a man who had promised not to beat about the bush, he was surprisingly willing to waste time discussing his own fanciful ideas. I could not tell whether he recognized my impatience but if he did, he did not express any irritation, but simply continued in his deliberate manner.

"'Thupten Gyatso, our Thirteenth Dalai Lama, is currently an adolescent boy who is being trained in seclusion to assume his duties.'

"'He has been the Dalai Lama since his birth, then?'

"'We believe he has been the Dalai Lama for considerably longer than that but, as you might say, Mr. Holmes, let us not waste time with trifles.'

"'Though Thupten Gyatso is the embodiment of Compassion, he is also a fifteen-year-old boy. In Tibet, that is a difficult age for many boys. Perhaps it is so in England also. Here in Tibet we discourage foreign visitors very strongly, but we know we must learn as much as we can about foreign ideas and customs, especially English customs since you are currently the master of the seas and therefore of the earth. You taught this lesson to our Chinese neighbors some years ago.

"'Your English educational system is one of the sources of your power, and we have attempted to incorporate some of it into the training of our Dalai Lama. Would it surprise you to learn that copies of *The Strand* magazine have found their way to our remote country? A committee of us read several of the stories and determined that they might make good diversionary reading for our Dalai Lama as they do for many English schoolboys. Further, the stories illustrate proper British virtues like energetic pursuit of the truth regarding the mysteries presented to us by our sense perceptions, careful reflection on the basic facts of existence, and a strong compassion which causes you to devote your life to helping the weak and suffering, a compassion which sometimes leads you to let the guilty go free.'

"'We had to edit some of the more lurid details of the stories (you should speak to your friend, Dr. Watson, about the excessive sensationalism), but the Dalai Lama has now read seven of the stories and, as you might expect, he admires you more than any of his teachers. His admiration for your type of rationality is so great that it threatens to hinder his training. Under the circumstances you can see how fortuitous it was that you decided to visit us at this moment 'of your own accord.'

"His eyes twinkled as he attempted to parody British speech. 'We would like to employ you, and to offer you a generous consulting fee, to assist our Dalai Lama in a spot of detective work. His quarry is hard to define but we think you would call it his 'soul' or perhaps his 'self.' We want you to help him track the beggar down.'"

"You know, Watson, that I have been involved in some strange cases and have dealt with some strange requests from clients, for example, in that nasty business of the Devil's Foot. Yet when the client is in earnest, as this man obviously was, I take all requests seriously. I said simply, 'Please explain further.'"

"'The ability to suspend judgment and keep an open mind is also a very rare skill which you will need in dealing with our Dalai Lama. Do you not suspect that I may be joking or mad when I make this request?'"

"'It is a capital mistake to theorize before one has all the data. I know already that you are not joking, and I will decide whether you are mad once you have explained your request more fully.' This response on my part provoked another child-like smile from the old man.

"'Well said! Well said!' he ejaculated. 'The right person has been sent to us.' Apparently he had forgotten or chosen to ignore my earlier remarks about coming of my own volition."

"'Let me ask you, what deductions have you reached concerning your "self" or "soul"? Do you believe that it exists or not?'"

"'I have not drawn, nor can I draw, any deductions on a subject which is not susceptible of rational proof.'"

"'Have you read the work of your countryman David Hume on this question, specifically, his *Treatise of Human Nature*?'"

"'David Hume is not a countryman of mine in the strict sense. He is a Scotsman and I have no more use for the Scottish school of philosophy than the German school. If you wish to know what my personal beliefs are, I believe we each have an immortal soul and this is our essence or self. I fail to see the importance of this line of inquiry.'"

"'I believe the King of Bohemia once told you the fate of his country depended upon your helping him to locate a photograph. I am now telling you that the fate of my country depends on your helping Thupten Gyatso to locate his essential nature. In return we can promise you a generous fee, and we may be able to help you solve your problems. Will you help us?'"

"'I must say at the outset that I have serious doubts about my ability to help in this matter, but as a guest I cannot refuse the attempt. Further, I cannot resist meeting a fifteen-year-old boy who is also a god in this country.'

"At this he winced. Something about my remark had apparently caused him more pain than his migraine had earlier. 'I know in your country he is called the God-King of Tibet. He is in truth neither a god nor a king. But he is more than a mere fifteen-year-old boy. Perhaps you would like to meet him to see if you agree with me.'

"'By all means,' I said excitedly. 'When can a meeting be arranged?'

"'Now.'

"'Do you mean this very moment?'

"'If not now, when?' he said, and, seeing my blank face he said, 'Or, if you prefer, there is no time like the present!'

"'If I am to instruct His Holiness, should I not be given time to prepare?'

"'Allow me to be precise. You will not be instructing our Dalai Lama. You will be helping him to inquire. You do not require any preparation.'

"'As you wish. Let us go and meet him.'

"'If you will wait one moment, he will come to us.'

"A moment later, a young monk appeared at the door. He entered the room so quietly and unceremoniously I at first thought he must be a young messenger sent to announce the arrival of His Holiness. However, the old Lama's deep bow, palms to the floor, told me that this was no messenger. I bowed my head slightly toward the boy.

"Ignoring me, he turned to the old man and asked, "Elder, why does the visitor not bow properly?'

"'Because he is not from our valley. He is a stranger. His letters of introduction say he is Leif Sigerson, a Norwegian explorer but this is not his true name or nature. Do you know his true name and nature, Younger Brother?'

"The boy looked at me with slight amusement. I saw on that face the look of a very bright schoolboy who has become bored with his lessons. 'His true name is emptiness and his true nature is an aggregation of five skandas,' the lad said with a flippancy which again made the older monk wince.

"'Please, Younger Brother, try to concentrate and apply the skills we taught you. If you can give us this man's true name it will please you.' Obviously, the boy had been over-indulged and wanted a sound caning, but the old monk was not one for caning. 'Please try,' he said again.

"The lad cast a bored glance in my direction and then with a shrug he looked directly at me with real attention. I saw his face lose the look of boredom and acquire a look of perplexity. Then, all at once, he broke into a wide grin which reminded me of the grin I had seen on the old man's face.

"'It is him! You brought him, just as you promised. Thank you, Elder Brother!' He dashed from the room and returned with several dog-eared copies of *The Strand*. 'You must tell me more stories,' he said.'

"Obviously, the lad had been told who I was and coached to pretend he did not know. I decided to play along.

"'Young man, you obviously know who I am. Rather than telling you a story I will work with you as I did with The King of Bohemia, Sir Henry Baskerville, and many others on a problem the Elder has set for you.'

"Instantly the little fellow's face took on the look of boredom again. 'I have already told my Elder Brother that I do not have a problem. I understand the basic teaching that all existences are void. I have no self.'

"'No man understands this truth until he has tried sincerely to find the self,' said the old monk, as though reciting a lesson he had told the young man many times. The young man rolled his eyes.

"'Young fellow!' I said somewhat sharply. 'You would do well to listen more closely to this man who has your own interests at heart. As it happens, I do not agree with, or even understand, the phrase "all existences are void." It sounds like daylight madness to me. If you are sure of your conclusion, let us employ my methods to see whether your deductions are sound. I will play Watson and you will play me. You will need this.' I handed the boy my pipe. He snatched it up and put it into his mouth as he has seen in the illustrations in *The Strand*, and furrowed his brow in a comical way.

" 'Now,' I said, 'tell me how you know there is no eternal soul or self.'

" 'My dear Watson,' said the boy with obvious relish. 'I did not say I know there is no self. I said, in accord with the teaching of the Holy Nagarjuna, that no self can be found. It would not be right to go to the opposite extreme and say that I can prove there is no self.'

"As he spoke I recalled myself at that age in public school, a bright student who learns his lessons almost too easily and may therefore lack real depth of understanding. Such students need to be challenged, and I felt I was up to the task.

" 'I must confess I am baffled. Surely the fact that I think proves I exist.'

" 'No, no, no, no,' he said, mimicking my own impatience which you have so accurately described in your stories. 'Surely you understand thought can exist without a thinking self. This is the most basic fact of existence. Not only did our Lord Buddha observe it but so did that German man who talked about "apperception of the manifold".'

" 'Immanuel Kant, Brother,' said the old man.

" 'Yes, yes , yes, yes. Immanuel Kant and that Englishman, Hume. Surely this is obvious. You have not thought things through.' The boy obviously was reciting lessons. He felt I had been sent to test him. I, on the other hand, was completely baffled.

" 'Young man, let us drop the poses and talk straightforwardly to each other.'

" 'Man to man,' he said.

" 'Yes. Surely you cannot be serious when you suggest that there is any question about whether we exist or have selves. We may or may not have immortal souls but the fact that we have selves is as obvious as the fact that we have bodies. It is impossible to conceive of existence without a self. It simply does not make sense. Even if it did, a strong conception of self is the basis for the self-discipline that makes it possible for a man to live in and contribute to his society. Personal responsibility is the basis for moral conduct. I have spent my life dealing with the criminal classes whose chief distinguishing feature is that they do not take personal responsibility for their actions. To attempt to convince people the self does not exist undermines civilization.'

"It was obvious I had shocked him out of some of his smugness. He stared at me for a very long time with his face full of perplexity.

" 'But how can you believe you have a stable self when you know that you change from year to year? What is the "self" that survives this change?' he asked with genuine curiosity.

" 'I believe it is a mental or spiritual entity which is the seat of my highest desires and aspirations,' I answered.

"'But do you not see that when you British try to "realize your highest aspirations," you are really trying to shore up your false conception of "self"? You always end by enforcing these aspirations with gun ships on people whose highest aspirations do not match yours.'

"'I admit we have made mistakes in our attempts to civilize the world. Yet despite our mistakes we have brought the entire continent of India into the nineteenth century and may yet do so with China.'

"'But you must understand that you have given both India and China a terrible weapon, which they will one day use against you. That weapon is your British concept of "self." The Indians will someday use this weapon to throw you out of their country. The Chinese, of course, will do far worse. Your gun ships woke them from a long period of lethargy. They were a great nation when London was a small village. In their history they have learned how to absorb foreign ideas and turn them to their own use. It will take them 100 years or more to absorb this notion of "self" which built the British Empire, but when they do, they will once again be a great nation. At that time, Britain will know some of China's present humiliation. Is it possible that you have not already deduced this yourself Mr. Holmes?'

"As he spoke I began to suspect that he might be suffering from the rigors of his training and seclusion. Though he spoke calmly, his words had the sound of a mystic's ravings. The future he foresaw was beyond belief. I said simply, 'I have no idea what you are talking about.'

"The lad fixed me in his gaze and his eyes slowly assumed a look of fatigue one sometimes sees in the eyes of very old men.

"'Your Holiness!' said the old monk sternly. He no longer used the expression "Younger Brother." 'Does Mr. Holmes really not understand that the self is void?'

"'He does not understand,' the young man replied with downcast eyes.

"'Then since you understand the concept why can you not explain it to this man whom you yourself told us is more clever than all the Elders put together?'

"'I do not know,' said the boy, and I could see tears welling up in his eyes.

"'Are you still sure the Buddha's teachings on this point are correct and that you understand them fully?' said the man with tears in his own ancient eyes.

"'I do not know,' said the boy, and began to weep in earnest now. These were not tears of frustration in a clever student who has gotten his homework wrong. These were tears of deep sorrow. His small body heaved with sobs. I have seen mothers weep in this way when their infants died.

"The old monk wept also as he said gently to the boy, 'Mr. Holmes has rendered you a great service, Brother, greater than either he or you realize at this moment. It would be appropriate for you to formally express gratitude to him.'

Holmes paused to refill his pipe. I realized that the story had taken less time to tell than it took Holmes to finish a single bowl of tobacco.

"Sadly, Watson, that is all there is to the story. The boy was too upset to continue that day, and the next day the old monk came to thank me for my 'help' and tell me that he had found lodgings for me with a local 'pious' family who would be willing and able to see to my needs as long as I cared to stay, even if that should be for years to come. I never again saw the boy who would later rule the country, but when I did leave two years later, he provided a small guard to escort me safely to the border where I was presented with a small package from His Holiness to Queen Victoria. I was instructed to deliver it through my brother Mycroft, who later told me that it contained an exceptionally fine piece of the semi-precious stone lapis lazuli and an extremely short letter saying in effect, "This jewel is a gift to the monarch of Great Britain. It symbolizes the gratitude of Dalai Lama Thupten Gyatso for the assistance rendered by Mr. Sherlock Holmes in locating the Great Jewel of Compassion.""

References

Aho, J. 1994. *This thing of darkness: A sociology of the enemy.* Seattle, WA: University of Washington Press.

Ahuja, M. and K. Carley. 1999. Network structure in virtual organizations. *Organization Science* 10:741–757.

Ainslie, G. 1986. Beyond microeconomics: Conflict among interests in a multiple self as a determinant of value. In *The Multiple Self,* ed. J. Elster. Cambridge: Cambridge University Press, 133–176.

Alba, J., and L. Hasher. 1983. Is memory schematic? *Psychological Bulletin* 93:203–231.

Albert, S., B. Ashforth, and J. Dutton. 2000. Organizational identity and identification: Charting new waters and building new bridges. *Academy of Management Review* 25:13–17.

Albert, S., and D. Whetten. 1985. Organizational Identity. In *Research in Organizational Behavior,* ed. L. Cummings and B. Staw. Greenwich, CT: JAI Press, 263–295.

Alloy, L. B., and L.Y. Abramson. 1979. Judgment of contingency in depressed and nondepressed students: Sadder but wiser? *Journal of Experimental Psychology: General* 108:441–485.

Allport, G. W. 1937. *Personality: A psychological interpretation.* New York: Holt, Rinehart and Winston.

———. 1943. The ego in contemporary psychology. *Psychological Review* 50:451–478.

———. 1961. *Pattern and growth in personality.* New York: Holt, Rinehart and Winston.

Alper, S., D. Tjosvold, and K. Law. 1998. Interdependence and controversy in group decision-making: Antecedents to effective self-managing teams. *Organizational Behavior and Human Decision Processes* 74:33–52.

Amason, A. 1997. Good and bad conflict in strategic decision making. In *Strategic Decisions,* ed. V. Papadakis and P. Barwise. Boston, MA: Kluwer Academic Publishers.

Amburgey, T., and A. Miner. 1992. Strategic momentum: The effects of repetitive, positional, and contextual momentum on merger activity. *Strategic Management Journal* 13:335–348.

Anderson, J. 1983. *The architecture of cognition.* Cambridge, MA: Harvard University Press.

Anderson, J. R. 1976. *Language, memory and thought.* Hillsdale, NJ: Erlbaum.

Anderson, J. R., and G. H. Bower. 1973. *Human associative memory.* Washington, DC: Winston.

Argote, L., P. Ingram, J. Levine, and R. Moreland. 2000. Introduction: Knowledge transfer in organizations: Learning from the experience of others. *Organizational Behavior and Human Decision Processes* 82:1–8.

Aronson, E. 1968. Dissonance theory: Progress and problems. In *Theories of cognitive consistency: A sourcebook,* ed. R. P. Abelson et al. Chicago: Rand McNally.

Aronson, E. 1984. *The social animal.* 4th ed. San Francisco: W. H. Freeman.

Ashforth, B., and R. Humphrey. 1993. Emotional labor in service roles: The influence of identity. *Academy of Management Review* 18:88–115.

Ashforth, B., and G. Kreiner. 1999. "How can you do it?": Dirty work and the challenge of constructing a positive identity. *Academy of Management Review* 24:413–432.

Ashforth, B., and F. Mael. 1992. "The dark side of organizational identification." Paper presented at the Academy of Management Meetings, Las Vegas.

Ashforth, B., and F. Mael. 1996. Organizational identity and strategy as a context for the individual. In *Advances in strategic management,* ed. J. Baum and J. Dutton. Greenwich, CT: JAI.

Astley, G., R. Axelsson, R. Butler, D. Hickson, and D. Wilson. 1982. Complexity and cleavage: Dual explanations of strategic decision-making. *Journal of Management Studies* 19:357–375.

Augustine. 398/1961. *Confessions.* ed. R. Coffin. Baltimore, MD: Penguin.

Axelrod, R. 1984. *The evolution of cooperation.* New York: Basic Books.

Baars, B. 1997. *In the theater of consciousness.* New York: Oxford University Press.

Banaji, M., and D. Prentice. 1994. The self in social contexts. *Annual Review of Psychology* 45:297–332.

Bandura, A. 1977a. Self-efficacy: Toward a unifying theory of behavioral change. *Psychological Review* 84: 191–215.

Bandura, A. 1977b. *Social learning theory.* Englewood Cliffs, NJ: Prentice-Hall.

Bandura, A. 1986. *Social foundations of thought and action.* Englewood Cliffs, N.J: Prentice-Hall.

Bantel, K., and S. Jackson. 1989. Top management and innovations in banking: Does the composition of the top team make a difference? *Strategic Management Journal* 10:107–124.

Barber, B. 1984. *Strong democracy: Participatory politics for a new age.* Berkeley, CA: University of California Press.

Barber, B. 1996. *Jihad vs. McWorld.* New York: Ballantine Books.

Barnard, C. 1938. *Functions of the executive.* Cambridge, MA: Harvard University Press.

Barnett, W., H. Greve, and D. Park. 1994. An evolutionary model of organizational performance. *Strategic Management Journal* 15:11–28.

Barr, P., L. Stimpert, and A. Huff. 1992. Cognitive change, strategic action, and organizational renewal. *Strategic Management Journal* 13 (special issue), 15–36.

Barry, D., and M. Elmes. 1997. Strategy retold: Toward a narrative view of strategic discourse. *Academy of Management Review* 22:429–452.

Bartlett, F. 1932. *Remembering: A study in experimental and social psychology.* Cambridge: Cambridge University Press.

Bast, J., P. Hill, and R. Rue. 1994. *Eco-sanity: A common-sense guide to environmentalism.* Lanham, MD: Madison Books.

Bateman, T., and C. Schwenk. 1986. Biases in investor decision-making: The case of John DeLorean. *Mid-American Journal of Business* 8:5–11.

Bateman, T., and C. Zeithaml. 1989. The psychological context of strategic decisions: A model and convergent experimental findings. *Strategic Management Journal* 10:59–74.

Bazerman, M., and M. Neale. 1993. *Negotiating rationally*. New York: Free Press.

Bem, D., and H. McConnell. 1970. Testing the self-perception explanation of dissonance phenomena: On the salience of premanipulation attitudes. *Journal of Personality and Social Psychology* 14:23–31.

Benedict XIV. 1749. *De servorum dei beatificatione et beatorum canonizatione*. Published in Rome.

Berger, P., and T. Luckman. 1967. *The social construction of reality: A treatise on the sociology of knowledge*. Garden City, NY: Doubleday.

Block, J., O. Flanagan, and G. Guzeldere. 1997. *The Nature of consciousness: Philosophical debates*. Boston: MIT Press.

Bloom, H. 1987. *Marcel Proust's remembrance of things past*. New York: Chelsea House.

Bodenhausen, G., and R. Wyler. 1985. Effects of stereotypes on decision making and information-processing strategies. *Journal of Personality and Social Psychology* 48:267–282.

Boje, D. 1995. Stories and the storytelling organization: A postmodern analysis of Disney as "Tamara-Land." *Academy of Management Journal* 38:997–1035.

Bourgeois, L. 1980. Performance and consensus. *Strategic Management Journal* 1:227–248.

Bourgeois, L. 1985. Strategic goals, perceived uncertainty, and economic performance in volatile environments. *Academy of Management Journal* 28:548–573.

Bower, G. H., and S. G. Gilligan. 1979. Remembering information related to one's self. *Journal of Research in Personality* 13:420–461.

Bower, J. 1970. *Managing the resource allocation process*. Boston, MA: Graduate School of Business, Harvard University.

Breckler, S. J., and A. G. Greenwald. In press. Motivational facets of the self. In *Handbook of motivation and cognition*, edited by R. M. Sorrentino and E. T. Higgins. New York: Guilford Press.

Breckler, S. J., A. R. Pratkanis, and D. McCann. 1985. "The representation of self in multidimensional cognitive space." Unpublished manuscript, Johns Hopkins University.

Brewer, M., and W. Gardner. 1996. Who is this "We"? Levels of collective identity and self representations. *Journal of Personality and Social Psychology* 71:83–93.

Brickson, S. 2000. The impact of identity orientation on individual and organizational outcomes in demographically diverse settings. *Academy of Management Review* 25:82–101.

Brockner, J. 1992. The escalation of commitment to a failing course of action: Toward theoretical progress. *Academy of Management Review* 17:39–61.

Brockner, J., J. Fine, T. Hamilton, B. Thomas, and B. Turetsky. 1982. Factors affecting entrapment in escalating conflicts: The importance of timing. *Journal of Research in Personality* 16:247–266.

Brockner, J., and J. Rubin. 1985. *Entrapment in escalating conflicts*. New York: Springer-Verlag.

Brockner, J., J. Rubin, and E. Lang. 1981. Face-saving and entrapment. *Journal of Experimental Social Psychology* 17:68–79.

Brockner, J., M. Shaw, and J. Rubin. 1979. Factors affecting withdrawal from an escalating conflict: Quitting before it's too late. *Journal of Experimental Social Psychology* 15:492–503.

Brown, S., and K. Eisenhardt. *Competing on the edge: Strategy as structured chaos.* Boston, MA: Harvard Business School Press.

Brown, A., and K. Starkey. 2000. Organizational identity and learning: A psychodynamic perspective. *Academy of Management Review* 25:102–120.

Buddhadasa, B. 1988. *Mindfulness with breathing.* Bangkok, Thailand: Pholpun Printing.

Butler, R. 1997. The process and context of strategic decision-making. In *Strategic Decisions,* ed. V. Papadakis and P. Barwise. Boston, MA: Kluwer Academic Publishers.

Butters, N., and L. S. Cermak. 1980. *Alcoholic Korsakoffs syndrome: An information processing approach to amnesia.* New York: Academic Press.

Caird, D. 1988. The structure of Hood's mysticism scale: A factor-analytic study. *Journal for the Scientific Study of Religion* 27:122–126.

Calkins, M. W. 1912. The self in recent psychology. *Psychological Bulletin* 9:25–30.

Calkins, M. W. 1916. The self in recent psychology. *Psychological Bulletin* 13:20–27.

Calkins, M. W. 1919. The self in recent psychology: A critical summary. *Psychological Bulletin* 16:111–119.

Calori, R., G. Johnson, and P. Sarnin. 1994. CEOs' cognitive maps and the scope of the organization. *Strategic Management Journal* 15:437–457.

Campbell, D. 1991. Methods for the experimenting society. *Evaluation-Practice* 12:223–260.

Campbell, D., and J. Stanley. 1966. *Experimental and quasi-experimental designs for research.* Chicago: Rand-McNally.

Campbell, J., P. Trapnell, S. Heine, I. Katz, L. Lavalle, and D. Lehman. 1996. Self-concept clarity: Measurement, personality correlates, and cultural boundaries. *Journal of Personality and Social Psychology* 70:141–156.

Carver, C. S., and M. F. Scheier. 1981. *Attention and self-regulation: A control theory approach to human behavior.* New York: Springer-Verlag.

Castells, M. 1997. *The Power of Identity.* Oxford: Blackwell.

Chandler, A. 1962. *Strategy and structure.* Cambridge, MA: MIT Press.

Chalmers, D. 1996. *The conscious mind.* Oxford, England: Oxford University Press.

Choi, I., R. Nisbett, and A. Norenzayan. 1999. Causal attributions across cultures: Variation and universality. *Psychological Bulletin* 125:47–63.

Churchman, C. 1966. Hegelian inquiry systems. Internal working paper, Space Sciences Laboratory, University of California, Berkeley.

Ciulla, J. 2000. *The working life.* New York: Times Books.

Claparede, E. 1911/1951. Recognition and me-ness. In *Organization and pathology of thought,* ed. D. Rapaport. New York: Columbia University Press.

Clapham, S., and C. Schwenk. 1991. Self-serving attributions, managerial cognition, and firm performance. *Strategic Management Journal* 12:219–229.

Coe, R. 1984. *When the grass was taller: Autobiography and the experience of childhood.* New Haven, CT: Yale University Press.

Cofer, C., D. Chmiekewski, and J. Brockway. 1976. Constructive processes in human memory. In *The structure of human memory,* ed. C. Cofer. San Francisco: Freeman.

Cohen, A. 1994. *Self consciousness: An alternative anthropology of identity.* London: Routledge.

Cohen, A., and N. Rapport (Eds.). 1995. *Questions of consciousness.* London: Routledge.

Colignon, R. 1989. The "holistic" and "individualistic" views of organizations. *Theory and Society* 18:83–123.

Collins, J., and J. Porras. 1996. Building your company's vision. *Harvard Business Review*, September/October, pp. 10–17.

Combs, A. W., and D. Snygg. 1948/1959. *Individual behavior: A perceptual approach to behavior*. New York: Harper and Brothers.

Conlon, E., and G. Wolf. 1980. The moderating effects of strategy, visibility, and involvement on allocation behavior: An extension of Staw's escalation paradigm. *Organizational Behavior and Human Performance* 26:172–192.

Cooley, C. H. 1902/1964. *Human nature and the social order*. New York: Schocken Books.

Cosier, R. 1978. The effects of three potential aids for making strategics on prediction accuracy. *Organizational Behavior and Human Performance* 22:295–306.

Cosier, R. 1980. Inquiry method, goal difficulty, and context effects on performance. *Decision Sciences* 11:1–16.

Cosier, R. 1981. Dialectical inquiry in strategic planning: A case of premature acceptance? *Academy of Management Review* 6:643–648.

Cosier, R., and P. Rechner. 1985. Inquiry method effects on performance in a simulated business environment. *Organizational Behavior and Human Decision Processes* 36:79–95.

Cosier, R., T. Ruble, and J. Aplin. 1978. An evaluation of the effectiveness of dialectical inquiry systems. *Management Science* 24:1483–1490.

Cox, T. 1994. *Cultural diversity in organizations*. San Francisco: Berrett-Koehler.

Crozier, M. 1964. *The bureaucratic phenomenon*. Chicago: University of Chicago Press.

Cummings, L., and B. Staw, eds. 1985. *Research in organizational behavior*. Greenwich, CT: JAI Press.

Cyert, R., and J. March. 1963. *A behavioral theory of the firm*. Englewood Cliffs, NJ: Prentice-Hall.

Daft, R. 1995. *Organization theory and design* (5th ed.). Minneapolis/St. Paul, MN: West.

Daft, R., and K. Weick. 1984. Toward a model of organizations as interpretation systems. *Academy of Management Review* 9:284–295.

Dandridge, T., I. Mitroff, and A. Joyce. 1980. Organizational symbolism: A topic to expand organizational analysis. *Academy of Management Review* 5:77–82.

Davis, T., and F. Luthans. 1980. A social learning approach to organizational behavior. *Academy of Management Review* 5:281–290.

Dawes, R., A. van de Kragt, and J. Orbell. 1988. Not me or thee but we: The importance of group identity in eliciting cooperation in dilemma situations. *Acta Psychologica* 68:83–97.

Deal, T., and A. Kennedy. 1982. *Corporate culture*. Reading, MA: Addison-Wesley.

Delorean, J., and T. Schwarz. 1985. *Delorean*. Grand Rapids, MI: Zondervan Books.

Dennett, D. 1991. *Consciousness explained*. Boston: Little, Brown, and Co.

Denzin, N. 1989. *Interpretive biography*. Newbury Park, CA: Sage.

de Rivera, J. 1968. *The psychological dimension of foreign policy*. Columbus, OH: Charles E. Merrill.

Dess, G. 1987. Consensus on strategy formulation and organizational performance: Competitors in a fragmented industry. *Strategic Management Journal* 8:259–277.

Dess, G., and N. Origer. 1987. Environment, structure, and consensus in strategy formulation: A conceptual integration. *Academy of Management Review* 12:313–330.

DeWoot, P., H. Heyvaert, and F. Martou. 1977. Strategic management. *International Studies of Management and Organization* 7:60–75.

Diggins, P. 1991. *The promise of pragmatism: Modernism and the crisis of knowledge and authority*. Chicago: University of Chicago Press.

Duhaime, I., and C. Schwenk. 1985. Conjectures on cognitive simplification processes in acquisition and divestment decision-making. *Academy of Management Review* 10:287–295.

Dukerich, J., R. Kramer, and J. Parkes. 1998. The dark side of organizational identification. In *Identity in organizations,* ed. D. Whetten and D. Godfrey. Thousand Oaks, CA: Sage.

Dunbar, R., J. Dutton, and W. Torbert. 1982. Crossing mother: Ideological constraints on organizational improvements. *Journal of Management Studies* 19:91–108.

Duncan, D. 1996. *River teeth.* New York: Bantam.

Duncan, D. 1998. The war for Norman's river. *Sierra Magazine* 83, #3 (May/June): 44–57.

Dutton, J., and J. Dukerich. 1991. Keeping an eye on the mirror: Image and identity in organizational adaptation. *Academy of Management Journal* 34:517–554.

Dutton, J., J. Dukerich, and C. Harquail. 1994. Organizational images and member identification. *Administrative Science Quarterly* 39:239–263.

Dutton, J., L. Fahey, and V. Narayanan. 1983. Toward understanding strategic issue diagnosis. *Strategic Management Journal* 4:307–323.

Dutton, J., and S. Jackson. 1987. Categorizing strategic issues: Links to organizational action. *Academy of Management Review* 12:76–90.

Eakin, P. 1991. *American autobiography: Retrospect and prospect.* Madison, WI: University of Wisconsin Press.

Economist, 1997 (December, 20, 1997). Environmental scares.

Eden, C., and F. Ackerman. 1998. *Making strategy: The journey of strategic management.* London: Sage.

Eden, C., and J. Spender. 1998. *Managerial and organizational cognition: Theory, methods, and research.* London: Sage.

Egan, S. 1984. *Patterns of experience in autobiography.* Chapel Hill, NC: University of North Carolina Press.

Ehrlich, P., and A. Ehrlich. 1996. *Betrayal of science and reason.* Washington, DC: Island Press.

Einhorn, H., and R. Hogarth. 1978. Confidence in judgment: Persistence of the illusion of validity. *Psychological Review* 85:395–416.

Eisenhardt, K. 1989. Making fast strategic decisions in high-velocity environments. *Academy of Management Journal* 32:543–576.

Eisenhardt, K. 1990. Speed and strategic choice: How managers accelerate decision-making. *California Management Review* 32:39–54.

Eisenhardt, K., J. Kahwajy, and L. Bourgeois. 1997. Taming interpersonal conflict in strategic choice. In *Strategic Decisions,* ed. V. Papadakis and P. Barwise. Boston, MA: Kluwer Academic Publishers.

Eisenhardt, K., J. Kahwajy, and L. Bourgeois. 1997. How management teams can have a good fight. *Harvard Business Review,* July–August: 77–85.

Ellinor, L., and G. Gerard. 1998. *Dialogue: Rediscover the transforming power of conversation.* New York: Wiley.

Elmes, M., and G. Gemmill. 1990. The psychodynamics of mindlessness and dissent in small groups. *Small Group Research* 21:28–44.

Elsbach, K., and R. Kramer. 1996. Members' responses to organizational identity threats: Encountering and countering the *Business Week* rankings. *Administrative Science Quarterly* 41:442–476.

Emery, F., and E. Trist. 1965. The causal texture of organizational environments. *Human Relations* 18:21–32.

Emsheff, J., and A. Finnel. 1978. "Defining corporate strategy: A case study in strategic assumption analysis." Working paper, Wharton Applied Research Center.

Engle, E., and R. Lord. 1997. Implicit theories, self-schemas, and leader-member exchange. *Academy of Management Journal* 40:988–1010.

Epstein, S. 1973. The self-concept revisited: Or a theory of a theory. *American Psychologist* 28:404–416.

Epstein, S. 1980. The self-concept: A review and the proposal of an integrated theory of personality. In *Personality: Basic issues and current research*, ed. E. Staub. Englewood Cliffs, NJ: Prentice-Hall.

Erchak, G. 1992. *The anthropology of self and behavior*. New Brunswick, NJ: Rutgers University Press.

Erikson, E. 1958. *Young man Luther*. New York: Norton.

Etzioni, A. 1988. *The moral dimension*. New York: Basic Books.

Fahey, L., and V. Narayanan. 1986. "Organizational beliefs and strategic adaptation." *Proceedings of the National Academy of Management*. Chicago: 7–11.

Fenigstein, A., M. F. Scheier, and A. H. Buss. 1975. Public and private self-consciousness: Assessment and theory. *Journal of Consulting and Clinical Psychology* 43:522–527.

Fiol, M., and A. Huff. 1992. Maps for managers: Where are we? Where do we go from here? *Journal of Management* 29:267–285.

Fischhoff, B., P. Slovic, and S. Lichtenstein. 1977. Knowing with certainty: The appropriateness of extreme confidence. *Journal of Experimental Psychology: Human Perception and Performance* 3:552–564.

Fisher, R. 1991. *Getting to yes: Negotiating without giving in*. New York: Penguin USA.

Fiske, W., and S. Taylor. 1984. *Social cognition*. Reading, MA: Addison-Wesley.

Fitzgerald, J. 1992. Autobiographical memory and conceptualizations of the self. In *Theoretical Perspectives on Autobiographical Memory*, ed. M. Conway. London: Kluwer Academic Publishers.

Freeman, R. 1984. *Strategic management: A stakeholder approach*. Boston: Pitman.

Friedman, M., and R. Friedman. 1999. *Two lucky people: Memoirs*. Chicago: University of Chicago Press.

Fromm, E. 1941. *Escape from freedom*. New York: Rinehart.

Gardner, W., C. Pickett, and M. Brewer. 2000. Social exclusion and selective memory: How the need to belong influences memory for social events. *Personality and Social Psychology Bulletin* 26:486–496.

Gates, W. 1999. *Business @ the speed of thought*. New York: Warner Books.

Genia, V. 1997. The spiritual experience index: Revision and reformulation. *Review of Religious Research* 38:344–361.

George, A. 1972. The case for multiple advocacy in making foreign policy. *American Political Science Review* 66:751–785.

Gergen, K. J. 1982. From self to science: What is there to know? In *Psychological perspectives on the self* (Vol. 1), ed. J. Suls. Hillsdale, NJ: Erlbaum.

Gergen, K. 1991. *The saturated self: Dilemmas of identity in contemporary life*. New York: Basic Books.

Giddens, A. 1991. *Modernity and self-identity: Self and society in the late modern age*. Stanford, CA: Stanford University Press.

Gioia, D., and J. Thomas. 1996. Identity, image, and issue interpretation: Sensemaking during strategic change in academia. *Administrative Science Quarterly* 41:370–403.

Gioia, D., M. Schultz, and K. Corely. 2000. Organizational identity, image, and adaptive instability. *Academy of Management Review* 25:63–81.

Gladwell, M. 2000. *The tipping point.* Boston: Little, Brown and Co.

Glick, W., C. Miller, and G. Huber. 1993. The impact of upper-echelon diversity on organizational performance. In *Organizational Change and Redesign,* ed. G. Huber and W. Glick. New York: Oxford Press.

Goffman, E. 1959. *The presentation of self in every day life.* New York: Doubleday.

Goffman, E. 1970. *The presentation of self in everyday life.* New York: Doubleday.

Goldschmidt, W. 1990. *The human career: The self in the symbolic world.* Cambridge, MA: Basil Blackwell.

Greeley, A. 1975. *The sociology of the paranormal: A reconnaissance.* Beverly Hills, CA: Sage.

Greenwald, A. 1980. The totalitarian ego: Fabrication and revision of personal history. *American Psychologist* 35:603–618.

Greenwald, A. G. 1980. The totalitarian ego: Fabrication and revision of personal history. *American Psychologist* 35:603–618.

Greenwald, A. G. 1981. Self and memory. In *The psychology of learning and motivation* (Vol. 15), ed. G. H. Bower. New York: Academic Press.

Greenwald, A. G. 1982a. Ego task analysis: An integration of research on ego-involvement and self-awareness. In *Cognitive social psychology,* ed. A. Hastorf and A. M. Isen. New York: Elsevier North Holland.

Greenwald, A. G. 1982b. Is anyone in charge? Personalysis versus the principle of personal unity. In *Psychological perspectives on the self* (Vol. 1), ed. J. Suls. Hillsdale, NJ: Erlbaum.

Greenwald, A., and M. Banaji. 1989. The self as a memory system: Powerful, but ordinary. *Journal of Personality and Social Psychology* 57:41–54.

Greenwald, A. G., M. R. Banaji, A. R. Pratkanis, and S. J. Breckler. "A centrality effect in recall." Paper presented at Psychonomics Society, Philadelphia, PA.

Greenwald, A. G., F. S. Bellezza, and M. R. Banaji. 1985. "Self-esteem, self-consciousness, and access to self-knowledge." Unpublished manuscript, Ohio State University.

Greenwald, A. G., and S. J. Breckler. 1985. To whom is the self presented? In *The self and social life,* ed. B. R. Schlenker, New York: McGraw-Hill.

Greenwald, A. G., and A. R. Pratkanis. 1984. The self. In *The handbook of social cognition* (Vol. 3), ed. R. S. Wyer and T. K. Srull. Hillsdale, NJ: Erlbaum.

Greenwald, A. G., and D. L. Ronis. 1978. Twenty years of cognitive dissonance: Case study of the evolution of a theory. *Psychological Review* 85:53–57.

Grinyer, P., and D. Norburn. 1977. Planning for existing markets. *International Studies of Management and Organization* 7:99–122.

Grove, A. 1997. Navagating strategic inflection points. *Business Strategy Review* 8:11–18.

Gustafson, L., and R. Reger. 1996. "Using organizational identity to achieve stability and change in high velocity environments." In *Proceedings of the National Academy of Management Meetings,* 464–468.

Hambrick, D., and P. Mason. 1984. Upper echelons: The organization as a reflection of its top managers. *Academy of Management Review* 9:193–206.

Hammer, M., and J. Champy. 1993. *Reengineering the corporation.* New York: HarperCollins.

Hanh, T. 1988. *The sutra on the full awareness of breathing.* Berkeley, CA: Parallax Press.

Hankiss, A. 1981. Ontologies of the self: On the mythological rearranging of one's life-history. In *Biography and society: The life-history approach in the social sciences,* ed. D. Bertaux. Beverly Hills, CA: Sage.

Hannigan, J. 1990. *Environmental sociology.* London: Routledge.

Hardin, G. 1968. The tragedy of the commons. *Science* 162:1243–1248.

Haslam, S., P. Oakes, K. Reynolds, and J. Turner, J. 1999. Social identity salience and the emergence of stereotype consensus. *Personality and Social Psychology Bulletin* 25:809–818.

Hastie, R. 1981. Schematic principles in human memory. In *Social cognition: The Ontario symposium* (Vol. 1), ed. E. T. Higgins, C. P. Herman, and M. P. Zanna. Hillsdale, NJ: Erlbaum.

Hatch, M., and M. Schultz. 2000. Scaling the Tower of Babel: Relational differences between identity, image, and culture in organizations. In *The expressive organization*, ed. M. Schultz, M. Hatch, and M. Larsen. Oxford, England: Oxford University Press, 11–35.

Hay, D., and A. Morisy. 1978. Reports of ecstatic, paranormal, or religious experience in Great Britain and the United States: A comparison of trends. *Journal for the Scientific Study of Religion* 17:255–268.

Hayek, F. 1944. *The road to serfdom*. Chicago: University of Chicago Press.

Hayes-Roth, F., D. A. Waterman, and D. B. Lenat. 1983. *Building expert systems*. Reading, MA: Addison-Wesley.

Hedberg, B. 1981. How organizations learn and unlearn. In *Handbook of organizational design*, ed. P. Nystrom and W. Starbuck. Oxford: Oxford University Press.

Hedberg, B., P. Nystrom, and W. Starbuck. 1976. Camping on seesaws? Prescriptions for a self-designing organization. *Administrative Science Quarterly* 21:41–65.

Herbert, T., and R. Estes. 1977. Improving executive planning by formalizing dissent: The corporate devil's advocate. *Academy of Management Review* 2:662–667.

Higgins, E. 1996. The "self digest": Self-knowledge serving self-regulatory functions. *Journal of Personality and Social Psychology* 71:1062–1083.

Hilgard, E. 1949. Human motives and the concept of the self. *American Psychologist* 4:374–382.

Hodgkinson, G., N. Brown, A. Maule, K. Glaister, and A. Pearman. 1999. Breaking the frame: An analysis of strategic cognition and decision-making under uncertainty. *Strategic Management Journal* 20:977–985.

Hofstadter, D. R. 1979. *Godel, Escher, Bach: An eternal golden braid*. New York: Basic Books.

Hofstede, G. 1980. *Culture's consequences*. Beverly Hills, CA: Sage.

Hofstede, G. 1997. *Cultures in organizations: Software of the mind*. New York: McGraw-Hill.

Hogg, M., and D. Terry. 2000. Social identity and self-categorization processes in organizational contexts. *Academy of Management Review*, 25:121–140.

Hood, R. 1975. The construction and preliminary validation of a measure of reported mystical experience. *Journal for the Scientific Study of Religion* 14:29–41.

Huff, A. 1983. Industry influences on strategy reformulation. *Strategic Management Journal* 4:119–131.

Huff, A. (Ed.). 1990. *Strategic argument mapping*. Cambridge, MA: Cambridge University Press.

Huff, A., and C. Schwenk. 1990. Bias and sensemaking in good times and bad. In *Strategic argument mapping*, ed. A. Huff. Cambridge, MA: Cambridge University Press.

Hume, D. 1739/1962. *A treatise of human nature*. New York: Meridian Books.

Hurley, S. 1998. *Consciousness in action*. Cambridge, MA: Harvard University Press.

Huxley, A. 1944. *The perennial philosophy*. New York: Harper and Row.

Iacocca, L. 1981. *Iacocca*. New York: Dell.

Iacocca, L. 1996. How I flunked retirement. *Esquire*, June.

Isaacs, W. 1995. Taking flight: Dialogue, collective thinking, and organizational learning. *Organizational Dynamics*: 24–39.

Isaacs, W. 1999. *Dialogue and the art of thinking together*. New York: Doubleday.

Jackson, J., and E. Smith. 1999. Conceptualizing social identity: A new framework and evidence for the impact of different dimensions. *Personality and Social Psychology Bulletin* 25:120–135.

Jacoby, L. L., and D. Witherspoon. 1982. Remembering without awareness. *Canadian Journal of Psychology,* 36:300–324.

James, W. 1890. *The principles of psychology* (Vol. 1). New York: Holt.

James, W. 1890/1950. *The principles of psychology*. New York: Dover.

James, W. 1902/1961. *Varieties of religious experience*. New York: Collier Books.

Janis, I. 1982. *Groupthink: Psychological studies of policy decisions and fiascoes* (2nd ed.). Boston: Houghton-Mifflin.

Janis, I. 1989. *Crucial decisions: Leadership in policymaking and crisis management*. New York: Free Press.

Janis, I., and L. Mann. 1977. *Decision-making*. New York: Free Press.

Jelinek, M. 1979. *Institutionalizing innovation: A study in organizational learning systems*. New York: Praeger.

Jervis, R. 1968. Hypotheses on misperceptions. *World Politics* 20:457–474.

Jervis, R. 1976. *Perception and misperception in international politics*. Princeton, NJ: Princeton University Press.

Ji, L., N. Schwarz, and R. Nisbett. 2000. Culture, autobiographical memory, and behavioral frequency reports: Measurement issues in cross-cultural studies. *Personality and Social Psychology Bulletin* 26:585–593.

Johnson, D., and D. Tjosvold. 1983. Constructive controversy. In *Conflict in organizations,* ed. D. Tjosvold and D. Johnson. New York: Irvington.

Kadar, M. 1992. *Essays in life writing*. Toronto: University of Toronto Press.

Kahneman, D., P. Slovic, and A. Tversky. 1982. *Judgment under uncertainty: Heuristics and biases*. Cambridge: Cambridge University Press.

Kaluphana, D. 1986. *Nagarjuna: The philosophy of the middle way*. Albany, NY: SUNY Press.

Kant, I. 1781/1966. *Critique of pure reason*. New York: Anchor Books.

Kapleau, P. 1965. *The three pillars of Zen: Teaching, practice, and enlightenment*. Boston: Beacon Press.

Katzenstein, G. 1996. The debate on structured debate: Toward a unified theory. *Organizational Behavior and Human Decision Processes* 66:316–332.

Kilduff, M. 1993. Deconstructing organizations. *Academy of Management Review* 18:13–31.

Kilduff, M., and A. Mehra. 1997. Postmodernism and organizational research. *Academy of Management Review,* 22:453–481.

Kim, W., and R. Mauborgne. 1997. Fair process: Managing in the knowledge economy. *Harvard Business Review,* July–August: 65–75.

Kim, J., and S. Nam. 1998. Exploring the concept of face in organizational behavior. *Organization Science* 9:522–533.

Kirchmeyer, C., and A. Cohen. 1992. Multicultural groups: Their performance and reactions with constructive conflict. *Group and Organization Management* 17:153–170.

Kitchener, K., and H. Brenner. 1990. Wisdom and reflective judgment: Knowing the face of uncertainty. In *Wisdom: Its nature, origins., and development,* ed. R. Sternberg. New York: Cambridge University Press.

Koberstein, P. 1997. Mountains of treasure, rivers of sorrow. *Cascadia Times,* June: 6–8.

Koffka, K. 1935. *Principles of Gestalt psychology*. New York: Harcourt.

Koriat, A., S. Lichtenstein, and B. Fischhoff. 1980. Reasons for confidence. *Journal of Experimental Psychology: Human Learning and Memory* 6:107–118.

Kotre, J. 1995. *White gloves: How we create ourselves through memory.* New York: Free Press.

Kotter, J. 1982. *The general managers.* New York: Free Press.

Kuhn, T. S. 1970. *The structure of scientific revolutions.* Chicago: University of Chicago Press.

Kuiper, N. A. 1981. Convergent evidence for the self as a prototype: The "inverted-U RT effect" for self and other judgments. *Personality and Social Psychology Bulletin* 7:438–443.

Kuiper, N. A., and P. A. Derry. 1981. The self as a cognitive prototype: An application to person perception and depression. In *Personality, cognition and social interaction,* ed. N. Cantor and J. Kihlstrom. Hillsdale, NJ: Erlbaum.

Kuiper, N. A., and E. T. Higgins (Eds.). 1985. Depression (Special issue). *Social Cognition, 3(1).*

Kuiper, N. A., M. R. Macdonald, and P. A. Derry. 1983. Parameters of a depressive self-schema. In *Psychological perspectives on the self* (Vol. 2), ed. J. Suls and A. G. Greenwald. Hilldale, NJ: Erlbaurm, 191–218.

Kunda, G. 1992. *Engineering culture.* Philadelphia: Temple University Press.

Lakoff, G., and M. Johnson. 1999. *Philosophy in the flesh: The embodied mind and its challenges to western thought.* New York: Basic Books.

Langer, E. 1975. The illusion of control. *Journal of Personality and Social Psychology* 32:311–328.

Langer, E. 1978. The psychology of chance. *Journal for the Theory of Social Behavior* 7:185–207.

Langer, E. 1983. *The psychology of control.* Beverly Hills, CA: Sage.

Langer, E. 1989. *Mindfulness.* Reading, MA: Addison-Wesley.

Langer, E. 1997. *The power of mindful learning.* Reading, MA: Addison-Wesley.

Langer, E., and J. Roth. 1975. The effect of sequence of outcomes in a chance task on the illusion of control. *Journal of Personality and Social Psychology* 32:951–955.

Langer, E., A. Blank, and B. Chanowitz, B. 1978. The mindlessness of ostensibly thoughtful action. *Journal of Personality and Social Psychology* 36:635–642.

Larwood, L., and W. Whittaker. 1977. Managerial myopia: Self-serving biases in organizational planning. *Journal of Applied Psychology* 67:194–198.

Lawrence, P., and J. Lorsch. 1967. *Organization and environment.* Homewood, IL: Irwin.

Lefcourt, H. 1973. The functions of the illusion of control and freedom. *American Psychologist* 28:417–425.

Leonard, D., and S. Straus. 1997. Putting your company's whole brain to work. *Harvard Business Review,* July–August: 111–121.

Levin, J. 1993. Age differences in mystical experience. *The Gerontologist* 33:507–513.

Lewicki, R., and D. Saunders. 1996. *Essentials of negotiation.* New York: Irwin.

Lewin, K. 1936. *Principles of topological psychology.* New York: McGraw-Hill.

Lewinsohn, P. M., W. Mischel, W. Chaplin, and R. Barton. 1980. Social competence and depression: The role of illusory self-perceptions. *Journal of Abnormal Psychology* 89:203–212.

Lifton, R. 1999. *The protean self: Human resilience in an age of fragmentation.* Chicago: University of Chicago Press.

Loevinger, J. 1976. *Ego development.* San Francisco: Jossey-Bass.

Loftus, E. 1996. *Eyewitness testimony.* Boston: Harvard University Press.

Lord, R., and R. Foti. 1986. Schema theories, information processing, and organizational behavior. In *The Thinking Organization*, ed. H. Sims and D. Gioia. San Francisco: Jossey-Bass, 20–48.

Lyles, M. 1988. Learning among joint venture sophisticated firms. *Management International Review* 28:85–98.

Lyles, M., and I. Mitroff. 1980. Organizational problem formulation: An empirical study. *Administrative Science Quarterly* 25:102–119.

Lyles, M., and I. Mitroff. 1985. The impact of sociopolitical influences on strategic problem formulation. *Advances in Strategic Management* 3:69–81.

Lyles, M., and C. Schwenk. 1992. Top management strategy and organizational knowledge structures. *Journal of Management Studies* 29:1–18.

Macken, C. 1910. *The canonization of saints.* Dublin: Hill and Sons.

Mael, F., and B. Ashforth. 1995. Loyal from day one: Biodata, organizational identification, and turnover among newcomers. *Personnel Psychology* 48:309–328.

Mander, J., and E. Goldsmith. 1996. *The case against the global economy.* San Francisco, CA: Sierra Club Books.

Manz, C., and H. Sims. 1981. Vicarious learning: The influence of modeling on organizational behavior. *Academy of Management Review* 6:105–114.

Margolis, J. 1986. *Pragmatism without foundations: Reconciling realism and relativism.* Cambridge: Basil Blackwell.

Markus, H. 1977. Self-schemata and processing information about the self. *Journal of Personality and Social Psychology* 35:63–78.

Markus, H., and S. Kitayama. 1991. Culture and the self: Implications for cognition, emotion, and motivation. *Psychological Review* 98:224–253.

Markus, H., and P. Nurius. 1986. Possible selves. *American Psychologist* 41:954–969.

Markus, H., and K. Sentis. 1982. The self in information processing. In *Psychological perspectives on the self* (Vol. 1), ed. J. Suls. Hillsdale, NJ: Erlbaum.

Markus, H., J. Smith, and R. Moreland. 1985. Role of the self-concept in the perception of others. *Journal of Personality and Social Psychology* 49:1494–1512.

Marquart, M. 1996. *Building the learning organization: A systems approach to quantum improvement and global success.* New York: McGraw-Hill.

Martin, J. 1982. Stories and scripts in organizational settings. In *Cognitive Social Psychology*, ed. A. Hasdorf and A. Isen. New York: Elsevier-North-Holland, 225–305.

Maslow, A. H. 1968. *Toward a psychology of being* (2nd ed.). Princeton, NJ: Van Nostrand.

Mason, R. 1969. A dialectical approach to strategic planning. *Management Science* 15:B403–14.

Mason, R., and I. Mitroff. 1981. *Challenging strategic planning assumptions.* New York: Wiley.

Maxey, M. 1997. Mining ethical issues: The new prohibitionists. *Engineering and Mining Journal.* October: 34–40.

May, E. 1973. *"Lessons" of the past.* New York: Oxford University Press.

McAdams, D. 1993. *The stories we live by: Personal myths and the making of the self.* New York: Guilford Press.

McClelland, D. C., J. W. Atkinson, R. A. Clark, and E. L. Lowell. 1953. *The achievement motive.* New York: Appleton-Century-Crofts.

McFarlin, D. B., and J. Blascovich. 1982. "Affective, behavioral and cognitive consequences of self-esteem." Paper read at symposium, "Functioning and Measurement of Self-Esteem," *American Psychological Association*, Washington, DC.

McGregor, I., and B. Little. 1998. Personal projects, happiness, and meaning: On doing well and being yourself. *Journal of Personality and Social Psychology* 74:494–512.

McGuire, W. J., and C. V. McGuire. 1982. Significant others in selfspace: Sex differences and developmental trends in the social self. In *Psychological perspectives on the self* (Vol. 1), ed. J. Suls. Hillsdale, NJ: Erlbaum.

McGuire, W. J., and A. Padawer-Singer. 1976. Trait salience in the spontaneous self-concept. *Journal of Personality and Social Psychology* 33:743–754.

Mead, G. 1934. *Mind, self, and society from the standpoint of a social behaviorist.* Chicago: University of Chicago Press.

Miles, R., and C. Snow. 1978. *Organizational strategy, structure, and process.* New York: McGraw-Hill.

Milgram, S. 1974. *Obedience to authority: An experimental view.* New York: Harper and Row.

Mill, J. S. 1859/1947. *On liberty.* (Albury Castell, ed.). New York: Appleton-Century-Crofts.

Miller, D. 1991. Stale in the saddle: CEO tenure and the match between organization and environment. *Management Science* 37:34–52.

Miller, D. 1994. What happens after success: The perils of excellence. *Journal of Management Studies* 31:325–358.

Mintzberg, H. 1983. *Power in and around organizations.* Englewood Cliffs, NJ: Prentice-Hall.

Mintzberg, H., D. Raisinghani, and A. Theoret. 1976. The structure of unstructured decision processes. *Administrative Science Quarterly* 21:246–275.

Mitroff, I. 1972. The myth of objectivity or why science needs a new psychology of science. *Management Science* 18:B613–18.

Mitroff, H., V. Barabba, and R. Kilmann. 1977. The application of behavioral and philosophical technologies to strategic planning: A case study of a large federal agency. *Management Science* 23:44–58.

Mitroff, I., J. Emshoff, and R. Kilmann. 1979. Assumptional analysis: A methodology for strategic problem-solving. *Management Science* 25:583–93.

Mitroff, I., and H. Linstone. 1993. *The unbounded mind.* New York: Oxford University Press.

Mitroff, I., and R. Mason. 1981. The metaphysics of policy and planning: A reply to Cosier. *Academy of Management Review* 6:649–652.

Mitroff, I., and R. Mason. 1982. Business policy and metaphysics: Some philosophical considerations. *Academy of Management Review* 7:361–370.

Morgan, G. 1986. *Images of organizations.* New York: Basic Books.

Murray, A. 1989. Top management group heterogeneity and firm performance. *Strategic Management Journal* 10:125–142.

Murrell, A., A. Stewart, and B. Engle. 1993. Consensus versus devil's advocacy: The influence of decision process and task structure on strategic decision making. *Journal of Business Communication* 30:399–414.

Nabokov, V. 1947. *Speak, memory.* New York: Putnam.

Nagel, T. 1970. *The possibility of altruism.* Oxford: Oxford University Press.

Narayanan, V., and L. Fahey. 1990. The evolution of revealed causal maps during decline: A case study of Admiral. In *Mapping Strategic Thought*, ed. A. Huff. Chichester, England: Wiley.

Neisser, U. 1976. *Cognition and reality.* San Francisco, CA: W. H. Freeman.

Neisser, U. 1982. *Memory observed: Remembering in natural contexts.* San Francisco: Freeman.

Newell., A., and H. A. Simon. 1963. GPS: A program that simulates human thought. In *Computers and thought*, ed. E. A. Feigenbaum and J. A. Feldman. New York: McGraw-Hill.

Nisbett, R., and L. Ross. 1980. *Human inference: Strategies and shortcomings of social judgment*. Englewood Cliffs, NJ: Prentice-Hall.

Noonan, H. 1989. *Personal identity*. London: Routledge.

Northway, M. 1936. The influence of age and social group on children's remembering. *British Journal of Psychology* 27:11–29.

Nuttin, J., and A. G. Greenwald. 1968. *Reward and punishment in human learning*. New York: Academic Press.

O'Brien, E. 1964. *Varieties of mystic experience*. New York: Mentor.

Olney, J. 1972. *Metaphors of self*. Princeton, NJ: Princeton University Press.

O'Reilly, C., and S. Flatt. 1989. "Executive team demography, organizational innovation, and firm performance." Working paper, Berkeley.

Organ, T. 1987. *Philosophy and the self: East and west*. London: Associated University Press.

Orwell, G. 1949. *1984*. New York: Harcourt-Brace.

Ostrom, E. 1990. *Governing the commons: The evolution of institutions for collective action*. Cambridge: Cambridge University Press.

Ouchi, W. 1980. Markets, hierarchies, and clans. *Administrative Science Quarterly* 25:129–141.

Parfit, D. 1984. *Reasons and persons*. Oxford: Oxford University Press.

Parker, S. 1995. Imitation, teaching, and self-awareness as adaptations for apprenticeship in foraging and feeding. In *Reaching into thought*, ed. A. Russon, K. Baird, and S. Parker. Cambridge: Cambridge University Press.

Parker, S., and R. Mitchell. 1994. Evolving self-awareness. In *Self-awareness in animals and humans: Developmental perspectives*, ed. S. Parker, R. Mitchell, and M. Boccia. Cambridge: Cambridge University Press.

Pascal, R. 1960. *Design and truth in autobiography*. Cambridge, MA: Harvard University Press.

Paul, I. 1959. *Studies in remembering: The reproduction of connected and extended verbal material*. New York: International Universities Press.

Pendell, S. 1990. Deviance and conflict in small group decision-making. *Small Group Research* 21:393–403.

Perrow, C. 1986. *Complex organizations: A critical essay*. New York: Random House.

Pfeffer, J. 1981. *Power in organizations*. Marshfield, MA: Pitman.

Pfeffer, J., and G. Salancik. 1978. *The external control of organizations: A resource dependence perspective*. New York: Harper and Row.

Popper, K., and J. Eccles. 1977. *The self and its brain*. London: Routledge.

Porter, M. 1980. *Competitive strategy*. New York: Free Press.

Porter, M. 1990. *The competitive advantage of nations*. New York: Free Press.

Pottruck, D., and T. Pearce. 2000. *Clicks & mortar*. San Francisco: Jossey-Bass.

Prahalad, C., and R. Bettis. 1986. The dominant logic: A new linkage between diversity and performance. *Strategic Management Journal* 7:485–501.

Pratkanis, A., and A. Greenwald. 1985. How shall the self be conceived? *Journal for the Theory of Social Behavior* 15:311–329.

Pratt, M. 1998. How do people identify with organizations? In *Identity in organizations: Building theory through conversations*, ed. D. Whetten and P. Godfrey. Thousand Oaks, CA: Sage.

Pratt, M., and P. Foreman. 2000. Clarifying managerial responses to multiple organizational identities. *Academy of Management Review* 25:18–42.

Priem, R. 1989. "Top management team demographic homogeneity, consensus, and firm performance in stable environments." Paper presented at the National Academy of Management meetings, Washington, DC.

Putnam, H. 1990. *Realism with a human face.* Cambridge, MA: Harvard University Press.

Quinn, J. 1980. *Strategies for change: Logical incrementalism.* Homewood, IL: Irwin.

Reedy, G. 1970. *Twilight of the presidency.* New York: World Books.

Reger, R., L. Gustafson, S. Demarie, and J. Mullane. 1994. Reframing the organization: Why implementing total quality is easier said than done. *Academy of Management Review* 19:565–584.

Reid, A., and K. Deaux. 1996. Relationship between social and personal identities: Segregation or integration? *Journal of Personality and Social Psychology* 71:1084–1091.

Reinert, D., and K. Stifler. 1993. Hood's mysticism scale revisited: A factor-analytic replication. *Journal for the Scientific Study of Religion* 32:383–388.

Robertson, B. 2000. *There's no place like work.* New York: Spence Publishing.

Robinson, D. 1990. Wisdom through the ages. In *Wisdom: Its nature, origins, and development,* ed. R. Sternberg. New York: Cambridge University Press.

Rogers, C. 1951. *Client-centered therapy.* Boston: Houghton-Mifflin.

Rogers, T. B. 1981. A model of the self as an aspect of the human information processing system. In *Personality, cognition, and social interaction,* ed. N. Cantor and J. Kihlstrom. Hillsdale, NJ: Erlbaum.

Rogers, T. B., N. A. Kuiper, and W. S. Kirker. 1977. Self-reference and the encoding of personal information. *Journal of Personality and Social Psychology* 35:677–688.

Rokeach, M. 1960. *The open and closed mind.* New York: Basic Books.

Rorty, R. 1979. *Philosophy and the mirror of nature.* Princeton, NJ: Princeton University Press.

Rorty, R. 1982. *Consequences of pragmatism.* Minneapolis, MN: University of Minnesota Press.

Rosch, E. 1973. On the internal structure of perceptual and semantic categories. In *Cognitive development and the acquisition of language,* ed. T. E. Moore. New York: Academic Press.

Rosenberg, M. 1979. *Conceiving the self.* New York: Basic Books.

Rosenberg, S., and A. Sedlak. 1972. Structural representations of implicit personality theory. In *Advances in experimental social psychology* (Vol. 6), ed. L. Berkowitz. New York: Academic Press.

Ross, B. 1991. *Remembering the personal past.* New York: Oxford University Press.

Rumelhart, D. 1980. Schemata: The building blocks of cognition. In *Theoretical issues in reading comprehension,* ed. K. Spiro, B. Bruce, and W. Brewer. Hillsdale, NJ: Erlbaum, 33–58.

Rumelhart, D. E. 1984. Schemata and the cognitive system. In *The handbook of social cognition* (Vol. 1), ed. R. S. Wyer and T. K. Srull. Hillsdale, NJ: Erlbaum.

Rumelt, R. 1974. *Strategy, structure, and economic performance.* Cambridge, MA: Harvard University Press.

Ryle, G. 1949. *The concept of mind.* Chicago: University of Chicago Press.

Salancik, G., and J. Meindl. 1984. Corporate attributions as strategic illusions of management control. *Administrative Science Quarterly* 28:238–254.

Santayana, G. 1923. *Skepticism and animal faith: Introduction to a system of philosophy.* New York: Scribner.

Sass, L. 1992. *Madness and modernism*. New York: Basic Books.

Schank, R. 1982. *Dynamic memory*. Cambridge: Cambridge University Press.

Schank, R. 1990. *Tell me a story: A new look at real and artificial memory*. New York: Charles Scribner's Sons.

Schank, R., and R. Abelson. 1977. *Scripts, plans, goals, and understanding: An inquiry into human knowledge systems*. Hillsdale, NJ: Erlbaum.

Scheier, M. F., and C. S. Carver. 1983. Two sides of the self. One for you and one for me. In *Psychological perspectives on the self* (Vol 2), ed. J. Suls and A. G. Greenwald. Hillsdale, NJ: Erlbaum.

Schlaim, A. 1976. Failures of national intelligence estimates: The case of the Yom Kippur war. *World Politics*, April: 355–378.

Schlenker, B. R. 1980. *Impression management*. Monterey, CA: Brooks-Cole.

Schlenker, B. R. (Ed.). 1985. *The self and social life*. New York: McGraw-Hill.

Schor, J. 1993. *The overworked Americans*. New York: Basic Books.

Schweiger, D., and P. Finger. 1984. The comparative effectiveness of dialectical inquiry and devil's advocacy: The impact of task biases on previous research findings. *Strategic Management Journal* 5:335–350.

Schweiger, D., W. Sandberg, and J. Ragan. 1986. Group approaches for improving strategic decision making: A comparative analysis of dialectical inquiry, devil's advocacy, and consensus. *Academy of Management Journal* 29:51–71.

Schwenk, C. 1982. Effects of inquiry methods and ambiguity tolerance on prediction performance. *Decision Sciences* 13:207–221.

Schwenk C. 1984a. Inquiry method effects on prediction performance: Task involvement as a mediating variable. *Decision Sciences* 1984, 15:449–462.

Schwenk, C. 1984b. Effects of planning aids and presentation media on performance and affective responses in strategic decision-making. *Management Science* 30:263–272.

Schwenk, C. 1984c. Devil's advocacy in managerial decision-making. *Journal of Management Studies* 21:153–168.

Schwenk, C. 1984d. Cognitive simplification processes in strategic decision-making. *Strategic Management Journal* 5:111–128.

Schwenk, C. 1985a. Giving the devil its due. *The Wharton Annual*, 104–108.

Schwenk, C. 1985b. The use of participant recollection in the modeling of organizational decision processes. *Academy of Management Review* 10:496–503.

Schwenk, C. 1985c. "The essence of strategic decision." Working paper, University of Illinois at Champaign-Urbana.

Schwenk, C. 1986. Information, cognitive bias, and commitment to a course of action. *Academy of Management Review* 11:298–310.

Schwenk, C. 1988. *The essence of strategic decision making*. Lexington, MA: D. C. Heath.

Schwenk, C. 1990. Effects of devil's advocacy and dialectical inquiry on decision making: a meta-analysis. *Organizational Behavior and Human Decision Processes* 47:161–176.

Schwenk, C. 1991. "Illusions of management control?" Working paper, Indiana University.

Schwenk, C. 1994. Management tenure and explanations for success and failure. *Omega* 21:449–456.

Schwenk, C. 1995. Strategic decision-making. *Journal of Management* 21:471–493.

Schwenk, C.1996. "Diversity is not enough." Working paper, Indiana University.

Schwenk, C. 1997. The case for weaker leadership. *Business Strategy Review* 8:4–9.

Schwenk, C., and R. Cosier. 1980. Effects of the expert devil's advocate, and dialectical inquiry methods on prediction performance. *Organizational Behavior and Human Performance* 26:409–424.

Schwenk, C., and A. Huff. 1986. Argumentation in strategic decision-making. In *Advances in Strategic Management*, ed. D. Lamb and P. Shrivastava. Greenwich, CT: JAI Press, 189–202.

Schwenk, C., and S. Rhodes. 1999. *Marijuana and the workplace: Interpreting research on complex social issues*. Westport, CT: Greenwood Publishing Group.

Schwenk, C., and H. Thomas. 1983a. Effects of conflicting analyses on managerial decision-making. *Decision Sciences* 14:467–482.

Schwenk, C., and H. Thomas. 1983b. Formulating the mess: The role of decision aids in problem formulation. *Omega* 11:239–252.

Scott, S., and V. Lane. 2000. A stakeholder approach to organizational identity. *Academy of Management Review* 25:43–62.

Senge, P. 1990. *The fifth discipline: The art and practice of the learning organization*. New York: Doubleday.

Senge, P., A. Kleiner, C. Roberts, R. Ross, G. Roth, and B. Smith. 1999. *The dance of change: The challenge of sustaining momentum in learning organizations*. New York: Doubleday.

Shaffer, G., V. Saunders, and W. Owens. 1986. Additional evidence for the accuracy of biographical information. *Personnel Psychology* 39:791–809.

Shaw, C. 1930. *The jack-roller: A delinquent boy's own story*. Chicago: University of Chicago Press.

Sherif, M., and H. Cantril. 1947. *The psychology of ego-involvements*. New York: Wiley.

Shrauger, J. S., and P. B. Sorman. 1977. Self-evaluations, initial success and failure, and improvement as determinants of persistence. *Journal of Consulting and Clinical Psychology* 45:784–795.

Simon, H. 1945. *Administrative behavior*. New York: Free Press.

Simon, H. 1969. *The sciences of the artificial*. Boston, MA: MIT Press.

Simon, J. 1996. *The ultimate resource*. Princeton, NJ: Princeton University Press.

Simons, T. 1995. "Top management team consensus, heterogeneity, and debate as contingent predictors of company performance: The complementarity of group structures and processes." *Proceedings of the Academy of Management National Meetings*, Vancouver, British Columbia.

Singer, J., and Salovey, P. 1993. *The remembered self*. New York: Free Press.

Skinner, B. 1953. *Science and human behavior*. New York: Free Press.

Slamecka, N. J., and P. Graf. 1978. The generation effect: Delineation of a phenomenon. *Journal of Experimental Psychology: Human Learning and Memory* 4:592–604,

Smith, J., G. Lyons, and E. Moore. 1998. *Global meltdown: Immigration, multiculturalism, and national breakdown in the new world disorder*. Westport, CT: Praeger.

Smith, J., G. Lyons, and P. Sauer-Thompson. 1997. *Healing a wounded world: Economics, ecology, and health for a sustainable life*. Westport, CT: Praeger.

Smith, K., K. Smith, J. Olian, H. Sims, D. O'Bannon, and J. Skully. 1994. Top management team demography and process: The role of social integration and communication. *Administrative Science Quarterly* 39:412–438.

Smith, M. B. 1984. "Metaphors of the self in the history of psychology." Paper presented at American Psychological Association, Toronto.

Snow, C. 1964. *The two cultures and a second look*. Cambridge: Cambridge University Press.

Snyder, M. 1974. Self-monitoring of expressive behavior. *Journal of Personality and Social Psychology* 30:526–537.

Snyder, A., and B. H. Campbell. 1982. Self-monitoring: The self in action. In *Psychological perspectives on the self* (Vol. 1), ed. J. Suls. Hillsdale, NJ: Erlbaum.

Sowell, T. 1995. *The vision of the anointed: Self-congratulation as a basis for social policy*. New York: Basic Books.

Srull, T. K. 1984. Methodological techniques for the study of person memory and social cognition. In *Handbook of social cognition* (Vol. 2), ed. R. S. Wyer and T. K. Srull. Hillsdale, NJ: Erlbaum.

Stace, W. 1960. *Mysticism and philosophy*. Philadelphia: Lippincott.

Staw, B. 1976. Knee deep in the big muddy: A study of escalating commitment to a chosen course of action. *Organizational Behavior and Human Performance* 16:27–44.

Staw, B. 1981. The escalation of commitment to a course of action. *Academy of Management Review* 6:577–587.

Staw, B. and J. Ross. 1978. Commitment to a policy decision: A multi-theoretical perspective. *Administrative Science Quarterly* 23:40–64.

Staw, B., and J. Ross. 1980. Commitment in an experimenting society: An experiment on the attribution of leadership from administrative scenarios. *Journal of Applied Psychology* 65:249–260.

Staw, B., and J. Ross. 1987. Behavior in escalation situations. In *Research in organizational behavior*, ed. L. Cummings and B. Staw. Greeenwich, CT: JAI.

Stifler, K., J. Greer, W. Sneck, and R. Dovenmuehle. 1993. An empirical investigation of the discriminability of reported mystical experiences among religious contemplative, psychotic inpatients, and normal adults. *Journal for the Scientific Study of Religion* 32:366–372.

Stokes, G., J. Hogan, and A. Snell. 1993. Comparability of incumbent and applicant samples for the development of biodata keys: The influence of social desirability. *Personnel Psychology* 46:739–762.

Stone, D., M. Sivitanides, and A. Margo. 1994. Formalized dissent and cognitive complexity in group processes and performance. *Decision Sciences* 25:243–261.

Strauman, T. 1996. Stability within the self: A longitudinal study of the structural implications of self-discrepancy theory. *Journal of Personality and Social Psychology* 71:1142–1153.

Suls, J. (Ed). 1982. *Psychological perspectives on the self* (Vol. 1). Hillsdale, NJ: Erlbaum.

Suls, J., and A. G. Greenwald (Eds.). 1983. *Psychological perspectives on the self* (Vol. 2). Hillsdale, NJ: Erlbaum.

Suzuki, S. 1970. *Zen mind, beginner's mind*. New York: Weatherhill.

Svendsen, A. 1998. *The stakeholder strategy: Profiting from collaborative business relationships*. New York: Basic Books.

Swann, W. B. 1983. Self-verification: Bringing social reality into harmony with the self. In *Psychological perspectives on the self* (Vol. 2), ed. J. Suls and A. G. Greenwald. Hillsdale, NJ: Erlbaum.

Tajfel, H. 1974. Social identity and intergroup behavior. *Social Sciences Information* 14:101–118.

Tajfel, H., and J. Turner. 1986. The social identity theory of intergroup behavior. In *The psychology of intergroup relations*, ed. S. Worchel and W. Austin. Chicago: Nelson-Hall, 7–24.

Taylor, C. 1989. *Sources of the self.* Cambridge, MA: Harvard University Press.

Taylor, S. E., and J. Crocker. 1981. Schematic bases of social information processing. In *Social cognition: The Ontario symposium* (Vol. 1), ed. E. T. Higgins, C. P. Herman, and M. P. Zanna. Hillsdale, NJ: Erlbaum.

Tesser, A., and J. Campbell. 1983. Self-definition and self-evaluation maintenance. In *Psychological perspectives on the self* (Vol. 2), ed. J. Suls and A. G. Greenwald. Hillsdale, NJ: Erlbaum.

Thomas, J., and D. Gioia. 1991. "Sensemaking, sensegiving, and action taking in a university: Toward a model of strategic interpretation." Paper presented at the Academy of Management Meetings, Miami.

Thomas, L., and P. Cooper. 1978. Measurement and incidence of mystical experiences: An exploratory study. *Journal for the Scientific Study of Religion* 17:433–437.

Thompson, J. 1967. *Organizations in action.* New York: McGraw-Hill.

Thompson, J. 1968. How could Vietnam happen? An autopsy. *Atlantic Monthly*, April: 47–53.

Tichy, N., and S. Sherman. 1993. *Control your destiny or someone else will. How Jack Welch is making General Electric the world's most competitive corporation.* New York: Doubleday.

Tjosvold, D. 1985. Implications of controversy research for management. *Journal of Management* 11:21–37.

Tjosvold, D. 1991. *The conflict-positive organization: Stimulate diversity and create unity.* Reading, MA: Addison-Wesley.

Tressalt, M., and S. Spragg. 1941. Changes occurring in the serial reproduction of verbally perceived materials. *Journal of Genetic Psychology* 58:255–264.

Tuchman, B. 1984. *The march of folly.* New York: Knopf.

Turner, M., and A. Pratkanis. 1998. A social identity maintenance model of groupthink. *Organizational Behavior and Human Decision Processes* 73:210–235.

Tushman, M., B. Virany, and E. Romanelli. 1989. "Effects of CEO and executive team succession on subsequent organizational performance." Working paper, Columbia University.

Tversky, A., and D. Kahnemann. 1974. Judgment under uncertainty: Heuristics and biases. *Science* 105:1124–1131.

Valacich, J., and C. Schwenk. 1995a. Devil's advocacy and dialectical inquiry effects on face-to-face and computer-mediated group decision-making. *Organizational Behavior and Human Decision Processes* 63:158–174.

Valacich, J., and C. Schwenk. 1995b. Structuring conflict in individual, face-to-face, and computer mediated group decision-making: Carping versus objective devil's advocacy. *Decision Sciences* 26:369–394.

Vallone, R., L. Ross, and M. Lepper. 1985. The hostile media phenomenon: Biased perception and perceptions of media bias in coverage of the Beirut massacre. *Journal of Personality and Social Psychology* 49:577–585.

Voyer, J. 1993. Pharmaceutical industry strategic groups based on cognitive maps. *Academy of Management Best Paper Proceedings*, 384–388.

Wall Street Journal, May 19, 2000, p. A3.

Wall Street Journal, May 23, 2000, A4.

Wall Street Journal, May 31, 2000, B1.

Wall Street Journal, June 9, 2000, B1.

Wall Street Journal, June 20, 2000, A26.

Wall Street Journal, July 7, 2000. A10.

Walsh, J. 1995. Managerial and organizational cognition: Notes from a trip down memory lane. *Organization Science* 6:280–321.

Walsh, J., and L. Fahey. 1986. The role of negotiated belief structures in strategy making. *Journal of Management* 12:325–338.

Walsh, M. 1987. *Thus have I heard: The long discourses of the Buddha.* London: Wisdom Publications.

Weeks, D., and K. Ward. 1988. *Eccentrics: The scientific investigation.* Stirling: Stirling University Press.

Wegner, D. M., and R. R. Wallacher. 1980. *The self in social psychology.* New York: Oxford University Press.

Weick, K. 1979. *The social psychology of organizing.* Thousand Oaks, CA: Sage.

Weick, K. 1995. *Sensemaking in organizations.* Thousand Oaks, CA: Sage.

Wells, H. 1919. *The sleeper awakes.* London: Classic Books.

West, C., and C. Schwenk. 1996. Top management team strategic consensus, demographic homogeneity, and firm performance: A report of resounding nonfindings. *Strategic Management Journal* 17:571–576.

Whetten, D., and P. Godfrey (Eds.). 1998. *Identity in organizations: Building theory through conversations.* Thousand Oaks, CA: Sage.

Wiesenfeld, B., S. Raghuram, and R. Garud. 1998. Communication patterns as determinants of organizational identification in a virtual organization. *Journal of Computer-Mediated Communication* 3:1–20.

Wicklund, R. A., and P. M. Gollwitzer. 1982. *Symbolic self-completion.* Hillsdale, NJ: Erlbaum.

Wixon, D., and L. Laird. 1976. Awareness and attitude change in the forced-compliance paradigm: The importance of when. *Journal of Personality and Social Psychology* 34:376–384.

Williamson, O. 1975. *Markets and hierarchies.* New York: Free Press.

Wood, D., and A. Bandura. 1989. Social cognitive theory of organizational management. *Academy of Management Review* 13:361–368.

Wood, M., and L. Zurcher. 1988. *The development of a postmodern self. A computer-assisted comparative analysis of personal documents.* Westport, CT: Greenwood Press.

Woodward, K. 1996. *Making saints: How the catholic church determines who becomes a saint, who doesn't, and why.* New York: Touchstone.

Wu, Pei-Yi 1990. *The confucian's progress: Autobiographical writings in traditional China.* Princeton, NJ: Princeton University Press.

Wylie, R. 1974. *The self-concept* (Vol. 1). Lincoln, NE: University of Nebraska Press.

Yankelovich, D. 1999. *The magic of dialogue.* New York: Simon and Schuster.

Yeats, W. 1986. The second coming. In *The Norton Anthology of English Literature,* Vol. 2, ed. M. Abrams. New York: W.W. Norton.

Zaehner, R. 1961. *Mysticism: Sacred and profane.* New York: Galaxy Books.

Index